QUICKSAND

Lulu Publishing, Raleigh, NC

ISBN 978-1-300-98803-8

QUICKSAND

To deny people their human rights is to challenge their very humanity.

Nelson Mandela

We must always think about things, and we must think about things as they are, not as they are said to be.

George Bernard Shaw

"Let your Sponsor and The Program do your thinking for you."

anonymous

ACKNOWLEDGMENTS

I'd like to thank Donna Y.-- without your encouragement, this book would not have been written.

I want to thank all the former 12-Step program members who shared their experiences and opinions-- especially, but not limited to, those who requested their stories be included in this book.

I also want to thank the experts and professionals in addiction, recovery, and related fields, who granted me permission to reference their material.

CONTENTS

Part 1: Introduction
Part 2: Quicksand
Part 3: Others share their stories
Part 4: References
Part 5: Afterword

part one

INTRODUCTION

"God and the United States government giveth... 12-Step programs taketh away..."

In looking back at my experiences with 12-Step programs, a very clear contrast comes to mind. As most people may recall from their elementary school years, one of this country's most important documents states: "We hold these truths to be self-evident: that all men are created equal; that they are endowed by their Creator with certain unalienable rights: that among these are **Life, Liberty, and the Pursuit of Happiness.**"

We can break these rights down to their basic definitions: the right to free will and self-determination, and the right to exercise these rights so long as they do not violate any laws or infringe upon the rights of others; the right to live peaceably, and to choose the course of one's life, without undue influence or intrusion; the right to privacy; the right to personal dignity. They are, in fact, the birthright of every human being.

For more than a decade, countless numbers of people have been coming forward, relating how their *unalienable rights* have been violated-- all within the context of 12-Step programs. Their experiences include everything from being denied the right to take medications prescribed by their own physicians for legitimate medical and mental health conditions, to 12-Step influences destroying their families, to sexual abuse and rape. Some have also spoken in behalf of former 12-Step program members who cannot speak for themselves, because the former members were murdered by others in the programs.

In 12-Step programs, many grant themselves the authority to take away the *unalienable rights* of other human beings. Regardless of what "the books" say, you may find you can no longer adhere to your own religious beliefs, or follow "the God of your understanding." You may find every aspect of your personal privacy, and self-determination for your own life, are violated. You may find anything from psychological manipulations to physical and sexual attacks. You may find you no longer have the personal dignity of a human being.

Second, if you become a part of a 12-Step program, you will find you are no longer in the real world. From the violation of your rights to what is expected of you, you will have an entirely different "place" than you had in the real world. You may be told your life, your mind, your memories, your priorities, and your future goals are no longer your own. You may see yourself as described by a quote from Dr. Martin Luther King, Jr.: *"I cannot adequately assume responsibility as a person, because I have been made the victim of a decision in which I played no part."** As explained by Dr. King, such a person is *"reduced to an animal,* with the *only resemblance* to a human being in *motor responses and functions."*

You may be expected to surrender your mind, your life, your freedom, your personal dignity-- not even to the God of your understanding, but to "Oldtimers," "Sponsors," and other members of the Program. To not do so can result in a variety of consequences. One common consequence, experienced by many, is if one refuses to either go along with the status quo of the Program in general, or refuses to cooperate with any individual member's unreasonable demands, is to be labeled *"sick."* Only in the context of a 12-Step program are stable adults who stand up for their rights and refuse to be intimidated deemed *'sick.'*

Third, a common saying in the Programs is *"It does not matter how you got here-- only that you are here."*

Not necessarily. Perhaps there are individuals who, due to their addictions, are so troubled or ill that they cannot make a rational decision for themselves. However, this does not describe the majority. As for the majority, the ability to make an informed, free will decision, is a basic human right.

In contrast, it often does not happen that way. Many are robbed of the right to make a free will decision for themselves by their health care providers-- who, themselves, are in 12-Step programs. Others are ordered into Programs by the courts. And then there are people like me: led to believe "working the steps" could bring about wonderful changes in my life, despite the fact that I never had any "substance abuse issues."

Yes, it matters very much "how you get there."

Fourth, another common saying is *"You are only as sick as your secrets."* While some take this statement as a way to legitimize violating other people's privacy and personal lives under the guise of 'honesty,' there is another approach to this concept, and it is the basis for this book.

Human beings have the right to privacy-- but the subject is not privacy. The subject is how 12-Step programs, and many individuals therein, consider the Programs to be a ready, easy cover for all kinds of sick behaviors and criminal actions. Whether individuals are "sharing" about such behaviors or crimes, or actively engaging in them, they know they are fully protected by their Programs.

Until now. Many individuals, including myself, are not willing to remain silent.

In this book, I have described my own experiences; situations I personally witnessed; and situations that were told to me by the individuals involved.

Although I stand by everything I have written as being one-hundred-percent true and accurate, you will not find any names, locations, or any other information that could easily identify any individuals or locations. While this may seem to protect the guilty along with the innocent, there is a reason for this approach: if anyone whose paths crossed with mine during these last nineteen+ years were to read this book and have the instantaneous reaction *"They're talking about **me**!"* then such individuals effectively admit and acknowledge their own guilt. After all, no one could think a statement or passage was about themselves unless they clearly see themselves *in it.*

To conclude this introduction, I will add an explanation about terminology I have used throughout the book. I struggled to find the correct word or term, and it was very difficult. As I have known people who belonged to or participated in 12-Step programs while continuing to be good people and decent human beings, the negativity I feel and express about 12-Step programs is not about such people.

Instead, it is about the percentage of the 12-Step population who "stayed sick, and/or got worse." It is about those who actively harm others, and use a "Program" as a cover.

The term I came up with for such individuals is *NRA*-- "Non-Recovered Alcoholics/Addicts." What I mean by that term is regardless of how many meetings they attend, how many people they "sponsor," or how many years or decades they have belonged to one or more 12-Step programs, such individuals have no interest in "recovery" or "change."

part two

IN MEMORY OF "BABY R."

A saying that was going around years ago was no person who wants help from a 12-Step program should ever hesitate in reaching out for that help due to shame, guilt, or embarrassment over anything he had done in the past. It went on to explain *"because there are many, many people who have done much worse things than yourself."* At the time, knowing nothing about the nature of drug addiction or alcoholism, I thought it made sense. All I took it to mean was there were people who had problems, many had made mistakes, and those who became involved in "programs" did so for the purpose of putting their lives on track. I found in most instances, the latter was not the case at all.

Quite a few years ago, I had the misfortune of my path crossing with an individual whom I will call "Bear." Bear had the habit of repeating one particular line to anyone who would listen: "*My wife killed my son.*" Assuming he must have been referring to some kind of tragic accident in which a child had been killed and Bear had blamed his wife, I asked him about it. He told me there had been no accident-- that the wife had intentionally suffocated the boy in order to get his life insurance money. He told me she managed to pass off the death as "S.I.D.S.," and there had been no further investigation. He said he did not turn her in for the crime, because he, too, wanted that money.

How did a mother get away with the cold-blooded killing of her child; how did the child's father get away with being an accessory-after-the-fact; or, the question that is even more pertinent: how did someone who had knowingly covered up the facts about his son's murder feel able to speak freely and frequently about it?

1. The factor of "anonymity." The general consensus is no matter what is said, those on the receiving-end of the information are not supposed to repeat it to anyone.

2. While individuals who truly seek help through 12-Step programs are able to acknowledge their problems and behaviors because they are aware that most people are not like themselves, those who are involved in programs for the wrong reasons do not seem to have this awareness; they prefer to associate primarily with others with whom they have much in common, and use this as an excuse to purport that "everybody" is like themselves.

3. Misusing what the programs teach about "acceptance." A 12-Step program uses the word to mean if a person has a drug or alcohol problem, "acceptance" is the first step in beginning to deal with it. However, some twist this word to mean something entirely different. You may hear "You cannot take someone's inventory." You may hear "You cannot judge others." The way these concepts are frequently manipulated, it comes to the person on the receiving-end being expected to condone all sorts of outrageous behaviors-- and the individuals who participated in those behaviors. After giving me the details of the crime and its aftermath, Bear went on to tell me about how he frequently beat his live-in girlfriend. He followed his remarks by sneering "So, ya gonna judge me *now*?!"

For a long time I struggled to find the correct word. In these situations, words I was familiar with did not apply. "Confess" was not an accurate term-- because when someone confesses something, it means he has acknowledged that the actions were wrong. For the same reason, "admit" would not have been an accurate word, either. I decided "dumping" or "unloading" more accurately described it.

An additional point I encountered was when one "dumps" even the most horrible tales on someone, they expect to hear nothing more from the person on the receiving-end than "*Thanks for sharing!*"

In other words, they expect involvement in a "program" to mean never being held accountable for their actions. While some delude themselves with the notion that all they need to do is "turn it over to God," others simply have no conscience at all. Bear was in the latter category. As a common factor amongst NRA's who misuse programs, Bear expressed no remorse or even regret about the child's murder or the cover-up, as well as no inclination to accept responsibility for his part in it. Instead, he made the mindboggling remark that every year on the child's birthday, he and his friends "got high."

The murder of a four-month-old child is not something they should get away with. "Baby R." would be alive today had it not been for his own parents-- and they should be held accountable for that child not having the chance to grow up and live his life.

DYING FOR IT

I was curious when I saw streams of men and women trudge into a building carrying small bags. The men and women-- adults in various age groups-- took their little bags up to various other individuals, and, after little whispery conversations, would shake their heads or shrug, and walk away. Some tossed their little bags into the wastebasket on their way out the door. When I became curious enough to ask, I was informed the bags contained over-the-counter or prescription medications, and the men and women were asking their 'sponsors' if they would be allowed to take the medications. Each time, the sponsors said no.

One of the many people affected by this was 'Randy.' I figured him to be somewhere between seventeen and twenty years of age. When I ran into him one evening, I was surprised by his attire: it was not especially cold, but he was wearing a very long, thick, wool coat. He was clearly ill, and told me why: his doctor had informed him he had an infection, and prescribed antibiotics. However, his sponsor told him 'antibiotics are drugs,' and forbid him to take them. The sponsor told Randy to eat licorice instead-- and the illness spread throughout his body.

12-Step program literature states that no one in the Programs has any authority whatsoever. The entire scope of any member, including sponsors, is to share 'strength, hope, and experience'-- what worked for them in their recovery process. The literature states neither members nor sponsors are professionals in any capacity, and the Program is not meant to replace professional assistance. Members and sponsors who claim they have special knowledge or authority are going against what is taught in their own Programs. However, for many, the Programs are nothing more than an arena where they can gain the upper-hand over other human beings.

There is Program literature that actually addresses this topic-- warning members to avoid individuals who claim to have 'special knowledge.' Lives can be ruined, health can be permanently damaged, and lives can even be lost, due to those who claim to know 'more, better, and different' than both the person himself and/or professionals with whom he has consulted.

Another individual was 'Jerry.' Jerry was at the end of his life, suffering from terminal cancer. The fact that he did not take any pain medication was applauded over and over again. This elderly man suffered needless agony, solely because of what individuals on power-trips told him he must do. When he finally died, they exclaimed '*Jerry died clean!*' as if his agony was cause for celebration.

In some instances, that upper-hand can cost people their lives. Not only are men and women not advised to seek professional assistance when they desperately need it, they are told they should not and cannot follow professional advice when they do receive it. Men and women are told they must ignore their own doctors' advice and do what 'Sponsor' says instead. Sponsors and other members of the programs state that they and only they can accurately diagnose others; that they and only they can recommend 'appropriate' treatment. Because of those who decide to go against what their own programs teach, there is needless suffering and even death.

WHAT IS A "WINNER"?

If you become involved with a 12-Step program, you are likely to hear the term *"winners."* The phrase *"Stick with the Winners!"* is often used. We can think about this term-- and see it is not necessarily what the programs say it is.

Within the 12-Step programs, a *"winner"* is someone with "quality clean time" or "quality sobriety." The catch: many have an entirely unrealistic view of what *"quality"* means. "Quality" does not mean devoting oneself to a Program at the cost to everyone and everything else in one's life. "Quality" also does not mean the only way a person can function, and the only way a person can avoid active drug or alcohol use, is by placing a Program as the focal point, and most consistent point, in their lives.

In all fairness, I have known people in 12-Step programs who could accurately be described as *Winners.* They have overcome their addictions, *and* proceeded to build better lives for themselves. However-- they are in the minority.

In contrast, most Winners I have known took different courses of action: there are those who found other programs that are not based on the 12-Step model, and other methods of recovery; there are those who made the choice to "moderate," and found it was within their ability to do so; and there are those who overcame their addictions without any outside assistance whatsoever. These people are Winners-- they are not "in denial," they are not "dry drunks;" they are simply people who found alternative methods of recovery-- methods that not only helped them overcome their addictions, but did not take away their lives the way 12-Step programs do.

The bottom line: it is neither "recovery" nor "winning" to trade one addiction for another. NRA's who give up alcohol or drugs, only to replace their substance-of-choice with *addiction* to a 12-Step program, are only fooling themselves. As a successful life is one in which a person can effectively live his or her own life, it is usually those who do so without a "program" who can be accurately described as *Winners*.

COMING OUT AS A "NORMIE"

It may be mindboggling to wonder how someone who never had any "substance abuse issues" ended up in not one, but two "12-Step programs." *(Author's note: actually there were three programs-- information about the third appears later in this book).*

Throughout much of my life, I'd had an ongoing battle with a relative. Not only did I never know how to effectively deal with the situation, neither did other family members and friends with whom I had discussed the situation. At a specific point in time, I met a person who offered hope and solutions. The woman, who was around my age, put it in terms I could understand: she said I was living a "second-rate life," and that there was no reason I should not be living a life of "choice" instead. She followed this by saying if I truly wanted a better life, what I needed to do was "work the Twelve Steps."

My new friend belonged to a 12-Step program called Alcoholics Anonymous. Without any literature to refer to, an essential point I missed was A.A.'s principle: 'the only requirement for membership is the desire to stop drinking.' At that particular point in time, I had not had a drink in more than six years. While drinking was something that for me had been moderate and relatively rare, I had stopped altogether when concern for an unborn child was my priority, and I had simply never taken up the habit again afterward. Unaware of any of this, my new friend presented A.A. and the Twelve Steps as the solution to anything that was standing in the way of a "choice" life.

Shortly after this woman came into my life, I found a longtime friend was in serious trouble due to drugs. Upon hearing about Narcotics Anonymous, I purchased some N.A. books for my friend. Reading the books myself to see if they offered any solutions, I noticed there were various points in the books that I could relate to. Although what I could not relate to was everything N.A. said about drugs and addiction, I hit on the saying "*Take what you need, and leave the rest*"-- and, believing what my friend had said about A.A., I assumed N.A. offered the same hope and solutions.

The catch: I overlooked the statement "an addict is someone whose life is controlled by drugs." The second catch, however, was I found individuals in Narcotics Anonymous who not only did not overlook it, but believed the statement applied to *everybody*-- and, to support that belief, were not only willing but determined to "go to any lengths" to claim *everybody* was in that category.

The first example of this illustrates something very important about 12-Step programs. One NRA, upon learning drug use had not been a part of my life, stated that an allergic reaction to a normal dose of cold medication meant I was 'a drug addict in denial;' and furthered this nonsense by saying if I were to 'go into denial about a relapse, I would end up with an eating disorder.'

Why was this important? What I learned through numerous experiences like this was individuals who have drug or alcohol problems and truly want to recover from their addictions are fully aware that most people are not like themselves. Whether it is an addiction itself, or the problems and lifestyles that often accompany it, people who want to recover realize that drug addicts and alcoholics are in the minority of the general population. In contrast, individuals who have no desire to improve their lives take an entirely different approach: they need to believe the entire population is "sick"-- and when they encounter people who are not, that's when the trouble really begins.

There can be two different reasons for this approach. First, individuals who assert that *everybody* is like themselves have no incentive to change anything about themselves. Second, however, are opportunists. Individuals who wish to take advantage of others, to exploit or harm others in some way, find the easiest way to do so is to claim the people are 'sick.' Not only can this result in manipulating someone who is healthy and stable, it can also result in discrediting such a person. A common tactic in programs, it is a common tactic for abusers in general.

While opportunists in 12-Step programs are not 'normal people' in any sense of the word, this particular subject is one in which abnormalcy is very clear. If you have the misfortune of meeting such individuals, you will learn it is "all about" getting something, getting their own way, and getting away with it-- and if you do not give them their own way, that's when the "psychobabble" comes out in full force. Mindboggling, isn't it, that only in the "world of 12-Step Programs" do NRA's claim that making decisions for one's own life and living one's own life, refusing to cave in to pressure or intimidations, and having a clear rational mind, are all very negative.

I also encountered an additional complication. Initially, I found it was pointless to either speak up in my own behalf or to try to explain anything, simply because most people did not understand. As anything I attempted to address was not in the range of their own personal experiences, they could not relate at all. It became much worse when I encountered a term and concept I had not been familiar with: one is not supposed to say anything that might "*offend*" someone. In the programs, and amongst those who are involved with programs, it comes to mean you must not tell the truth about yourself-- for if you go as far as to "admit" you are not an addict, not an alcoholic, do not have any of the problems common amongst this segment of the population, and have never participated in their way of life, they will be "offended" by it.

In other words, I have learned A.A. and N.A. likes liars-- when it comes to expecting people to portray themselves in a very negative light when a negative light is not accurate. Unable to come to terms with this type of deception and dishonesty, the only approach I was ever able to take was "think whatever you think- believe whatever you believe." In most instances, this approach backfired-- very few saw me as I really was, and were concerned about the truth. As one friend accurately worded it: *"They rewrite your life history."* And I have heard similar remarks from many other people who shared about their experiences in 12-Step programs.

You can pick any topic, and they are all equally valid. The 12-Step program slogan that comes to mind is *"The sicker you are, the more we love you."* It is not nearly as benevolent as it may sound. While there are too many NRA's who need weak, vulnerable people to take advantage of, you can even find members who take the same approach with no wrongful motives whatsoever.

With a wide variety of experiences, one topic that especially bears noting in this section is the topic of addicts and/or alcoholics. If a person who does not have these issues refuses to say he or she does, the person is up against a whole host of negativity. It ranges from snide remarks to feigned sympathy for the 'poor poor sick person who cannot admit his or her problem.'

In contrast, 'admitting' something that is not true can bring some stunning results: big wide smiles, the 'thumb-up' sign, and heads nodding happily. In other words, amongst the A.A. and N.A. populations, one cannot easily admit that one is not an addict nor an alcoholic. Not only is this an issue with the A.A. and N.A. populations in general, but even more so in "Open Meetings" that are allegedly open to anyone and everyone, regardless of their positions on addiction or alcoholism.

Another complication I encountered in 12-Step programs was the saying "*Act as if.*" The reason I didn't buy into this nonsense was one specific benefit of my upbringing: even as a child, pretense was not a part of my life-- and I never developed it afterward. Refusing to buy into pretense was another factor that put me "on the bad side" of individuals in the programs-- I would not say something was o.k. when it was not, I would not say something was right when it was wrong, and I would not say I was fine with something when I was not fine with it at all.

So when it comes down to it, there are three categories of individuals who make up A.A. and N.A.: there are those who try to recover from their addictions and related problems but cannot manage to do it; there are those who try and succeed; and there are the opportunists. In the latter category, a quote from a program spells it out quite clearly: they "manipulate people, and manipulate situations." If one is not familiar with this term, it means to be sneaky, devious, underhanded-- and 12-Step programs are filled with them.

Actually, there is a fourth category: those who managed to "escape" the 12-Step programs. While most people in this category are men and women who have struggled with alcohol or drug problems, they all found 12-Step programs to be places where they were taken advantage of, harmed in a variety of ways, and even witnessed and experienced criminal behavior. As for myself, the destruction and damage caused in my life by 12-Step programs is insurmountable. For anyone who has any kind of life situation that does not involve drug or alcohol dependency, a 12-Step program is not the place to find assistance-- and for anyone who does have any of these problems, and wants to move on to a better life, a 12-Step program is not the right place for you, either.

I think back to when I first heard that word: *'normies.'* Without elaborating on her point of view, a middle-aged woman had spoken the word with hostility, distaste, disgust. In more recent years, I noticed the term was often preceded by *"don't trust _,"* and *"don't associate with _."* And those who hold the viewpoint that 'normies' are "the enemy," it goes to show they're only fooling themselves about believing they are "recovering."

In fact, the refusal to acknowledge that 'normies' exist, and/or that we are not 'the enemy,' is so commonplace that I met very few people in 12-Step programs who did not have these viewpoints. There were a few who, after asking detailed questions about my history, came to the logical conclusion that I was neither an alcoholic nor an addict, and there were even those who seemed to know this without asking for any details. One incident stands out in my mind, as it took a very long time for me to grasp what the person was talking about. Noting how I was dealing with a crisis, the person remarked that I "wouldn't make a very good addict"-- because clear-minded was my way of approaching whatever was going on in my life.

A long time later, I encountered the terms "use (or 'pick up') over it" and "drink over it." Individuals who had various difficulties-- from minor problems to crises-- would comment "but I won't use over it" or "I'm not going to drink over it." Before these incidents, I wasn't even aware that drinking or using drugs was the way addicts and alcoholics approached difficulties in their lives-- and that to not do so was considered some kind of personal victory. In contrast, throughout my lifetime it never occurred to me to diminish my clear state of mind with any mind-altering, mood-altering substances.

To be completely fair and honest, I do not believe my initial A.A. friend had any wrongful motives when she urged me to 'work the steps;' I believe she felt her Program was useful in her own life, and that it could be equally useful to *everybody*.

However-- the most important point I learned from my involvements in 12-Step programs: *They do not result in a life of "choice"-- they take it away.*

THE MODEL

Quite a few years ago, some people taught me about a Program concept known as 'the model.' With 'the model,' a person is to describe "What it used to be like, what happened, and what it is like now."

Prior to becoming involved in programs, the only oddity and/or negativity in my life had been one overbearing, impossible-to-deal-with, parent. If I had taken to heart one of the programs' popular sayings, my life would not have taken a downward spiral. The saying: "There are many many people who have done much worse things than yourself." If I had paid due attention to this, and carefully examined "the exact nature of my wrongs," what would I have found? Well, when I was twenty-one years of age, a couple of friends lent me their car to drive to the laundromat, and I did so even though I didn't have a driver's license. When I became involved with programs, if I'd examined all of the "wrongs" in my past, all I would have found were a few examples on that level.

Individuals in programs were different from any people I had ever known before. When I lived in one certain area, for example, many of my friends had entirely different ways of life than myself-- yet it was always a matter of mutual respect. My friends did not ridicule or attack me over my slightly-conservative ways, nor did I treat them poorly because of their more liberal ways. It has only been amongst addicts and alcoholics in 12-Step programs that I have been ridiculed, accused, attacked-- and worse.

While individuals who approach 12-Step programs usually do so when their use of drugs or alcohol cause them to "hit rock-bottom," my own rock-bottom had nothing to do with drugs or alcohol. When I approached people in programs, I was looking for friends and for answers-- and the first person I met offered both. My own rock-bottom occurred as a *result* of the harm and damage done to me and my life by Program members-- mainly those who would be classified as 13th-Steppers.

I was not personally familiar with, nor knowledgeable about, the "sleazy side of life" prior to finding 12-Step programs. In fact, there was much I was not familiar with before I became involved with programs: being homeless, sexual assault, needing to call the police for help, restraining orders, lies against my reputation and stability and morality-- these were only a few things I only experienced after I became involved with 12-Step programs.

With the NRA population, I also learned the beliefs, values, and way of life that had been mine throughout my lifetime were not valid in this "new environment." First, treating people fairly and decently was manipulated, twisted to mean condoning and even participating in their lifestyle. Second, all of my positive attributes were taken as negative-- being "nice," being straightforward, being a law-abiding citizen-- these attributes were deemed cowardice, dishonesty, and even manipulation. One can consider it a twist on a phrase often heard in 12-Step programs: "If you always do what you've always done, you'll always get what you've always gotten." No, that is not true at all-- prior to "programs," "doing what I'd always done" was always considered positive, and had positive results; only after becoming involved in programs did I meet individuals who took it all as negative, and often turned it against me.

I was also on the receiving-end of attacks on my self-esteem, my self-image, and my place to make the decisions for my own life, family, and home. Similar to sick individuals anywhere, "they" attempted to build themselves up by tearing me down.

I had "the right heart, but blind eyes." That's me: a conscience, caring about other people, and trying to do the right thing. I found sick individuals take such attributes, and try to twist them into something altogether different.

While I met some good people along the way, for the most part my experiences with these programs have been of pain, loss, and trying to hold myself intact while the craziest did their damnedest to tear me apart and destroy everything I had.

Although they were by no means the only examples, the cold-blooded manipulativeness of the first and last NRA's I had the misfortune of encountering can sum up the nightmare that has gone on since I first became involved with *Programs.* Both individuals were "Oldtimers" claiming long "clean and sober time" in 12-Step programs. One individual stated: *"I hope you die alone in your own private hell;"* and another stated: *"I guess the only way we'll end up together is if one of your kids ends up dead."*

And these are only two examples of the sickness I've attempted to cope with-- and survive through-- because of 12-Step programs. From my experiences, a large percentage of so-called Oldtimers could accurately be described by an old saying from generations past: *They go through life with a chip on their shoulders, and an ax to grind--* wanting to make life as miserable as possible for "Others." And while such individuals certainly wreak havoc on people whose lives are already in disarray, they pull out no stops when they encounter people whose lives are basically happy.

WHAT DO THE 12-STEP PROGRAMS TEACH?

I used to believe both of the programs I was familiar with were excellent resources for individuals who both need and want recovery. The only "catch" is, as program literature states, "it works IF you work it"-- and this means "following THEIR path." What is "their path"? everything you need to know about these programs is clearly stated in their own literature. Those who do not gain true recovery, as well as those who wreak havoc on others, ignore what the literature says.

First, the programs have "twelve steps, and twelve principles." The steps are written in plain, clear language which anyone can understand; if there is any confusion, each step is thoroughly explained. Anyone who is truly interested in recovery can see what is expected of him, and what he must do to achieve his goal. The principles are equally clear.

Second, the programs say the individual who wants to recover must change his "attitudes, beliefs, and behaviors." They state that alcohol/drugs are only a symptom of a much larger problem, and that recovery must involve a complete overhaul of a person's outlook and way of life.

Third, the programs clearly set forth the scope of a 12-Step program. One aspect of this is the scope of all members: to share the "strength, hope, and experience" of what worked for them in their own recovery. Another aspect is the scope of sponsors: a sponsor is no more and no less than "a guide through the 12 Steps."
The programs also bring up two additional points on this subject: first, that the programs are not intended to replace professional, outside assistance-- medical, psychiatric, legal, and financial concerns are to be addressed to outside professionals; and second, that no one in a program has any authority or any special knowledge on these or other topics.

Fourth, the literature of these programs is written in easy-to-understand, plain English. The programs do not use psychobabble or street slang.

Fifth, you may read the phrases "Honesty, Open-mindedness, and Willingness," and "rigorous honesty." You may also see the phrase "To thine own self be true." The person's approach to the program, his stepwork, and to himself, are to be based on these principles.

Sixth, the programs say one must be prepared to look at his past, see it for what it was, and move past it.

Seventh, the programs provide very clear definitions and examples of what alcoholism/addiction is, and what it is not. One program states an alcoholic is a person who has a 'bodily allergy' to alcohol, and so cannot 'drink normally like other people;' Another program states that an addict is someone whose 'life is controlled by drugs;' it also adds that alcohol can be in this category, as alcohol is a substance that alters one's mind and mood.

These are some of the most important, clear concepts set forth in these 12-Step programs.

In contrast, some of my earliest introductions to these 12-Step programs should have clued me in that it was a dangerous place with dangerous people. The reason it did not was because, with no knowledge of addictions, and my earliest experiences being one-to-one with individual alcoholics and addicts, I was in the position of viewing any and every oddity as only representing the individual it came from, rather than the entire NRA population. In other words, it was a very long time-- *years*-- before I learned countless "oddities" are very common in these programs. And it was longer yet before I heard nearly every lousy experience I had echoed by others who had managed to get away from the programs.

One oddity I encountered were some extremely inappropriate approaches NRA's in the programs take toward people they do not know. I encountered two specific angles that these individuals use: one is to ask the person intensely personal, inappropriate questions; and the other is to tell the person a variety of equally-personal, equally-inappropriate information about themselves.

Whether there was ever any truth in the latter or not, is not even the issue. I have learned the *reason* NRA's habitually give personal information about themselves to people they do not know is to attempt to gain the person's trust and confidence-- when such trust and confidence is definitely *not* in the person's best interest. In such situations, you may hear total strangers "sharing" about their childhoods, their personal relationships, abuse and sexual abuse experiences, and so forth.

The former situation is completely out-of-line, too. When total strangers ask you what kind of relationships you have with your parents/children/siblings/spouse, what your childhood was like, and so forth, they are intruding into areas where they have no business-- and it is *never* with good intentions.

While I had numerous experiences with both tactics, clearly the one that was the worst was an NRA who did not simply ask questions-- but *demanded* the information. Interrogating me with questions that were none of his business, he often punctuated it by asserting he 'had *the right'* to the information he was demanding from me.

Again, for the longest time it did not occur to me that either of these approaches were anything more than individuals who did not know what was and was not appropriate. I learned, however, that when anyone uses these tactics, they always have some kind of wrongful motives in mind.

A second oddity was the insidious approach to *"the past."* I have found NRA's who want to coerce others into doing something or going along with something haul out this subject. Similar to the topic I discussed above, hearing this garbage from *individuals* initially led me to believe it was only an oddity of individuals, rather than a common occurrence. The approach is that a person would like, want, and/or go along with *anything and everything* unless some 'traumatic experience *in the past'* prevented one from doing so.

Similar to other oddities I experienced, my first experience with this particular subject was rather minor. Distressing, yes, but minor. The situation: as I was prone to hypoglycemic migraines, any type of flashing lights could bring on a migraine; I commented about this when there was a large colorful plastic planter in a window-- spinning back and forth, reflecting the sunlight. However, I was told it was something entirely different: that there must have been 'something in my past' that caused a 'negative reaction to spinning objects.'

If this situation was not bad enough, I later encountered similar remarks about everything from my decision to be single and unattached to objecting to sexual advances: allegedly none of it was my personal decision, it was 'because of something in the past.'

In other words, NRA's refuse to acknowledge human beings *as* human beings-- with human characteristics such as preferences, medical conditions, and free will; and, instead, attempt to bypass one's rights and personhood by claiming everything is 'about' the past.

These common oddities are not covered in the programs-- and, regardless of what one's opinion is of 12-Step programs in general, these types of situations clearly show NRA's have wrongful motives that have nothing whatsoever to do with their "programs."

An example of the clear contrast came from one of the first women I met who belonged to a 12-Step program. One of the first topics she brought up: "What are your hobbies? What are your interests- what you like to do in your spare time?" While the woman had many problems, at least she was able to recognize what was and what not appropriate topics of conversation. 'What kind of hobbies do you have?' or 'What kind of work do you do?' are appropriate subjects coming from someone you do not know-- your personal and family relationships, your childhood, and similar topics are not only inappropriate, but ways to get under your skin and look for weak spots they can exploit.

**12-STEP PROGRAMS ALSO TEACH HELPLESSNESS
AND DEPENDENCY**

This subject is addressed throughout this book, but it deserves its own special section. 12-Step programs do not assist people in becoming self-reliant, independent, strong human beings, but actively *discourage it--* and, whenever possible, actively *prevent* it.

When a person becomes involved with a program, he is urged to view himself as "powerless" over his addiction-- and that his addiction has caused his life to become "unmanageable." Whether there is any validity in this viewpoint or not, further participation in a program often results in the person being expected to a) become completely dependent on "the program" *and* others in it, and b) give up any independence and self-reliance that he *has* had.

Individuals are consistently beaten down with the teaching that they must remain participating members of their "program" for the rest of their lives, and if they do not, they will drink/use or die. Thus, you will find NRA's who have made their program-of-choice a part of their daily lives for decades fully believing their lives are on the line if they do not continue to do so.

Second, for the many who fall into this trap, "the program" takes priority over everything and everyone else in their lives. At the top of the list, families are affected, children are neglected, and marriages end, all due to one family member's devotion to "their program."

Learning helplessness and dependency goes further than attending meetings and focusing on the program: individuals are told they cannot do anything in their lives or make the smallest decision for themselves without first checking it out with, and gaining the approval of, their "sponsors." Individuals are told they require "support" for everything they do, and everything that is occurring in their lives. In other words, individuals-- adults-- are actively discouraged from making their own decisions, relying on themselves, taking their personal situations to their family members or close friends, and living their everyday lives without interference.

All of this was brand new to me, and the fact that I refused to buy into it never ceased to irk or stun NRA's. As one example, dealing with a difficult task brought the reaction: "You did that *all by yourself?!"* A second example occurred when a minor difficulty resulted in dealing directly with the difficulty, rather than 'going to a meeting and sharing about it.'

While I never failed to be stunned by the sense of helplessness of longtime NRA's, there were those who took it a few steps further. "You're only independent because you've always had to be-- because nobody ever cared about you," was one outrageous remark. "When your mother dies, you will need counseling" was another. These kinds of statements are designed to cause a person to doubt his or her ability to effectively deal with his or her own life. Such attributes as personal strength and maturity, and the place of family members and close friends in one's life, are not seen as positive, but that they get in the way of 'the Program.'

"TWELVE STEPS INTO THE EGYPTIAN RIVER"

If you have had any involvement with a 12-Step program, or interactions with members of such programs, you may have heard the slogan: *"Denial is not a river in Egypt."* The slogan is tossed around regularly, and appears on everything from posters to coffee mugs.

The 12-Step program fiasco began with Alcoholics Anonymous. Years later, A.A. granted permission for its steps and other concepts to be used in the formation of Narcotics Anonymous. Although people have successfully overcome their addictions, resolved their problems, and moved on to better lives by participating in these programs, a large percentage fail-- if not by actively relapsing, by having the same attitudes and behaviors as before they came to the programs.

It gets worse. While A.A. and N.A. have been held up as recovery programs for individuals with alcohol or drug issues, it was essentially a breeding ground for a wide variety of other programs. You could probably pick any topic in existence, and find a 'program' for it.

The catch: "the blind leading the blind" approach in the initial 12-Step programs may have had some degree of success because they addressed alcoholism and drug addiction. Attempting to apply such a 'program' to various other issues is a recipe for disaster.

One example includes 12-Step programs for individuals who have psychiatric or emotional problems. Rather than being directed to appropriate mental health professionals, individuals who participate in these programs are led to believe 'recovery' is possible, simply by interacting with others who have the same problems.

A second example includes programs for "sex addicts." Rather than addressing the issue as something that requires mental health assistance-- and sometimes legal intervention-- individuals get themselves off the hook by interacting with others who have the same attitudes and behaviors as themselves. This approach can be destructive enough when the subject is alcohol or drugs, but is far worse when the subject is one's inability to control his sexual urges.

To make matters worse, one of these programs presents itself as a recovery program for individuals who are "addicted" to sex *and love*. As there is logically no such thing as a 'love addict,' all this does is further the confusion for those who are already confused.

There are also programs for incest survivors. It is another example of individuals who need mental health assistance being led to believe they can achieve "recovery" by "sharing" and "working steps."

Another example of potentially-destructive programs are programs for "loved ones" *of* alcoholics and addicts. First, these programs teach individuals that they are as 'sick' as their alcoholic or addicted family member. Second, regardless of how destructive the relationship may be, "loved ones" are never urged to leave the relationship. This includes women who are on the receiving-end of physical abuse from addicted or alcoholic husbands. The course of action recommended to loved ones of alcoholics or addicts: to *'work their own program.'* They are told they should not try to 'control' someone else's behavior-- even when they are on the receiving-end of violence.

The bottom line: even if some people can achieve success and better lives through Alcoholics Anonymous or Narcotics Anonymous, many other 12-Step programs are a breeding ground for disaster. From issues that require professional help to those that should be dealt with with basic common sense, "joining a program," "sharing," and "working steps" does nothing but make matters worse.

WHY SOME RECOVER AND OTHERS DO NOT

I believe one statement the Programs say: that nearly everyone who truly wishes to recover, can. I also believe what a recovering addict/alcoholic said years ago: that everyone deserves a chance. Unfortunately, too many are unwilling to do what it takes to achieve recovery.

Over the years, I have known good people, and I have known "lost souls." There are those who try, and succeed; and those who are unable to succeed despite trying. However, individuals in these categories are the minority. I have learned: most want to stay the way they are-- and use every rationalization to do it.

Whether the reader of this book is someone who wants recovery from drug or alcohol addictions, or is someone who frequently deals with addicts/alcoholics, I am hoping what I have learned can benefit others. One important aspect of it is "why some recover, and others do not." In the latter category, I have learned there are generally three common factors:

First, for those who do not proceed into true recovery, it is often a matter of "the blind leading the blind." While only individuals who have experienced drug addiction and/or alcoholism can fully understand what an addict or alcoholic is going through, those who do not proceed into true recovery limit his or her interactions to those who have had these experiences, as much as possible. They do not want to be around "normies," or step into the "normal" world. If they do interact with normal people, they will insist it is the "normies" who have the problems, and individuals in programs are the ones who are 'sane.'

Second, with this self-imposed limited view, they insist everybody is like themselves. Whether it is drug or alcohol abuse or the lifestyle oddities that accompany it, they assert everybody has had these experiences and problems.

Third, one cue as to whether someone is recovering or not is the way in which he or she "shares" his or her experiences. For those in this latter category, it is like "Step 5 gone awry." There are actually two parts of a legitimate Step 5: acknowledging 'the exact nature of one's wrongs,' and admitting them to 'another human being.' Those who do not care about recovery go completely off-base on both parts. Not only do they not acknowledge their behaviors and actions as wrong, they essentially use them as bragging rights to anyone who will listen. Some simply call it 'sharing;' with others, it is a misguided-- and often intentionally misguided-- approach to 'honesty.'

Every person is the sum-total of his or her life-experiences. This does not mean the impact is the same for all people. In addition to the above-mentioned Step 5 process, Programs have more to say on this topic: recovery means being able to put the past in the past and move forward-- but they also say a person must look at those experiences and see them for what they were. While exaggerating and lying do not cut it, neither does "staying stuck in the past."

NRA's who do not proceed into true recovery constantly rehash and rehash "the past." Part of it is every single wrong or slight-- real or imagined-- ever done to them. The other part is misdeeds that they still cannot see as wrong. Regardless of what they did or did not do with their first three Steps, these factors stand in the way of any real progress or any real change. They go through their adult lives as "rebels without a cause"-- fighting losing battles, and often taking down everyone in their midst.

In contrast, those who succeed take the recovery process seriously. Rather than turn to or listen to fellow addicts on topics such as medicine, psychiatry, law, or other professional subjects, they seek outside help from real professionals. Rather than staying stuck in their pasts, they see wrongs done to them as something that heals, and misdeeds as something to not do again. And they learn from "normies," rather than resent us.

The bottom line regarding why some recover and others do not: go back to the first paragraph in this section. Almost anyone who truly wants to recover *CAN*. You can take this section, and most of the other sections in this book, and see exactly what is and is not meant by *'truly wants to.'*

Recently, I heard a statement that sums it up: *The best predictor of future behavior is past behavior.* And it is accurate.

"MIND GAMES"

One of the first individuals I met who claimed membership in a wide variety of 12-Step Programs acquainted me with another concept I was not familiar with before; he called it "mind-games."

On a canary-yellow legal pad, the individual listed approximately thirty-five topics in this category, and then proceeded to describe what each one meant.

Some of the most common "games":
My Truth is the only truth;
Your Truth is the only truth;
What you heard is not what I said;
The way you experienced something is not the way it really happened.

The purpose of "mind-games": an individual who participates in this behavior seeks to gain the upper-hand over others. He does this by knowing the "buttons" to push, to get the reaction he desires. The purpose of mind-games is to cause the person on the receiving-end to doubt himself-- to doubt his perceptions, his memories, and even his own sanity.

In the late '60s and early '70s, a popular pastime was taking apart a psychiatric technique and using it for this type of manipulation. The technique was called "Transactional Analysis." The concept, however, goes further back. Many decades ago, there was a play titled "Gas Light;" the theme of the play was a husband who attempted to convince his wife and other people that she was insane-- that she was only imagining the things that were occurring.

Thus, the term gaslighting can be used to cover these so-called "mind-games." Far from being a harmless diversion, quote: *Gaslighting is a form of psychological abuse in which false information is presented with the intent of making a victim doubt his or her own memory and perceptions.*

"THEY REWRITE YOUR LIFE HISTORY"

I have heard this statement so often from people who have separated themselves from 12-Step programs that it deserves its own section. From my own experiences, also, it is one-hundred-percent accurate.

The first NRA I ever met summed it up with a very odd remark: "Tell the truth- and then later, revise it." It would have been more accurate to add 'and if you don't, *they will.*'

Within the programs you may find many individuals who insist your mind is 'wrong,' your memories are 'wrong,' your perceptions are 'wrong;' and that they 'know' everything that you do not. Not only is this approach obviously dangerous, it is a very commonplace occurrence in 12-Step programs.

The late Margaret T. Singer**, who began studying brainwashing in the 1950s, was, throughout her career, known as the world's #1 cult expert. In her words:
The tactics of a thought-reform program are organized to:
- Destabilize a person's sense of Self;
- Get the person to drastically reinterpret his or her life's history and radically alter his or her worldview and accept a new version of reality and causality.

Many individuals who left 12-Step programs related these experiences in context of the programs; what I experienced was by no means unique. The only actual difference was, as I had very little formal involvement in 12-Step programs, the experiences I was on the receiving-end of came directly from *individual members* of the programs. Consequently, it was not until quite recently that I learned exactly how common "thought-reform" actually is within these programs.

I have included detailed references at the end of this book, but perhaps the subject necessitates explanations from those of us who have experienced it. The general consensus would logically be "How could these things possibly happen?" I was surprised to find the experiences of many other people were remarkably similar to my own: a person can be destabilized by putting the person in a suggestible state, planting seeds of doubt, and creating the illusion that the speaker is "the only one who 'knows the truth'," and is "the only one who can be 'trusted'." As for the first topic, not only individual people but quantities of material I have since read on the topic, included such factors as limiting or eliminating the person's access to opposing information, dietary changes, and sleep deprivation.

To illustrate the outrageous extremes perpetrators in the programs can go to when attempting to achieve their goals, I will include some examples from my own experiences. Some of the things I was told: When I was a small child, my parents "drugged" me with a powerful narcotic; My parents "abused" and "sexually abused" me; I was "raped" by my mother; My eldest brother "sexually abused" me; My entire family-of-origin (parents and two older siblings) were all "drug addicts;" My eldest brother had been killed in the Vietnam war; My niece had committed suicide; I had a wide range of "traumas in the past" that I "just did not remember;" and other outrageous examples.

To add fuel to the fire, stating that these and similar events did not occur was said to be a matter of being 'in denial.' In other words, if you do not 'admit' things that are not true, and do not 'remember' things that did not happen, perpetrators claim it means you are 'sick'-- because there is no surer way of gaining power than to get a person to doubt his or her own mind.

In addition to "rewriting your history," attempting to instill self-doubt also comes in the form of "rewriting your present." Not only do they scrutinize everything about you and call it something else, some are prone to doing something their own programs tell them they cannot do: attempt to replace health care professionals by claiming they know more than said professionals. Earlier in this book we covered individuals who tell people to not go to health care providers, and not do what health care providers say, but some take it a few steps further: telling people their doctors are wrong, and that 'only they' know the facts. I, personally, was 'diagnosed' by uneducated nonprofessionals as having "post-traumatic stress disorder," "multiple personalities," and "chronic fatigue syndrome." The fact that professionals had said I did not have any mental health conditions or medical conditions only brought the response that the doctors were all 'wrong.' To further illustrate how outrageous these situations can be: one NRA who claimed she could diagnose me was someone whom I had never met in person and never spoken with, and another had much less than a high school education.

The bottom line: the sickest individuals in the programs need people to be weak-- because it is the only way they can attain power. And if you are not weak, they will do everything they possibly can to make you vulnerable.

Trying to create vulnerability by attempting to create doubts can extend to every*thing* and every*one*. One example involved my remarks about disliking a very negative environment, my wish that I was living in a former environment, and my desire to eventually do so. I was told none of my previous environments-- nor the people who lived there-- were the way they seemed. I was told environments that seemed good, happy, and positive, were actually all 'hiding something very dark,' and that the people I'd known and liked in those places were all 'in denial.'

The terminology was asinine enough, but the topics the NRA's were addressing led it to be even more asinine. *Denial*-- any person who had ever used any 'drug,' including correct use of medication for legitimate medical issues, was a *Drug Addict;* and any person who had ever consumed any alcohol was an *Alcoholic.* And what was everybody allegedly hiding? *abuse,* naturally. I cannot even imagine what the reactions would be from all the decent people I knew throughout my life, if they'd heard that they were not only all 'drug addicts and alcoholics,' but that their homes, marriages, and families were one big mass of *'abuse.'*

Another example involved my comment that I liked myself-- the person I was. I was told that was a stupid viewpoint, and virtually everything about me was 'bad.'

From numerous experiences with this subject, it is a common approach NRA's take to people they wish to gain power over-- the approach that everyone, everything, and everyplace is negative and harmful, and if you do not see it that way then you do not have a clear view of 'reality.' Personally, while I continued to retain the facts about every situation, NRA's persisted in trying to change my *perceptions and interpretations* of the facts.

One approach can be summed up in the words of author Philip K. Dick: *The basic tool for the manipulation of reality is the manipulation of words. If you can control the meaning of words, you can control the people who must use the words.*

Throughout this book, and in the references section, you will find sources as diverse as Codependents Anonymous and a leading cult authority providing examples of this approach. NRA's misuse words and terms of their own 12-Step programs, as well as what is commonly known as psychobabble, for the purpose of making themselves look like authorities, screw with other people's perceptions, and control other people's behaviors.

And the point to bear in mind is you are not dealing with professionals who use these words and terms in a legitimate manner.

"DO YOU REALLY HATE YOUR LITTLE BROTHER?"

As you will read in the examples throughout this book, there is much about 12-Step programs that could accurately be described as bad and dangerous. However, while a wide variety of *abuses* occur within the programs, there is one that bears special noting. I was granted permission to quote this short passage by a person who goes by the screen name "Agent Orange"-- if you check the References section at the end of this book, you will find a link to his site which, resulting from many years of his hard work and research, is probably the #1 site of its type on the Web:

*"Cults and other mind-manipulators will tell you that you cannot trust your own mind and your own thinking (so you should let them do your thinking for you). If you buy into that idea, it will really cripple you. You won't be able to think anything without also thinking that it must be wrong, because you thought it. (But then the thought that your thinking is wrong should also be wrong... So your thinking must be right... But if your thinking is right, then it must be wrong..".****

Many people may be familiar with one particular form of 'bad parenting' which is not as commonplace as it was in the distant past: the approach of essentially nullifying a child's thoughts, feelings, and beliefs, by claiming the child *does not really have* those thoughts, feelings, and beliefs. The purpose was to 'convince' a child that his thoughts, feelings, and beliefs were actually one-in-the-same as whatever his parent (or other adult) *wanted* him to think, feel, or believe.

As a random example, a youngster who stated that he hated his little brother, instead of being told it was wrong, or asked why he thought or felt that way, was likely to be admonished with *"You do not really* hate your brother-- *you really* love your brother-- *say* you love your brother..."

Similarly, in the Programs, people are consistently told their thoughts, feelings, and beliefs are not real, *and* that they must 'trust' *Others* to provide them with information about their 'real' thoughts, feelings, and beliefs. In other words-- forgive the vocabulary here-- *adults* are prodded to give up 'their Truth' and 'their Reality' in favor of someone else's.

And, similar to the situation with the child, they are generally given positive reinforcements for blind compliance, and negative reactions if they refuse.

While the entire approach is dangerous enough, think about this very clearly: *who, exactly, are 'Them' and 'They' who use this approach?* As 12-Step literature itself states, *no one* in a 12-Step program has 'special knowledge' about other people or other people's lives, *no one* in a 12-Step program has any authority over anyone else, and *no one* in a 12-Step program has a professional role such as a medical doctor, legal adviser, mental health practitioner, or any other professional role.

So what it comes down to is you have Oldtimers in 12-Step programs whose only point of difference between themselves and either 'rock-bottom' newcomers or 'normies' is they may have abstained from drug or alcohol abuse for a specific period of time. As such, the only knowledge or authority they claim to have is only in their own minds.

An Oldtimer in a 12-Step program-- an NRA-- is really no different from a total stranger you may happen to meet in a grocery store. With that in mind, how would you react if the latter approached you, telling you he or she 'knows' what you *really* think, feel, believe? If you would not take medical, legal, psychiatric, or other professional 'advice' from such a person, you should be equally cautious when someone says they 'know' you better than you know yourself.

While it is an ongoing issue when there are 12-Step program Oldtimers in or around your life, NRA's often use the same tactics on other people in your life. While they are attempting to convince you that they know you better than you know yourself, they can, at the same time, be working the same manipulations on the people in your life-- often those who have been a part of your life for years or decades. With enough manipulation, can even get your loved ones who have lived with you all of their lives to believe they do not really know you at all-- that you are not the person they've always known you to be. NRA's-- including individuals who have just met you and know nothing about you-- can get your loved ones to fully believe they know you in ways your own loved ones do not.

"MEN HELP MEN, AND WOMEN HELP WOMEN"

There are many mistakes people who are truly interested in recovery should not make. One example which many dismiss is best addressed by a program mailout: a 12-Step program is not a "dating club." Unfortunately, people do fall into these types of situations-- and there are others who seek them out intentionally.

"Men helping men and women helping women." This is not only true in Sponsorship, but other interactions as well. It does not mean individuals in the programs must completely avoid members of the opposite gender-- but it does mean the programs actively discourage intimate interactions.

NRA's who do not take recovery seriously dismiss these cautions. Instead, they look at the programs as a place to form 'relationships,' or a place to find casual 'hook-ups.'

First, newcomers are cautioned to not make any significant changes in their lives during the first year of recovery. However, there are those who have stated, with variations, "My Sponsor told me to avoid relationships-- but that it does not mean I can't have sex!" In other words, "Sponsors" are advising newcomers to continue their old ways of living-- or advising them to take on unhealthy approaches that they did not even have before-- including casual sexual activity that is completely separate from relationships.

Second, NRA's who have been in programs for a considerable length of time often take advantage of newcomers. A newcomer-- regardless of age or gender-- is often seen as "fair game" for those who wish to take advantage of them. Whether it proceeds by manipulation, or direct rape or sexual assault, it occurs much more often than many people realize.

Third, NRA's who are not interested in recovery seek out other alcoholics/addicts with the belief that doing so means they will never need to be accountable for past wrongs nor change their ways in the present or the future. When someone says they are looking for someone 'who can understand' them, that is what they mean-- they are looking for someone who is 'sick,' so they never need to change themselves.

Fourth, while there are numerous ways individuals get around the "men help men, women help women" principle, there is one method that is especially alarming: those who try to get around this principle by claiming they were "abused" or "sexually abused" by members of their own gender, and therefore "do not trust" members of their own gender.

While the programs clearly state that recovery from alcohol or drug addiction is the only scope of a recovery program, and that all other issues-- personal, legal, medical, financial-- must be avoided, the topic of interpersonal relationships is amongst the most bothersome. Whether someone is looking for casual sex or a codependent relationship, it can destroy everything from basic self-esteem to human lives.

Yet it is another example of the many who do not take recovery seriously. They do whatever they want, with no concern about the consequences to others. Similar to all of the other topics they dismiss, they run not on "recovery" but on "self-will."

"THE POSTMAN IS NOT YOUR FRIEND"

No, this is not a negative remark about mail carriers; what it is is a caution about one specific aspect of 12-Step programs that is not well known. There were three programs I was aware of that offered the option of interacting, by mail, with people in the programs. Designed to be a type of pen-pal exchange for individuals who, for whatever reason, did not attend meetings in person, it was my first experience with 12-Step programs-- years before I met any program members in person, and many years before I attended a meeting.

What I learned: there are individuals who lie on a wide range of topics; individuals who misrepresent themselves; and individuals who actually do attend meetings, but simultaneously use this by-mail method to "troll" for prospective victims. All of these points are important, but the third is one you should think about very carefully. I personally knew of two such individuals-- both attended meetings regularly in their hometowns, but used the pen-pal option as a special way to seek out "pigeons."

What I learned: if you make the mistake of becoming involved with any of these by-mail options, you are at a definite disadvantage primarily for one reason: when all you have to go on is whatever an individual writes, you have no way of assessing either the person or the situation. In other words, you cannot assess such things as body language, mannerisms, speech patterns or tone of voice, eyes, or eye contact. Even those of us who are generally experts with "gut instincts" can find our gut instincts shut off, or are at least minimized, because we cannot see or hear the individual on the other end. And, NRA's who use the by-mail methods for wrongful reasons take full advantage of others' inability to assess what kind of people they are, what they are after, and what they are really like.

An additional point about these by-mail options covers the 12-Step program concept of "Sponsorship." While it is not in your best interests to give your personal information to anyone in a 12-Step program, the subject of by-mail "sponsorship" should be underlined-- many times over.

During the period of time that I received these mail-outs, I had a number of experiences with this subject. The first was a male who was somewhat older than myself; not only was he violating the 'men help men, women help women' rule, I was not directly involved with any 12-Step programs whereas he claimed he had been a member for approximately a decade. "Playing the victim" and telling me he "hated men," he asked me to be his "sponsor."

The second odd experience came from a woman who was also somewhat older than myself; although I was not directly involved in the programs, she said she and I should "Sponsor each other."

Another experience involved a woman who lied about everything from her age to her marital status; not only was she "trolling" the mail-out offering to "sponsor" people, she was doing the same thing at her meetings.

There is another issue covering these by-mail options that I had not even considered at the time: while a subscriber to a mailing is not required or obligated to do so, he is advised and encouraged to provide his contact information. If you follow this advice, your mailing and/or home address, email address, etc., are immediately visible to anyone who reads the mail-out. As the mail-outs are sent upon request to anyone who asks for them, dangerous and potentially-dangerous situations can occur: you do not know *who* obtains your contact information, or what an individual might do with it.

WHAT IS A "SPONSOR"?

Program literature states that a sponsor is no more and no less than a guide through the Twelve Steps. A sponsor and sponsee are supposed to be the same gender. A sponsor is supposed to be chosen by a prospective sponsee, based primarily on the prospective sponsor's "quality" clean/sober time. The main headquarters of one 12-Step program also stated a sponsor is supposed to prevent harm from coming to the sponsee whenever possible, and help the sponsee if any problems do arise from the 12-Step meetings.

Unfortunately, the horror stories I've been told about sponsors make it appear as if none of those individuals had a clue about their role-- from telling sponsees they could not take prescription medication, to unconscionable interference in sponsees' personal and family lives. I have even heard from former program members who related that sponsors had informed them *they* (sponsors) would be selecting 'appropriate' spouses or partners for the sponsees!

To illustrate how out-of-balance and absolutely outrageous a so-called sponsor/sponsee arrangement can be, one individual related that he wanted to buy a car, but could not do so unless his "sponsor" gave him permission.

Another individual told me a sponsee is never supposed to address his or her sponsor by name, but always by that "title," as if the sponsor is some kind of authority figure.

It really should not take much effort to realize how destructive and damaging these types of situations can be-- especially if a sponsor is untrustworthy, delights in having power over others, and/or has a "personal agenda."

"WHAT PART OF 'NO' DON'T YOU UNDERSTAND?!"

Unfortunately, by the time a super-intelligent friend advised me to use this line, the advice came too late. As it is a common problem within 12-Step programs, this issue cannot be stressed too strongly. Although I use the term "13th-Stepping" in the broadest sense-- referring to any situation in which "Oldtimers" take advantage of new people-- this section is devoted to the more common usage of the term: NRA's who prey on people whom they perceive as vulnerable.

In the real world, people realize that other people have rights, and generally respect other people's rights-- including the right to say 'No.' While this knowledge is not as common within the programs, there is an additional factor that needs to be addressed. In the real world, turning someone down is nothing more nor less than asserting your free will; and, even at its worst, would be taken as nothing more than a personal rejection. However, while you may find this type of experience in the programs, you may also find something much worse.

One expert in the field uses the term "pathologicals." This term is defined as "mentally disturbed" and/or a "diseased mind." One reason such an individual does not take 'no' for an answer is such an individual does not even see it as a personal rejection, but as you asserting your free-will rights which the individual fully believes you do not have and should not have.

Amongst the sickest NRA's, not only does nothing matter but their own wishes, nothing even exists except their own wishes. Their sense of entitlement extends to a sense of entitlement over other human beings.

Using the word 'no' or its variations in response to an NRA *will* result in retaliation. You may find yourself on the receiving-end of inappropriate anger, or of manipulations, or of other attacks. Amongst the mentally disturbed NRA's, no one has rights except themselves-- although the 'rights' they concoct are only in their own minds.

I had quite a few experiences with this subject.

One early experience I had occurred at the meetingplace where I first attended a meeting. A guy who was around my age asked if I would go out for coffee with him the next evening.

The next evening, however, he said he really did not have time to go for coffee, and suggested we simply go to his place instead. When I replied that I was not interested, his reaction was outrageous: first his head, and then his entire body, shot backward, as if he had been hit; with his eyes bugged out, he hollered: "No? *NO*?!" as if he had never heard the word before. I shook my head, shrugged, and walked away.

Years later, after I was invited into a meeting in a different location, I had similar experiences with NRA's who did not seem to realize human beings have the right to say no. In each instance, my refusals resulted in either of two responses: there were NRA's who, like the first guy, became extremely angry; and others who asserted that my lack of interest in them was some kind of defect on my part.

The bottom line is NRA's both expect and demand *compliance.* Not only do they believe they have rights and others do not, and that their wishes count while others' do not, from my experiences these individuals are *accustomed to* compliance. Like the first guy, they respond to the word "No' and its variations as if they were totally unfamiliar with the concept.

THEY ARE NOT YOUR FRIENDS-- NOR ARE THEY CLASSIFIED ADS

I look back and wonder *"What in the universe was I thinking?!"* I suppose most people would have the same viewpoint: *"You stupid, stupid person, you!"* When it comes to that question and viewpoint, I have only one "defense": when I became involved with 12-Step programs, individuals in programs, and most especially NRA's, I had nearly four decades of life behind me-- decades and life that had consisted of a wide range of people, nearly all having one factor in common: they were *honest.* I will immediately clarify that: straightforward, direct, and without any hidden motives. The result: I made the mistake of assuming NRA's were the same way.

Long ago, I had a friend who assessed the situation very clearly. She said there are those who seek out vulnerable people, and then "swoop in like vultures." While there can be numerous ways a person can be vulnerable, this is one topic NRA's focused on.

In each instance, my main concern was I needed a job to support myself and my family. In each instance, NRA's lured-- or attempted to lure-- me into dangerous situations by offering jobs. The fact is in all the years I was involved with programs, there was only one person whose "job offer" was legitimate: the person had a business, asked for help with it, and was in no way scamming me. In the other instances, NRA's held 'jobs' like a carrot on a stick-- solely for the purpose of getting me into dangerous situations where I was flat-broke, had no options, and could not defend myself.

If I had any knowledge or experience with the underhanded ways of NRA's, I may have seen the situations for what they were, and walked in the opposite direction. I did not. The first two NRA's, for example, initially took different approaches *before* they zeroed in on my need for work.

The first NRA approached me with the desire for a 'relationship;' when I informed him this was not going to happen, he changed his tactic to presenting me with a wonderful job offer: I would be able to work in a field where I had plenty of experience, earn and save money, and move myself and my family back to California.

The second NRA, upon learning my young-adult son was away at an out-of-state college, began expressing great interest in my youngest child. Although I had no plans for moving at that particular time, she said she lived in a very nice area and that I should consider moving there. When I said I did not think it would be a good idea, she waited until I was desperately in need of a job, and then came up with a "job offer" to encourage me to do so.

These were only two examples of how NRA's, upon finding someone is in need, exploit that need for their own wrongful purposes. While these two examples involved NRA's whom I had never even met, many people have come forward with their own similar "horror stories" involving NRA's whom they had met in 12-Step meetings. These types of NRA's all have something they want-- and exploit whatever a person's need may be in order to make that person vulnerable.

"HONESTY": THE REAL WORLD VS. 12-STEP PROGRAMS

In the real world, honesty is positive. It is good for the individual person, and good for the people in his or her life. As someone who had lived for decades in the real world before stepping blindly into the quicksand of 12-Step programs, I learned the NRA use of this word is much different from the way it is used by the average population. More recently, I learned countless numbers of other people have had the same experiences.

In the real world, *honesty* reflects a person's attitudes toward, and interactions with, other people. It involves such attributes as presenting oneself as one actually is, being truthful in what one says, and being straightforward about one's motives.

In contrast, while NRA's lack these attributes, there is an additional, entirely different, angle on the subject. The approach NRA's take is that "no stone can be left unturned." It comes to an intentional violation of personal rights and personal dignity. Not only does it violate one's right to privacy, information that NRA's have no legitimate reason to have is often twisted to appear as if it were something entirely different, or used for gossip.

Completely dismissing what is and is not appropriate, this kind of pressure comes from individual NRA's, sponsors, and groups. If one does not comply, one is accused of ' not being honest' or 'not working the program.'

As one example, a woman who had discussed her most private issues with her sponsor was later horrified, stating her "Step 4" had been spread throughout the city by the next day.

As a second example, an individual who was in an Alcoholics Anonymous meeting stated, when it was his turn to 'share': "I'm a incest survivor- my sponsor told me I had to say that!"

Another example that occurred in an A.A. meeting: "I'm supposed to tell you all: I had sex last night!"

There are only two approaches to the subject of honesty that are legitimate in so-called recovery programs. First, there is the idea if a person hides a horrible secret, the guilt and other negative feelings may cause him or her to drink or use drugs again. Unfortunately, in all my years of involvement with programs, I never met *anyone* who felt guilt, shame, remorse, or regret over their destructive behaviors and actions. Second, there is the approach that one must be honest in one's dealings with others. Unfortunately, the NRA's were everything *but* honest. The majority were underhanded, manipulative liars.

The bottom line is within 12-Step programs, NRA's are clueless about honesty. Whether they are practicing underhandedness themselves, extracting information from others, or both, the true concept of honesty is something they have never learned.

LIVING IN THE PAST

It is one of those catch-all psychobabble terms that is frequently tossed around by individuals in 12-Step programs; yet, as with most such terms, it is usually misused and misunderstood. And, similar to other catch-all terms, it can be harmful.

When I first started meeting individuals who belonged to 12-Step programs, it was one of the first subjects that often left me shaking my head in disbelief: it was never a matter of anyone casually mentioning an incident, but rather their entire focus and concentration being on their *pasts*. Regardless of whether their stories contained an element of truth, were completely made up, or any other variation, I found individuals who made no real progress with 'recovery' consistently emphasized two themes: their childhoods, and their adolescent years.

Initially, the individuals I met were all in their thirties and forties-- yet childhood and the teenage years were virtually all they ever talked about. I duly noted all of the childhood experiences were about "abuse"-- real, imagined, or exaggerated; and the adolescent stories were all about sexual exploits-- real, imagined, or exaggerated. A number of points occurred to me: first, these topics were entirely inappropriate coming from individuals I had just met and barely knew; and second, they were entirely consumed by these subjects to the exclusion of everything else. Eventually I met others in the programs, ranging from people in their twenties to people in their late sixties-- all expressing the same theme: their *pasts*.

Actually, 12-Step literature does not promote this approach-- and even discourages it. They say if a person truly wishes to recover, he is to acknowledge his past for what it was, deal with it, and move on. Consequently, those who insist on rehashing and rehashing their childhoods and adolescent years not only do not make any real progress with recovery, they also do not make any progress with their lives in general.

Naturally, as with any topic pertaining to 12-Step programs, it becomes complicated and it becomes worse. NRA's who persist in this approach cannot recognize that the majority of the general population does not do this, and have no reason to do it. If a non-NRA does not persist in rehashing and rehashing his past, he is accused by NRA's as being "in denial," "not being honest," or even having "repressed memories." In addition, those who persist in this approach appear to not understand what it means. While non-NRA's are accused of "living in the past" if they enjoy music from a different era or mention an incident that occurred yesterday, they evidently do not grasp that their universal focus on childhood and adolescence is what living in the past really means-- nor do they grasp that it is standing in the way of them effectively functioning and living in the present.

For many, the everyday world is something they deal with as little as possible. Whether their everyday worlds include jobs they hate, families they ignore, normies they resent, or any other average factor, the NRA approach is that the everyday world is little more than an inconvenience to cope with or dismiss so they can get back to what they feel is truly important: *the past.*

The repercussions of this approach affects everyone: the NRA, and everybody in his life. I am sure I am not unique in taking a very negative view of it all. Such individuals should make a concentrated effort to *grow up.* If there is something in their pasts they are truly unable to deal with, or if they are truly unable to function in the present, they need professional help-- not 12-Step programs where they are consistently amongst others making the same mistakes. The bottom line is whether they are actually unable to function appropriately in the present, or whether it is a matter of "choice," they are wasting and ruining their own lives-- and attempting to lead others to do the same.

THE ILLUSION OF REALITY

The most obvious and most relevant factor in an NRA's 'disease' is his "illusion of reality." While it is detrimental to the addict himself, it pales in comparison to the effect it has on other people who are in or around his life. It cannot be stressed too strongly that it is the primary factor which comes to mean you-- the "outsider," the "normie,"-- are "living in the addict's disease."

What is an addict's illusion of reality? One example is he defines "others" by the same means as he defines himself.

While some do this intentionally, with full knowledge of the facts, the majority of the NRA population simply have no other frame-of-reference. When they define other people and other people's situations in the same terms as they define themselves, they lack the ability to recognize, acknowledge, or process whatever is in front of them that is Normal.

"Everybody is an alcoholic! Everybody is an addict! Everybody has some kind of mental problems!" I have heard these outrageous statements from numerous NRA's in programs-- and it is this lack of touch with reality that stands between them and true recovery.

While some fall into this delusion through no fault of their own, and others subscribe to it with full knowledge of the facts, the result is the same: the inability or refusal to acknowledge the majority of the adult American population is indeed not like themselves.

Recent statistics show:
8% of American adults who have made alcohol a part of their lives are alcoholics;
4.9% of American adult women and 8.7% of American adult men are illegal-drug users;
approximately 6% of American adults have a serious mental illness;
approximately 1% of American females and 3% of American males have a sociopathic personality.
"Everybody"?

This is one subject in which "sticking to one's own kind" is detrimental. It validates one's own weaknesses and failings, by allowing the NRA's to continue with the delusion that "everybody" possesses those problems and histories.

What happens when "Normies" enter the picture? In some cases, the person is ostracized-- a normal person is seen as a threat. In other cases, a normal person is attacked: "You're in denial," "You're just not ready to see it," "You're lying." And, in yet other cases, NRA's go to great lengths to try to drag Normies down to their own level.

This is one clear sign of whether an alcoholic/addict is on the road to recovery, or whether he is not. Those who have a healthy grasp on reality are fully aware most people do not have the substance dependencies, mental problems, and lifestyle histories that they have. When NRA's merrily dance down denial road, they miss one extremely important point often quoted in the 12-Step programs: "It was your best thinking that got you here."

The entire mess can be summed up with a quote from a well-known singer: *"Like everybody else in the world, I do what I can get away with."*

This outrageous and far too common viewpoint is a lousy influence on younger generations, and it illustrates the denial of NRA's-- *everybody* approaches illegal drug and alcohol abuse in terms of 'what they can get away with'? Nope-- only the tiniest minority.

I have encountered two different angles on the 'everybody' illusion: there are NRA's who fully believe "everybody" is like a carbon-copy of themselves; and there are NRA's who are fully aware of differences, yet go out of their way to claim otherwise. In other words, for those in the former group it can be nothing more than an honest mistake, while those in the latter group intentionally lie.

One of the many examples I encountered: an NRA approached me about a new habit I had acquired. He said "I saw you *always wearing those sunglasses-* so I figured you'd been *smoking crack."* I was beyond 'offended'-- I was absolutely *livid* that someone had thought I was a drug user. Not only had I never smoked crack, I'd never even *seen* the drug.

The truth: I'd had an eye infection, and was using eye drops; because of this, my eyes were very sensitive to light, so I'd borrowed a pair of sunglasses and wore them both indoors and outdoors until the infection cleared up.

Yet-- to an NRA, the only possible explanation for a person wearing sunglasses was *drug use.*

If it is not bad enough when this occurs with NRA's who simply do not know the facts and misinterpret unintentionally, it shows something entirely different when NRA's do know the facts and elect to "call it something else." One of the many examples of this was an NRA who, upon noting my preference for not wearing shoes, took watching where I was going so I would not step on sharp objects to begin telling people it meant I had "self-esteem issues." A second idiotic example involved my habit of going into a rest room after eating-- the basic manners of not using toothpicks at a table where people were eating, and excusing oneself to do so in a rest room, was gossiped about as 'she must have an eating disorder.'

Over the years, I have experienced many situations like this-- where individuals misinterpreted what they *thought* they saw, or what they *thought* was going on, based on *their* addictions, lifestyles, and problems, rather than on the facts.

WHAT IS A DRY-DRUNK?

"Dry-drunk" is another clear sign that individuals do not always "work the program." To clarify: dry-drunk does not simply mean an alcoholic is not drinking; it does not mean a person is not attending 12-Step meetings; dry-drunk is a term often used to describe a person whose attitudes, beliefs, behaviors, thought-processes, and lifestyle have not improved or changed, regardless of how long he has abstained from drinking. It is equally appropriate when describing a drug-user.

Dry-drunk is often described as *"the three I's"*: Irresponsibility, Immaturity, and Impulsiveness. A 12-Step program also uses the term "self-will."

Dry-drunk is a sign that the NRA is not taking the necessary steps in his own behalf to leave his destructive ways behind and put himself on the path of true recovery. It does not matter how many years or decades he has kept alcohol or drugs out of his life, or how long he has claimed membership in a program-- when he is continuing to exist with the same attitudes, beliefs, thoughts, and behaviors he existed with in the past, "recovery" is like a book that has never even been opened.

"SUFFER THE LITTLE CHILDREN"

My point of view is human beings *matter*-- and children matter the *most*. It is for this reason that while every section of this book has been difficult to write, this topic is the most difficult. Although the infant referred to as Baby R. was the only fatality I was aware of (and I will stress: the only one I was *aware* of), the years of 12-Step programs brought to my attention many other youngsters who were abused, neglected, abandoned-- and it does not even begin to address the countless numbers of youngsters who suffer greatly due to parents who are still actively addicted.

The bottom line is youngsters suffer when adults are actively addicted-- and many continue to suffer when active addiction turns into quote, "recovery," unquote.

I have heard countless members of 12-Step programs speak of their children-- or, more to the point, their *absent* children. While drugs or alcohol abuse initially took priority over their children's well-being, the *Programs* essentially replaced substances as the priority. When asked about their children, one remark was common: *"They're being well taken care of."* I learned this meant taken care of by someone else-- virtually anyone else-- other than by the parents themselves. Youngsters were dumped on relatives, the foster care system, or whatever resource was available. There were those who lost their children because of their drug or alcohol abuse-- and those who willingly abandoned them. A statement by one NRA clarifies the shift in priorities is not making one's children one's priority: "I'm glad my kids were taken away-- because now I have more time for my Meetings!" This NRA, as many others, had simply shifted her priority to the 12-Step programs-- rather than her own kids.

Another common scenario I have heard numerous times involved middle-aged males who claimed they did not even know how many children they had. True to program form, none were making any attempts to "make amends"-- either to the children or the children's mothers. I have heard those who virtually bragged about such situations, as if they were examples of their misguided sense of masculinity, and others who brushed it off as "the past."

Also true to program form was the degree of resentment "dead-beats" assigned to their own children. Specifically, after abandoning children, they could not grasp why they were unable to successfully manipulate the children to take them back into their lives. Without any attempt to make up for abandonment, they believed the now-adult children should accept money and expensive gifts as a way to be bribed into "forgive and forget."

Children are vulnerable and impressionable-- not only one's own children, but children in general. It should not come as a surprise that individuals who claim membership in programs without doing any of the "footwork" do not take vulnerable, impressionable children into consideration when they claim they are "recovering" addicts/alcoholics. Those who use "Step 5" as nothing more than a platform for bragging about their numerous wrongs do not look at wrongs-- or the people they have harmed.

One NRA, for example, "shared" about how he had grossly harmed a number of young children. First, he "shared" about how he had abused his girlfriend's children-- that he had sexually abused the woman's toddler-aged girls, and had beaten her toddler-aged son almost to the point of unconsciousness. However-- he claimed the little girls "actually liked" being molested, and the little boy "wasn't hurt too badly."

Second, he "shared" that he had raped a four-year-old boy. However-- he claimed he'd stopped in the middle of the rape because the child's screaming bothered him.

Needless to say, none of these incidents were anything he felt the need to "make amends" for. Similar to Bear, he believed claiming membership in 12-Step programs automatically absolved him of any guilt, had no remorse for the effects his sick behavior had had on the children involved-- and, similar to Bear, was never held accountable for what he did. He simply felt free to "share" about it-- and believed nobody had the right to judge him.

Another individual, claiming long "clean and sober" time, made the outrageous statement: *"Kids- some live, some die, and there's really nothing anybody can do about it."*

In addition to abandonment, neglect, and various other forms of abuse, I have known individuals who used drugs with their young children, drank with their young children, and even prodded preteens to become sexually active. It does not seem to matter whether the parents are actively addicted or claiming they are "in recovery"-- children continue to suffer. Adult-aged NRA's who did so well at fouling up their own lives move on to encourage youngsters to take on the same behaviors.

The messiest subject I ever encountered with the NRA population was the contrast. On a totally ludicrous note, I used to figuratively beat myself up occasionally, truly feeling I had been a failure as a parent because of two specific topics: first, when my kids were growing up, I could never afford to take them to Disneyland; and second, we never had a family vacation. Because of these two topics, I actually felt that I had failed my kids.

Instead, though, I gave them a solid base on which to grow into healthy stable adults. In addition to making sure they never went without anything they needed, I gave them my time and guidance. And when it comes down to it, this is the main reason NRA's resented me-- sometimes to the point of all-out attacks, and worse.

LOST HEARTS

Of the wide range of problems experienced by people who become involved with programs, one of the most heartbreaking and devastating is the destruction of marriages and other important relationships. I never cease being stunned whenever I hear people relate their experiences. The issues come from a number of different angles. And, whether it is the individual himself/herself who belongs to a program, or whether it is his/her spouse or partner, the experiences and effects are equally horrible.

On one side, there are those who have lost their spouses or partners directly due to the behavior of others in the programs. Some include program members who have no reservations about initiating affairs or one-night-stands with people who are married or in committed relationships. In other instances, sponsors and other members urge individuals who are in relationships to "dump" their spouses or partners-- pushing them to believe their "significant others" are "bad for them," "unhealthy or sick," or that it is a "codependent relationship."

On the other side there is the program itself. While you may be familiar with the concept that one's "sobriety must come first," this is usually not the issue at all. It is often not about individuals who are teetering on the edge and need 24/7 help to get clean and sober or stay clean and sober. What it *is* about is *The Program* completely taking over a person's time, energy, efforts, and focus.

You may be tempted to look at the subject in terms of "a meeting takes approximately an hour-- so you have approximately twenty-three hours left in that day" to live your own life and tend to your own priorities. Unfortunately, for many, *The Program becomes* their lives and their priorities. Whether a person attends a meeting each day, once per week, or on some other timetable, the *remainder* of his time is also consumed by his Program. When he is not in a meeting, he is on the phone with his sponsor or other members, "hanging out" with his "social circle" of program members, participating in Program activities, and so forth. Many who become involved with the programs soon see their Program as the be-all and end-all of their entire lives, their entire existence.

For this reason, marriages and other personal relationships come apart-- often permanently-- even when it does not involve affairs or meddling. When a Program takes over one's life, there is no time, energy, effort, or focus left for one's partner.

These kinds of experiences have been related by many, many people. I, personally, did not have any experiences like this, but my own experiences were no less heartbreaking. I am not referring to incidents that were pointless, destructive, and generally misunderstood by others. Instead, I am referring to learning the hard way-- twice-- that truly caring for another human being, and 12-Step programs, are a disastrous combination. The bottom line: addiction *wins*-- regardless of any other facts, regardless of the particular situation. And what that comes to mean is those of us who are not addicts or alcoholics, and have no legitimate need for a 'recovery program,' we are the ones who lose.

The first situation occurred well over a year after I boarded that bus on Chestnut Street. When I became acquainted with my first 12-Step meetings, I also become acquainted with many people who participated in the meetings, most of whom had been doing so for a long time. One person, who had many good qualities in general, had a characteristic I did not see in much of the 12-Step population: he was *respectful*. First, he was respectful toward *me*-- from his attitudes to his behavior; and second, he was respectful in terms of my family-- understanding they were *my* family, and not there for anyone else to "barge in and take over."

The problem: when I say his addiction "won," I'm not talking about drugs; I'm referring to the way he approached and viewed *The Program*. Not only did he believe it was the answer to everything, even worse, he believed Oldtimers were automatically honest, trustworthy, and on the right track simply because they *were* Oldtimers-- and regardless of what kinds of underhanded, dishonest, abusive practices they were engaging in.

So it came to losing a solid-gold human being-- because when it came to *The Program*, he could not see reality.

Nearly five years later, it was almost like "history repeating itself," although there were differences. A person I met that summer also had qualities and characteristics that were uncommon in the programs: he was *genuine*-- there was not a phony or dishonest bone in his body; and he was *kind*.

The problem: the fact was we lived in two different worlds. For either of us to try to enter or become a part of the other's world would have been a complete disaster. My "world" was family and stability; his was addiction and recovery. Neutral ground, where we were "friends," was the only sensible conclusion. As such, he never came to my home, never met anyone in my family; and, to the best of my ability, as much as possible, I avoided the "people, places, and things" with whom he associated.

There is also the other side of the issue. Quite a few years ago, without bringing up specific situations or specific people, I happened to mention a part it to a longtime acquaintance in a 12-Step program. Unfortunately, as the qualities and characteristics those two men had were qualities and characteristics I was familiar with, and what I saw in the majority of 12-Step members were characteristics I was not familiar with with prior to programs, I could not even find the correct word. While the word I said to the acquaintance was "aggressive," the word I was actually looking for was "arrogant"-- and, in fact, both sum up the majority of NRA's.

Amongst the majority of NRA's-- male and female, regardless of age-- I have never seen such *arrogant* individuals in my entire life. To make matters worse, it's one of the many subjects on which it is impossible to get through to them. In one instance, for example, I chided an NRA for being "nervy;" the individual acted as if it were a *compliment!* There is nothing positive about being nervy, arrogant, not knowing one's place-- and it is certainly not a compliment.

The bottom line: whether a person belongs to a program, or whether one's "significant other" or prospective significant other does, it is a surefire path to heartbreak. I cannot even imagine the misery of those who related about their marriages and other personal relationships being broken up or destroyed completely because of the programs, but the two experiences I had were bad enough.

It all comes down to an accurate assessment by a long-ago acquaintance. She said for any relationship to work, both parties involved must have the same *values*. I did not think much about it at the time, because before I became involved with programs, most people I knew in general did have the same values as myself.

In the programs, though, it is usually much different-- from right vs. wrong to personal rights and dignity, and the entire lifestyle. If you want to be used, treated like a doormat, watch someone attempt to take away your rights and dignity, *The Program* is for you. For me, though, it was not.

"PRINCIPLES BEFORE PERSONALITIES"

One statement you may hear in the Programs is *"Principles Before Personalities."* You can look at it as similar to the comment I heard at a New Year's Eve party: *"Everybody deserves a chance."* In actuality, though, you may find something entirely different if you become involved in the programs. You may find a core group of NRA's who feel they have the authority to determine who deserves a chance and who does not. From my experiences, these groups can seem like Junior High cliques-- those who are 'in,' versus those who do not count at all.

One example was an individual who appeared to be mildly retarded; after he 'shared' in meetings, louder and more obnoxious members would make snotty remarks about what he said, and laughed at him. Another example was a guy who could not manage to kick his drug habit; an Oldtimer approached him, handed him some money, and told him to go buy himself some crack. Another example was an individual who rarely failed to bring liquor with him when he attended meetings, and drank during the meetings; while no one commented about his drinking, they verbally attacked him because he didn't do 'shares' during the meetings. Yet another example involved a young person who was gay; not only did some of the Oldtimers laugh at him when he spoke in meetings, one member went as far as to say 'If he comes near me or speaks to me, I'll beat his head into the ground.'

The older they are, the worse they are-- meetings, and after-meetings gatherings are like popularity clubs for middle-aged adolescents. They believe it is their place to decide who matters and who does not-- with no concern whether 'unpopular' people never manage to get clean and/or sober, or stay clean and/or sober, or whether their lives fall completely apart, or whether they die. It is not an exaggeration-- I witnessed situations that involved 'unpopular' people dying, with Oldtimers laughing, smirking, or shrugging. As the older generation used to say: *Some people simply have no respect for human life.* .

REBELS WITHOUT A CAUSE

One of the errors made by those who do not move toward recovery is the inability to grasp and apply one of the most important parts of recovery: to see the Past for what it was, deal with it, and move on. Consequently, you have countless numbers of NRA's in all adult age groups, existing in the present day as nothing but a reaction to their "pasts."

One aspect of this can label them "rebels without a cause." They glom onto various experiences of their childhoods, and spend their adult-aged lives attempting to "turn the tables" on those experiences. One example involved an individual who, nearly forty years later, was still reacting to an experience he'd had as a young child: as a youngster, there had been one isolated incident in which an adult had yelled at him for wearing a purple shirt, saying it was not appropriate for boys to wear purple.

Throughout his entire adult life, he refused to buy a single article of clothing or even a household item unless it was purple.

There have also been numerous instances in which NRA's in various adult age groups stated they had not been allowed to be 'demonstrative' when they were children; in each instance, they followed their childhood stories by exclaiming they *will* be that way *now*-- whether those on the receiving-end are o.k. with it or not. These are only a few examples of how many continue to live in their pasts-- even when it involves others in the present day who are not o.k. with it at all.

Second, they are ridiculously hung-up on the topic of age. They constantly ask other people the inappropriate question "how old are you?" and constantly feel the need to inform others of their own ages. While they act like young adolescents in adult-sized bodies, their vocabularies often reflect it-- constantly yammering about 'when I was seventeen,' or 'when I lived in Florida,' or 'I'm acting like I'm sixteen!' Not only do they not grasp that normal people their age have nothing in common with them or their "lifestyles," many NRA's prefer the company of kids because they cannot relate to normal adults.

Third, the inability to feel, recognize, process, and express normal human thoughts and emotions is so extreme that there are actually 12-Step programs devoted to this problem. It should not be a surprise to hear that many are domestic abusers, because anger and self-will both win-out when individuals do not know what 'normal' is. However, the lack of empathy likely occurred long before drugs and alcohol abuse became a part of their lives. In every story I've been told, the foundation for this problem began in early childhood. Every human being-- but especially little children-- needs to know they count, needs to know they matter. When neglect in early childhood runs rampant, adult-aged individuals with no empathy toward other people is the result-- with or without drugs and alcohol.

The first experience I had with this was many years ago. In this particular instance, I was very ill, and an NRA who was present later said he fully believed I would die during the night. However, what was his response to believing I would die?: he said he left to watch television so he would not have to think about it. When I replied by saying if he'd thought I was ill enough to die he should have called a doctor or paramedics, his voice turned cold and he answered: "Waaa waaa, it's all about you, isn't it?"

I have heard from quite a few other former program members who had been 'hit' with that line; if one either expresses a legitimate need, or asserts oneself, that line is used in an attempt to make you feel as if you are selfish and self-centered. The reason: NRA's are like unsocialized little children who have never outgrown the belief that they are the center of the universe, and that other people's needs and preferences do not count.

While that was my first experience with this subject, it was far from the last. I learned: when the shit hits the fan, count on everyone to vanish; if you express a need or ask for help, be prepared to be ridiculed or brushed off. One of the most recent examples involved a minor medical emergency for which I needed medical attention; one of the EMTs looked at me and asked: "What kind of neighbors do you have, anyway, that nobody would even drive you to the hospital?" Similarly, I met the same response of no response at all when I reached out to a number of NRA's for help with a serious situation a few years ago: no one I left messages for ever returned my messages, and the one individual I approached in person simply gave me a blank stare.

These are the addicts and alcoholics who have been products of their environments. Environments where little children are forced to fend for themselves, ridiculed or punished if they have a need, expected to be completely obedient yet completely unbothersome, are environments where individuals do not become human beings with compassion and concern for others.

From what I have seen, heard, and experienced, these factors are even more relevant than drug and alcohol abuse. While psychobabble tells them to 'not stuff their feelings,' their normal feelings were essentially obliterated long before they began drinking and using drugs. In fact, it is quite likely that this is one reason many began drinking and using drugs in the first place-- the idea that normal thoughts and feelings are not to be acknowledged and expressed, they are to be shut down and shut off.

One may be tempted to think of Adolph Hitler's "goal" of turning human beings into emotionless animals-- and the comparison would not be very far off.

A saying that seems to be quite popular amongst NRA's is *"You can't go along to get along."* The way this would be approached in the real world is not the same as the NRA approach. To average people, all it would mean is one should not "follow the crowd" in order to fit in when what "the crowd" is doing is wrong.

While that is a logical approach, the NRA approach is not. Instead, it is not about doing the right thing when confronted with opposition, but going out of one's way to be difficult, uncooperative, and different. Whether it comes to breaking laws or rules solely to prove the point that they can get away with it, or being obnoxious and difficult solely because they *can*, it can be described as pointless rebellion that has no place in mature people's lives, and would rarely have a place in younger people's lives.

Rebelling for the sake of rebelling is something I have found very common in the NRA population. Whether it is in terms of laws, society's expectations, interpersonal relationships, or some other arena, the theme is "because I *can*," "because I can *get away with it*," and "nobody can tell *me* what to do!" Not only is it an immature stance, it has the potential of being destructive.

From what NRA's related during my 12-Step program involvement, it was what they started out with early in life, carried through active addiction, and never changed. NRA's who never developed standards and values continue to sabotage their own lives-- and wreak havoc on everyone around them. They simply never learned there is a difference between what is reasonable and what is unjust, nor did they learn there is a difference between a right and a whim. When you have countless numbers of NRA's in various adult age groups, it can make 12-Step programs very messy.

Because of my background, this was one of the many issues on which I often "butted heads" with NRA's in the programs. As my growing-up years involved always having a

70

"say," I never felt any need to rebel for the sake of rebelling, nor to be difficult solely to prove any points. At home, in school, and in the community, it was nothing more nor less than following rules that were reasonable and sensible, and speaking up whenever I disagreed with something.

One example comes to mind. With biology as one section of my ninth-grade science class, one task we students were expected to perform was dissecting a frog. I told the teacher I was not going to do this-- I was not queasy, did not have any particular fondness for frogs, but simply felt unnecessary killing was wrong. When I related this to the teacher, he looked at me as if I were an idiot: "But the frog is already dead!" he said. I politely replied that if I did not dissect the frog, it would be one less frog that would have to be killed-- that he could either give it to another student, or send it back.

My viewpoint was this was a ninth-grade science class, not a college pre-med, so there was no legitimate reason for the dissections. Upon realizing I was serious, and not about to budge, he told me if I would not do the task I would have to write a very long, detailed report on the bubonic plague instead. I willingly wrote the report, and gave it to him.

The point: people who are not naturally obnoxious or troublesome are usually taken seriously when we *do* take a stand for something. Unfortunately, in the NRA world, this is not considered a positive attribute. One is expected to either blindly and silently comply-- even if something is wrong-- or go out of one's way to be obnoxious and difficult, even if there is no reason for it.

Although there were many situations that I either fell into or was sucked into because I had no idea what I was getting into, and no idea how to deal with, my refusal to blindly and silently "go along to get along" never ceased to irk NRA's. If a person has his or her own mind, the ability to make sound judgments, and the strength and courage to stand for what is right, these attributes that are positive in the real world lead to a whole host of negativity in the NRA world.

As examples, we can contrast these situations. As a thirteen-year-old student, I had no trouble standing my ground with a school teacher, telling him I would not do something that I felt was wrong. In the programs, however, you will find NRA's who, despite rebelling for the sake of rebelling, refuse to acknowledge that people have their own minds, adhere to standards and values, and will not "go along to get along" even when ordered to do so.

DARKNESS

One of the creepiest things I learned about dealing with the NRA population is you often have no way of knowing whether the odd things they say are intentional lies, contain some element of truth, are mental delusions, or are delayed drug flashbacks. I learned the only way you can ever know for sure is if someone else who has the facts can tell you-- and, of course, this is unlikely to happen very often.

One of the weirdest examples was a guy who, for years, had been telling everyone who would listen that he witnessed his father shoot his mother to death. He described the crime in detail, point by point. Not only had he related this story to many people-- it truly seemed as if he believed it himself. He was completely stunned when he was presented with a copy of the death certificate, showing that she'd died in the hospital of natural causes, with these facts later being verified by someone who had been present.

In another instance, a guy talked about the horrible damage caused to members of his family by "nuclear testing" in the area where they had lived. An informed source later stated no such "nuclear testing" had ever occurred in that area. The tale reminded me of another NRA, who insisted his mother and father were each other's brother and sister; and yet another NRA, who claimed his brother was actually his son.

In yet another instance, an individual related that in his early childhood he'd been sexually abused-- by his mother, father, stepmother, stepfather, uncle, and family friend. As he was one of the first people I met who belonged to the programs, I did not know what to make of it-- until I later started hearing similar stories from other alcoholics/addicts.

In another instance, a young woman also claimed she had been "sexually abused" by virtually everyone she had ever known. Familiar with this young woman's history, it was one of my first encounters with this kind of "darkness"-- because I knew none of the incidents she related could possibly have happened.

I have heard outrageous stories about abuse, sexual abuse, murder, cults, baby sacrifices, other instances of violence, and similar tales. While there have been numerous instances in which I had no way of knowing whether there was any truth in the stories, in the majority of cases there was not. While there should be compassion and hope for those who experienced horrible things, it bears noting the majority of "stories" you may hear from the NRA population are not true at all. Whether someone is "playing the victim" in order to make other people feel sorry for him, or is simply too messed up to know the difference between fact and fiction, it is wise to take any outrageous stories with "a grain of salt."

When I was a young adult, I had a few friends who engaged in a practice I called "fabricating." Their general approach was to make up stories to make themselves look important. However, while I found their habits to be annoying, there was nothing beyond their desire to look "big." The NRA population, though, seemed to have an entirely different "agenda"-- looking back, the purpose of their fabrications was to see if the listener was gullible enough to believe the tales.

Examples I heard from NRA's: one NRA stated she had been present at, and witnessed, the fatal car crash that took the life of actress Jayne Mansfield; one NRA claimed it was actually a friend of his who had written one of the famous songs of the rock group Fleetwood Mac; one NRA stated he was in a gang that murdered people, cut them open, and ate their hearts; one NRA said to scare him when he had done something wrong, his father took him to a top-secret institution that housed beings who were the consequences of breeding between humans and various animals. And these are only a few of the tales I heard from NRA's-- along the line of 'if you're gullible enough to believe this, you're gullible enough to believe anything.'

To make matters worse, there was yet another part of the darkness that never failed to be a problem: NRA's who fabricate, lie, and tell tall stories, do not believe other people when the other people are telling the truth. You can say something about yourself, and whether it is something basic and minor or something important, and an NRA will insist you are lying. To the NRA population, it seems like The Truth does not exist.

"THE YARDSTICK"

Frankly, I think it was one of the most difficult-- or even the most difficult, aspects of my involvement with 12-Step programs and involvements with members of those programs. I have reached the conclusion that it is human nature for people to base their own conclusions on what they are familiar with, even when what they are familiar with has nothing to do with a particular situation. In other words, people tend to judge others based on their own 'yardsticks.'

Although this has been a distressing issue ever since I became involved with the Programs, and covered virtually everyone I met in the Programs, in most cases there was no malicious intent on the parts of the program members. They simply believed whatever was true for themselves was equally true for everybody. And it was yet another example of 'if you tell the truth, you will offend them-- and some will not believe you at all.' Why do some not believe the truth? For no reason other than it is not in their own range of experiences. To use pop-psych terminology, it's not their 'reality.' I have known countless numbers of 12-Step program members who claimed they never knew anyone who did not have drug or alcohol problems, who did not have mental health issues, who did not have criminal histories; in other words, they had never known anyone who had had the lifestyle I have had throughout my life.

One particularly distressing example came from a guy who was somewhat older than myself. Reflecting on adult-aged kids, he sadly remarked "That is the way they punish us." The word 'us' bothered me, because the person was placing me in the category of individuals who did not spend their kids' growing-up years doing right by their kids.

A second example came from a middle-aged, female neighbor. I met this person as I was on my way out for the day, and she asked me what I was doing. When I replied I was going out to put in job applications, she acted as if it was something she had never heard before. "Why do you want to work- can't you get Disability?" When I replied that I was not disabled, she followed it with "Aren't you on meds- not *anything?*" In an area where individuals with drug and/or alcohol issues are deemed 'disabled,' put on psychiatric medication and given SSDI, she was only one of the many who could not seem to grasp that anyone was not in that category.

Drug and/or alcohol addiction, mental health issues, criminal histories, and the entire lifestyle that often accompanies it, set me apart from "others." If I said nothing, they jumped to the wrong conclusions, believing I was like them. But if I told the truth, they were 'offended.'

It led me to think about the area where I grew up, and all the people I knew in that particular area. For the most part, virtually everything about me, and virtually everything about my life, was one-hundred-percent average. In fact, there were only two subjects that set me apart as "different" from most of the locals: I did not own my own house, and I was not married. Other than those two subjects, I was exactly like everyone else: I had a clean, moral lifestyle, and my priority was my family.

Unfortunately, while the largest percentage of 12-Step program members did nothing more than base their conclusions on honest mistakes, there were NRA's who had an entirely different approach. Rather than believing something negative because they did not have the facts, they portrayed me to others in the most negative lights possible while being fully aware of the facts. In other words, the truth that I have led a clean, moral lifestyle with my family as my priority did not fit into their agenda. So they told lies, mainly focused on the lie that these 'truths' did not represent me at all.

When it comes down to it, there is only one 'truth' that I am concerned about, only one that matters. In assessing everything about myself and my life, there is one and only one reason members of my own family have just-cause to be angry. And that reason is that I exposed them to the 12-Step programs and horrible NRA's who belonged to those programs. Because of my mistake, we went from a stable life to years of ongoing, constant chaos. We went from a 'world' consisting of decent people to a world of twisted NRA's who had an ax to grind, wrongful motives, and no conscience about how their behaviors affected us. Not only have nearly two decades of my life been in the quicksand, so have the lives of my family members and my family itself. And when it comes down to it, that is the only mistake that I need forgiveness for-- for it is the only way I wronged my family. Long ago, a 12-Step program member said "God forgives us, and gives us a second chance"-- but what about members of my own family- will they ever be able to take that approach?

To clarify: unlike NRA's I have known, I did not spend my kids' growing-up years using drugs, abusing alcohol, wh*ring around, or claiming they were 'well taken care of- by someone else.' I was a decent human being and a good parent who never abused or neglected my family. Unfortunately, though, when young people are influenced by the ever-present world of NRA's, they may not necessarily remember the way it was-- the way I was, the way our lives were-- before we all fell into the quicksand.

THE DARKEST PART OF THE QUICKSAND

My "formal' experience with 12-Step programs was minimal: in one location, I attended a meeting to celebrate an acquaintance's birthday; in a different location, an NRA with her own personal motives drew me into her 12-Step group; and in the other location, I was "invited in for a cup of coffee," without even knowing it was a 12-Step meeting. Consequently, the majority of my 12-Step program experiences were with individual people who were members of programs. Because of this, I initially assumed the negativity I experienced was solely the workings of individual people, and had little to do with the 12-Step programs. Eventually, though, I learned otherwise-- from many people who had suffered horrible experiences during their more formal participation in the programs.

There was, however, an exception. While I, and many others, have experienced countless situations in which NRA's attempted various forms of psychological manipulations, there was an instance in which I encountered this from an actual 12-Step program. I happened to come across some literature for the program, specifically a brochure that had a long, long list of topics. Each of these topics was purported to be "symptoms" of sexual abuse. Two items that were listed come to mind: the brochure advised the reader to ask himself if he had ever experienced nightmares, and if he feared death. I'd venture to say there has probably never been anyone alive who never had a nightmare, and very few people who look at death in a positive light.

As with anything pertaining to 12-Step programs, it gets more complicated: while the literature advised readers to consider anything on the list to be signs that they had been sexually abused, they took it further: one should not say 'sexual abuse,' but instead should say 'incest.' And the literature was very clear that the dictionary-definition of the word was irrelevant.

The point: all it can take is *planting seeds of doubt* for a person to begin questioning his or her own memory or memories.

While planting seeds of doubt is one of the most common forms of psychological manipulation in 12-Step programs, it was the only time I'd seen it coming from a program itself rather than coming from individuals. This particular program went further to claim that any person can be the victim of sexual abuse at any point in time after they are *conceived*. Yes, you read that correctly: they claimed a newly-conceived embryo in its mother's uterus can be "sexually abused."

While any form of sexual abuse is horrible and must be condemned, I believe this and other stories I have heard on the subject makes something crystal clear: a large percentage of stories about sexual abuse that one hears within 12-Step programs are not based on reality. I will go further to say it is probably the main reason statistics covering sexual abuse are so high-- not only have there been unscrupulous mental health practitioners leading people to believe abuse that did not happen actually did happen, but 12-Step programs are a breeding-ground for the same issue.

Not only was the longtime "cult-classic" *"Sybil"* exposed as a fraud, and legitimate mental health professionals exposing "repressed memories," "multiple personalities," etc., as largely frauds, celebrities began attention-seeking tales to confuse the general public even further. As one example, well over a decade ago, a popular celebrity came forward to say *no one can know* whether or not he or she was sexually abused-- that if anyone presents the question, the only 'truthful' answers are either "Yes," or "I don't know." More recently, another popular celebrity came forward with the story of her ongoing, adult-aged "incestuous relationship" with her father. While most of her family members refuted it as an obvious lie, she said her 12-Step program urged her to approach it in terms of how a parent has "power" over an adult.

Obviously I have compassion for any individual who was ever sexually abused. However, with nearly two decades of experience with 12-Step programs and their members, I have found in the majority of cases "childhood sexual abuse" or "incest" did not happen. The previous section where an NRA claimed six different members of his family "sexually abused" him during his early childhood is only one example. This kind of darkness is not like individuals who went through their lives struggling with the after-effects of childhood sexual abuse, but instead, individuals in various adult age groups claiming they were 'just now remembering' incidents.

There are people who are so messed up from drug and alcohol abuse that they do not know fact from fiction, as well as those who are prodded to use terms such as 'abuse' and 'sexual abuse' when they are not appropriate, but there are also NRA's who use insidious forms of psychological manipulation for their own purposes. What I experienced were NRA's who wanted to make others weak and vulnerable-- and there is no surer way to accomplish this goal than to lead you to doubt your own mind and memories- or to claim a person is 'so *sick'* that he or she *'does not even remember'* horrible incidents that never occurred.

My experiences with these types of NRA's involved the pressure to believe 'abuse' or 'sexual abuse' is *the answer to* everything, and *the reason for* everything. One absolutely ludicrous example involved my poor math skills. Without the facts, it might seem odd that while I did quite well with algebra and geometry in High School, I'd never mastered some of the basics of arithmetic. I didn't think much about it until I had a couple of conversations with an acquaintance on subjects covering American history. At first, it was a little surprising to find the acquaintance knew more about certain aspects of American history than I knew.

The facts: during the period of time those topics were being taught in my elementary school, I may as well not have gone to school at all. Actually, there were quite a few times that I didn't. The reason: during that period of time, I had one-- and only one-- concern: my much-older brother was in the United States Marine Corps, serving in Vietnam.

When I was in school, I could not have cared less about arithmetic, American history, or anything else that was being taught. In addition, I became troublesome to the teachers, and, although I had been an Honor student, my grades fell to just barely passing. When I was not at school-- including staying home for this one particular purpose-- I was glued to the television watching news reports, or listening to it on the radio.

It became worse when my brother was reported Missing in Action; and it became worse when one of his friends was killed in a horrible tragedy in Vietnam. The reason I stayed home from school whenever I could was the fear I would come home to find "two Marines in dress-blues" at the door-- the way the military informed "the family" that they had lost their loved one.

Yet-- doing poorly in school, not learning those basics, was pounced on by NRA's as alleged "proof" that I'd been "abused" or "sexually abused." It was one of the many examples of how NRA's "rewrite people's life histories" in an attempt to cause people to believe situations occurred that never occurred at all.

On this subject, or the subject of psychological manipulation in general, I was initially tempted to say it does not matter whether NRA's have the facts-- the truth about any given situation-- or not. After thinking about my experiences, though, I concluded that is not exactly the case. Instead, it is more like the more facts they have about any given situation, the more information they have to twist, change, alter. This is why, whether an NRA asks for information or demands it, it is a good idea to consider their motives.

For the sickest individuals in the programs-- those who attempt to weaken others with psychological manipulations-- this topic is often the base-line from which they start. One example, which showed the individual was completely disregarding what his own program teaches, was a statement that most women who become alcoholics do so because of sexual abuse. Actually, what A.A. teaches is people-- female or male-- become alcoholics because they have a "bodily allergy" to alcohol. A second example was a statement that *most women* have been raped-- followed with *most women* have been raped *multiple times.*

These are only two of the many examples I have heard on this topic. It should not take much to realize how anyone who is impressionable for any reason, upon hearing these kinds of statements, would begin to question or doubt their own memories-- the "seeds of doubt" of *'it has happened to so many others- perhaps it happened to me, too.'* And these seeds of doubt are exactly what NRA's with ulterior motives count on.

Near the beginning of this book, I stated I had been involved in three 12-Step programs. While the first two were designed for people who had "substance abuse issues," the third did not apply to me, either. This third 12-Step program was one of numerous programs designed for individuals who had survived sexual abuse-- specifically, incest.

While it is extremely important-- and potentially dangerous-- I did not address the subject when I first began writing this book. The reason: this particular 12-Step program takes "anonymity" to an entirely different level than Alcoholics Anonymous and Narcotics Anonymous. While these two well-known programs emphasize the anonymity of their members, the program for sexual abuse survivors places its highest priority on the program itself. In fact, even its website threatens lawsuits if anything about the program is mentioned anywhere.

This is not o.k.-- silencing people is not o.k.

Looking back, it seems the main reason for this approach is this particular program intentionally tries to 'recruit' people who do not belong there-- primarily by deception. I will relate my own experiences later in this book, but I will not be relating the name of this program. However, unless a program is fully aware their approaches are underhanded and deceptive, they would not be putting "gag orders" on their members or former members.

Much of "the darkest part of the quicksand" can be summed up with a subject that has been highly controversial and extensively researched in recent decades: *False Memory.* As virtually every adult in America who was alive and tuned in to the news and media in the mid-1980s was aware of, the incident that brought this topic to the public light was the McMartin case in California. Based on allegations brought forth by one disturbed parent, it involved years of investigations and criminal trials. While the McMartin school staff was eventually cleared of the accusations against them, many lives were destroyed-- from the reputations of those who were wrongfully accused, to children who later realized they had been led to 'remember' incidents that had not occurred. In another widely-publicized case, a California father was incarcerated for six years before he was eventually cleared of the charges against him: twenty years after the death of her best friend, his daughter claimed to have experienced a 'memory'-- a 'flashback'-- in which she had 'seen' her father rape and murder the little girl. It is yet another example of the destruction that can occur-- to human beings, families, lives-- from false memories. And after these cases led to nationwide hysteria on the subject of sexual abuse, decades of research concluded 'recovered' memories are very rarely based in reality.

By far, the most accurate assessment on the subject has come from Elizabeth F. Loftus, PhD., who has done an extensive amount of research on human memory, and produced a wealth of articles and books. A statement from her UCIrvine faculty page: *memories can be changed by things that we are told.*

Within the context of 12-Step programs, though, there is a difference. While false memory is often the result of tactics by unscrupulous mental health practitioners, NRA's in the 12-Step programs have no such credentials. Instead, many use what they learn through years or decades in the programs for their own wrongful purposes-- and, in fact, some 12-Step literature actually warns newcomers and other members about this issue.

"Memories can be changed by things that we are told"-- leading questions, individuals being in suggestible states, NRA's claiming they have 'special knowledge' that the individuals do not have about themselves, and the caution to 'not trust' oneself or anyone else, are some of the most common examples.

We can begin with an average newcomer to a 12-Step program. First, such an individual is not likely to be physically or psychologically at his or her best-- a newcomers is likely to be struggling with the physical and psychological effects of longterm alcohol or drug abuse. Second, such an individual is likely to be desperate for help-- desperate for someone he or she can trust. These issues make such a person an ideal candidate for altering memories, changing memories, planting false memories. While no one is immune to these tactics, individuals who have no idea what they are up against are especially vulnerable.

Personally, I experienced these tactics on a number of occasions. In addition to a number of individual NRA's who were Oldtimers in 12-Step programs, there was another incident in a different type of 12-Step program setting. In this particular situation, I occasionally waited for a friend to finish and come out of her "group counseling" sessions. The group leader noticed me hanging around in front of the building, and asked if I would like to join their group. Between basic curiosity and hoping some of the local group members might be able to help me with job leads, I took her up on her offer. However, while I knew the group consisted of individuals trying to overcome drug and alcohol problems, I was surprised by what the group leader did next: as soon as I entered the room, she presented me with a copy of *"The Courage to Heal: A Guide for Women Survivors of Child Sexual Abuse."* Although the group leader-- who was a recovering addict and alcoholic-- knew nothing about me, this was her initial approach.

A writer named Meredith Maran addressed this in her book *"My Lie."* Not only can vulnerable people be "singled out" by NRA's with wrongful motives, people can also begin to develop false memories when they are consistently surrounded by the subject. As Ms. Maran described the nightmare she and her family went through after ongoing exposure to the subject resulted in her own false memories, I have seen the same thing within the context of the 12-Step programs. When you hear sexual abuse happened to so many people, you may begin to wonder 'did it happen to me, too?' And whether it comes from reading quantities of material on the subject or hearing claims from other people, you actually can start doubting and questioning your own mind and memories.

And, as I have stated, with the exception of the young woman who struggled with the after-effects of a childhood attack throughout her life, every other person who claimed they had been victimized by sexual abuse during their childhoods only started reaching these conclusions after becoming involved with the programs. It is not a matter of individuals 'recovering' memories-- but being led to develop 'memories' that have no basis in fact.

"WHAT TANGLED WEBS THEY WEAVE"

It is one of the many subjects that I still have difficulty finding the correct word for; and, with no prior experiences, when I was smack-dab in the middle of it, I had no way to defend myself against it.

"Lie" would not be the correct word; for if someone 'lies,' he or she simply says something that he or she knows is not true. What I am referring to is something entirely different-- and it seems accurately summed up by the lines of an old famous poem: what tangled webs they weave, when first they practice *to deceive.*

With a wide range of different angles, one that was especially troublesome was frequently being told 'this this and this is what *people* think and/or say *about you.'* In some instances, the alleged 'people' were unnamed; in others, they were individuals whom I had met briefly; and in others, it involved people whom I had never even met at all. Yet all of these 'people' allegedly had plenty of negative things to say about me.

The first difficulty associated with this was the message that I should not trust anyone-- along the lines of 'after all, look at the horrible, untrue things they're saying about you.' When it involved individuals I'd personally met, I duly noted I no longer had access to them, so I could not bring the issues up to them directly.

The second difficulty: when you're in a *'WTF?!'* state over something like this, it's where your *focus* is; you may not even realize shifting your focus to this type of asinine situation is *intentional*-- so you are less likely to notice other, more important things that are going on.

Well, I was frequently 'treated' to this kind of b.s., both in vague terms and specific remarks that probably never came from the individuals who were 'quoted.' While there were many examples, the one that stands out most prominently was one acquaintance's description of a specific incident. The incident: one evening, on my way home, I stopped to rest for awhile and, while sitting on a bus bench near the edge of town, this acquaintance drove up. We chatted for a few minutes, and then I accompanied him to his house where we talked about the program for awhile, and then he drove me home.

An average situation, nothing unusual-- but that was not the way it was related to me at a later date. Instead, I was told the acquaintance claimed he had found me standing on the top of the bridge that was located approximately a half-mile away, preparing to commit suicide by throwing myself off the bridge.

To further complicate matters, I was resting on the bus bench because I'd been having a vertigo attack caused by an inner-ear problem; but although I had the attacks frequently, I didn't know what it was all about because I hadn't yet sought medical attention. However, when the story was related to me, I was told the acquaintance had said I was in very bad condition because I'd had a fight with my 'boyfriend.' This lie only added fuel to the fire-- I didn't have a 'boyfriend.'

So what it came down to was the speaker claimed my acquaintance had put a very negative and untrue light on both my mental stability and my general morals.

Although I did not know this acquaintance very well, I was fairly certain these lies had not come from him; instead, it was the speaker's "game" of trying to cause me to distrust and dislike people *because* they were allegedly telling these kinds of lies. And, while I feel this particular incident was especially noteworthy, it was an ongoing thing-- covering people I'd briefly met, and people I'd never met at all.

It goes beyond lying-- and the "game" of creating tangled webs of deception certainly says a lot about the ways oldtimers approach "rigorous honesty."

"She's so confused!" *"She doesn't know what she wants!"* *"She's prone to depression!"* *"She's only hurting herself!"* *"She's very insecure!"* were some of the remarks that were attributed to other people-- including people whom I had never even met. Now, there was obviously no way of knowing if 'the people' actually said any of these things-- but if they did, it should bear wondering where they got these ideas... or from whom. *"They think you're a drug dealer!"* was another example of the asinine garbage I was up against. Again, it is quite likely that none of 'the people' ever said or thought these things-- but if they did, the

only possible source was someone who wanted to damage my reputation by telling lies.

I will also add: from my experiences, there were two "categories" of "web-weavers." First, there were those who were accurately summed up by a long-ago friend: *"shit-starters."* These peculiar NRA's, who had nothing of worth in their own lives, 'compensated' for it by wreaking havoc on others. The general method was to pit people against each other for no legitimate reason, truly enjoying the discord they created. It was like tossing a stink-bomb into a population, and watching the reactions with a weird sense of glee.

The others, though, had their own personal motives-- something to gain by causing people to think the worst about others, when 'the worst' had no truth in it whatsoever. I guess they could be called shit-starters, too, but the consequences were even worse.

Actually there was one incident long before I became involved with 12-Step programs. Whether the liar was involved with a Program or not, and whether he or she was an addict/alcoholic or not, is something I never knew. The reason for this is the individual went to great lengths to remain 'anonymous,' and managed to remain so.

The incident involved a guy whom I had recently met, receiving a typed, unsigned letter in the mail. It was evident that the individual who wrote it had some kind of 'beef' against me, and concocted lies to ruin my reputation. The letter told the recipient that I frequently 'went off my rocker,' and had spent a considerable amount of time in a local hospital's 'locked psychiatric ward.' The catch: there was no truth to any of it.

However, while the recipient of the letter simply brushed it off as garbage, it continued to chew on me: "Who would do such a thing?!" Awhile later, I presented it to my Aunt, and she was equally baffled and angry.

The other catch, though: the letter included a tactic that is common amongst the NRA population-- NRA's often back up their lies by adding "some something" to make it appear credible, so a reader or listener assumes they have some kind of "inside information."

In this particular instance, for example, whomever wrote the letter did not say "a hospital," but named a hospital that was a few miles away from where I had lived. As I was living in a different state at the time, it was obvious the letter had come from someone in my previous location.

However, the "some something" that can make blatant lies appear credible can be either very specific or extremely vague. The problem, naturally, is liars can reach their goal of getting people to believe the most outrageous things, simply by applying these underhanded tactics. They have no qualms about "bearing false witness" when they have a goal in mind.

I was surprised, but probably should not have been, to find this particular topic addressed in Dr. Robert Hare's book *"WITHOUT CONSCIENCE: The Disturbing World of the Psychopaths Amongst Us."* (There will be further information about Dr. Hare and his work later in this book). Dr. Hare, who has been Canada's authority on psychopaths and psychopathy for decades, received this information directly from psychopaths he studied. Individuals who plant a word, a name, or some other factual word or term, in order to cause the listener to believe everything he or she says is credible.

As for vagueness, it evidently works the same way-- *'certain people* say...,' *some kind of* problem...,' etc.

When unsuspecting people are on the receiving end of these tactics, they are less likely to question the lies they are told.

I think it also bears noting that a long-ago member of the programs who actually did take his program seriously put a great deal of effort into explaining what *The Program* means by "rigorous honesty"-- terms that are sprinkled throughout Program literature.

My friend said the most accurate approach is the way it is set up in "the fourth step": that individuals who are truly 'working the program' must consistently examine their attitudes, beliefs, behaviors, and approaches to other people, to make sure their motives are honest; and, if they find they are dishonest, to examine 'the exact nature of their wrongs.'

Logically, weaving webs of deception-- either for 'entertainment value' or personal gain-- does not fall into the category of "rigorous honesty." And for whatever wrongful reason such individuals participate in a 12-Step program, 'working their own programs' is obviously not a part of it.

THERE IS NO 'YOUR PART'

There is one subject that is very common in 12-Step programs, but I heard very little about it until quite recently. People who are involved in the programs are told, in any situation, to "look at *your part*" in it. These situations often involve individuals who are on the receiving-end of violence and other criminal behaviors. Not only does this outrageous approach lead to victims feeling unnecessary and inappropriate guilt over being victimized, it also gets the offenders "off the hook."

One of the most common situations is rape and other forms of sexual assault. It is a throwback to the olden days when rape victims were blamed, rather than the perpetrators. It should not take much effort to understand the power a perpetrator feels in getting away with it, *or* how harmful it can be to the victim.

In the distant past, my only experience with this horrible aspect of 12-Step programs was a young friend who, at age two, had been raped by a family member. Not only had her family members blamed *her* (a two-year-old child!) for the attack, her participation in the program made it worse: her sponsor told her she must directly *forgive* the offender. After carrying this misery with her throughout her life, she did what the sponsor told her to do. While she did not tell me what the results were in terms of the offender, the act of "forgiveness" turned a troubled woman into a completely broken human being. Rarely did I hear a statement from her that did not include the word *"ashamed"*-- frequently saying she was "so *ashamed"* over what had happened *to* her.

Logically, this is not o.k. In any situation, individuals who have been victimized have nothing to feel "ashamed" about-- and there *is no 'your part'* in it.

However, most people who have related their experiences with this subject were not referring to childhood experiences-- they were talking about incidents that occurred *within the programs.* After being victimized by other members, they found there was no source of help-- nor even compassion. While those of us who have spent our lives in the civilized world are nothing less than appalled to find this approach in the so-called modern era, it is the "blame the victim" mentality that often accompanied sexual crimes in generations past.

The repercussions of this outdated, inhumane approach: first, when a victim knows she will either be blamed for a crime committed against her, or not believed at all, she is unlikely to speak up and demand justice. Whether a victim suffers in silence or blames herself, is it destructive to the person and to her life. Second, when individuals who perpetuate crimes-against-persons know they can get away with it, those who seek easy prey find it in the programs-- because, whether a prospective victim is vulnerable or strong, predators know they will not be held accountable for their actions.

In other words, NRA's in the programs have not joined the civilized world, or civilized society.

HOW CRAZY ARE THEY, REALLY?

As I had no prior experience with NRA's, I made quite a few mistakes. One mistake in particular often resulted in wasting my time and draining my energy. Assuming many people in my position could make the same mistake, I believe it should be addressed. It was the mistake of trying to figure out something that never seemed to have an answer: are NRA's really as crazy as they present themselves to be, or is it only a "game"?

The subject usually came up in terms of "crazy" things they said or did-- along with their inability to recognize it as abnormal or wrong. While it covered a wide variety of topics, ranging from inappropriate physical or sexual advances to inappropriate comments and questions, one that I am still shaking my head over is the habit of "putting people on the defensive."

From individual people who left the programs to websites cautioning about the dangers of 12-Step programs, I have learned this is a widespread issue. There is even a wide range of "pat" phrases used for this purpose. You may hear such phrases as *"I'm not God- and neither are you," "Opinions are like a*sholes- everybody has one, and they all stink," "You need a check-up- from the neck-up,"* or one that I frequently heard that never failed to irk me: *"Have a nice day- unless you've already made other plans."*

Once, I went as far as to remark that these individuals could simply buy a tape recorder, as it would save them time and energy from needing to consistently repeat the same nonsensical lines. The catch, though: these lines, and many others like them, are *intended* to put the listener on the defensive-- they are *intended* to cause strong, negative reactions. And, as is the case with thought-stopping vocabulary in general, one's focus immediately falls on one's *reaction*.

However, my mistake was wasting time and energy wondering whether this garbage was something they were taught in the programs, learned in the programs, believed, or were simply mouthing-off in order to appear ignorant. But whether they were merely parroting phrases they'd heard in the program or inventing something of their own, what I learned is it is a fruitless endeavor to try to make the determination between intentional and crazy. Whether they believe the nonsense they say or are only putting on an act, the worst approach is to try to figure it out.

The question is: are their brains so disordered that they actually believe they're on-target and the rest of the world is not, or is it all a "game"? The smartest approach is to not wonder, because there is really no way of knowing.

The title of a blog post almost jumped out at me: *How Sociopaths twist other people's words and actions.* Nearly all of the examples gave me a figurative knot in the stomach. While this is not to say all NRA's are sociopaths, experiences I have heard from other former members as well as my own make it crystal-clear that this issue does cover a considerable part of the NRA population. Whatever you say, whatever you do, the sickest will twist it to sound like or look like something entirely different.

BRICK WALLS AND OTHERS

One of the first oddities I noticed when I began associating with members of 12-Step programs was they did not communicate like normal people; in fact, they did not communicate at all.

Communication involves two or more individuals engaging in a give-and-take process. In contrast, I have seen two entirely different approaches, neither of which could be described as communication.

The first non-communication oddity I noticed was people who 'spoke'-- either briefly or at length, either on something very basic or a serious topic-- but did not want input, feedback, comments, or questions. When this involved one-on-one non-communications with individuals, it was really no different from what one encounters in a 12-Step meeting. In a meeting, an individual 'shares,' and those who listen are expected to either remain silent or toss a pat phrase such as 'thanks for sharing!'

The second oddity was that other forms of one-on-one communications did not exist, either. In the real world, people may 'ask questions;' NRA's do not ask questions-- they interrogate you, demanding answers. In the real world, people may 'make requests;' NRA's do not request anything-- they demand it.

These are some examples of how NRA's do not grasp the meaning of communication. It is like that old saying: "like talking to a brick wall."

BLURRING THE LINES

When it comes to appropriate vs. inappropriate, there is another term that is overused, and often misused; and doing so can lead to confusion and unnecessary problems. The word is "friend." While it is tossed around with great regularity on "social networking" sites and in the everyday world, it can take on entirely different connotations when it is used in the context of 12-Step programs.

Upon becoming involved with programs, it was one more subject on which I found myself dismissing everything I had learned and known in the past, and taking on "the ways" of those in the programs instead.

At its worst, to apply the word *friend* where it is unwarranted can lead to trusting those who should not be trusted. Whether or not one does this oneself, it can result in the *appearance* of trust to those who witness it.

When it comes to the 12-Step programs, there are those who simply do not know the difference, those who want to be or appear more important than they actually are, and those who exploit the entire subject for their own personal reasons.

What is a *friend*? The way I have come to describe it is a friend is a person with whom there is a mutual emotional investment. Equally important-- if not more important-- a friend is someone who has *earned* your trust. And, equally important, trust is not earned through underhanded, deceitful approaches-- it can only be earned in a straightforward, honest manner.

What did I dismiss when I made the mistake of taking on the NRA approach to the word? I dismissed the fact that there is a difference between a friend and an acquaintance. There may be many people in your everyday life-- at your job, school, or in your neighborhood-- but even if you interact with them, communicate well with them, and get along well with them, they do not automatically reach the status of *Friend* unless they have earned your trust in a straightforward, honest manner, and your relationship with them is of mutual importance.

In contrast, the approach that everyone you know is your "friend" can range from negative to dangerous. In the programs, specifically, not only can you be urged to place everyone in this category, your family members and others in your life can be urged to do the same.

It is yet another example of how NRA's in 12-Step programs dismiss what is said in their own programs. First, people are cautioned to draw the line between who is and who is not a *friend.* In addition to not automatically applying the word to one's fellow members or group, the program states one's sponsor is not automatically in that category, either. They underscore this by saying if someone is your friend, that person is not necessarily your best choice for sponsor.

Second, the 12-Step programs I became acquainted with were very clear about their scope. 12-Step programs are neither 'dating clubs' nor social circles. By their own descriptions, one might say a 12-Step program is a business arrangement-- the "business" of recovery from alcohol or drug addiction.

A program states that one's sponsor is one's guide through the steps; it is also stated that the sole scope of all who participate in the programs is 'sharing one's strength, hope, and experience' of what 'worked for them in their own recovery process.'

The catch: not only did I, personally, have years of experiences with NRA's who seemed to be completely clueless about all of this, countless numbers of former program members have related experiences similar to mine. Men and women have related how individuals in the programs have interfered in and taken over their families, interfered in and broken up their relationships, and a wide variety of other inappropriate behaviors. Unlike examples you may read in the literature of longtime program members intervening to help someone who cannot stop drinking or using drugs, they have been examples of inappropriate interference, intrusion, and meddling in other people's lives. And the point: the programs neither promote nor condone this type of behavior.

The bottom line: while one may be capable of making friends and having friends amongst others in the programs, the majority of individuals one meets in the programs are not one's "friends"-- and, if one is actually "working the program" they are not intended to be.

Did I have any true friends in the 12-Step programs? I'd like to think so, but it is something I cannot say for certain. For the most part, it was like virtually everything else during those years: I met good people along the way, but also lost good people along the way. What I mean is people I met in other locations are people with whom I am no longer in contact, although I have no way of knowing if they ever considered me a real friend or not.

12-STEP PROGRAMS, NRA'S, AND FAMILIES

The effects of the programs and NRA's on my family is my deepest, most painful regret. There are some effects that have continued, long past my involvement with the programs.

There was one particular issue that needs to be addressed in this book, especially since other former members have reported similar experiences. The "divide and conquer" approach is common. One issue that I experienced on a number of occasions involved NRA's who looked at my family unit and did their damnedest to tear it apart. My family unit consisted of three individuals: a single mother, a young adult, and a preteen. The first oddity involved NRA's deeply resenting the young adult for one reason and only one reason: unlike themselves, this person had not wrecked his life with alcohol or drugs, nor the "lifestyle" that often accompanies alcohol or drug addiction. Their resentment was to the extreme of an all-out vicious *hatred*. As I had never experienced or witnessed anything like it before, it took a very long time to understand what was going on and why.

The second oddity involved the warped beliefs and practices the NRA's had on the subjects of influence, power, and protection. Directly to the point, the NRA's believed the young adult had the ability to influence my decisions and actions, and to protect the family, simply because he was male. I learned all of these ridiculous beliefs about status are very common in the programs.

Consequently, NRA's who intended to harm or damage the family began by attempting to remove this person from the picture. They believed he was not only the strongest, but the only strong member of our family unit, and without his presence there would be nothing standing in the way of them getting what they were after-- that the remaining members would be helpless, "sitting ducks." My numerous experiences with this topic led me to conclude the sickest NRA's have both factors in common: both a deep hatred toward anyone who did not go the wrong way in life, and a warped view of status. And it is a very dangerous combination.

True to NRA form, there were those who employed the tactic "use big words they've heard, to feign knowledge and/or authority." One NRA, for example, used this tactic on a regular basis. On this particular subject, though, I nearly choked trying to stop myself from laughing when she clearly-- intentionally or not-- misused two terms I was familiar with from my long-ago psychology classes: "dependent personality" and "emotional incest." To explain it in clearer, layman's terms, the former refers to someone who cannot adequately function in his or her own life without the consistent guidance, support, and input from another person. The cliche of a housewife who cannot make the most basic decisions without first asking her husband is an example. The latter term describes an adult who puts a child in a position where he or she relates to the child as if the child were his or her partner. An example would be a mother who tells her young son he is "the man of the house," and relates to him as such. It is not much different from "covert sexual abuse," in which an adult exhibits such behavior as sharing the details of his or her intimate or personal life with a youngster.

The point, though, is this kind of behavior occurs quite regularly amongst NRA's: whether they "read a book" or "saw something on the internet," they claim this as authoritative knowledge; and whenever they wish to manipulate someone, they haul out this type of vocabulary. In this instance, specifically, the NRA saw the young adult as a threat, and attempted to portray an adult child and parent who got along with each other as something warped and sick.

Other former members have related how NRA's have pitted their family members against each other, totally wreaking havoc in their families and in their lives. As is the case with much that I experienced, wreaking havoc on people's families is evidently very common in the programs. For some NRA's it's simply a matter of resenting solid families because they do not have it themselves; for others, "divide and conquer" is the approach they use because there is something they wish to gain.

The bottom line is while it should sound logical, it often is not clear enough: if anyone in a 12-Step program begins interacting with your children, or any other members of your family, be very suspicious, because There is no *legitimate* reason for it.

There was an additional angle to this subject that also must be addressed. In recent years, I have heard from quite a few former program members who talked about oldtimers who 'single out' single women who have children. One mistake most of we mothers make is, as we love our kids and are proud of them, it is often one of the first subjects that comes up. If you are in a normal, decent environment, this is not necessarily negative-- but 12-Step programs are not PTA meetings or a local ballpark. And while many NRA's who target single mothers are male, this is not *always* the case.

As I have mentioned, my introduction to 12-Step programs came in the form of pen-pals who belonged to the programs. Initially, the subject was casual, and, for all intents and purposes, average: a few of my pen-pals had children, and loved talking about them, so I saw no reason to not do the same.

Eventually, though, there was a change. Rather than parents who seemed to be similar to myself-- happy with raising their kids of various ages-- I encountered a very odd and very different approach. One NRA who began writing to me-- and bear in mind this was someone whom I had never met-- expressed that if I were to die, *he* wanted guardianship of my youngster. The creepiest thing he said-- bearing in mind he had never met the child in question, and had no connection to our family-- was "Nobody could possibly love that child as much as I do!"

While it should have been an automatic "red flag" that there was something seriously wrong with this individual, and there being no legitimate reason for me to provide any information whatsoever about my family's personal situations, I informed the NRA that in the event of my early death, guardianship of my youngster had already been settled: my oldest child, a young adult, had agreed to take care of the youngest sibling if anything were to happen to me. And, although the NRA had not met any of us, that was his reply: that even the child's sibling could not possibly 'love' the child as much as he, a total stranger, did.

However, while hearing about this incident is enough to make a person's blood crawl, it was far from being the only incident of its kind. And, while each NRA who approached the subject had his or her own 'agenda,' the one point they all had in common was they were individuals whom I did not even know-- individuals who came up with this garbage while not knowing my family or anything about us. *Total strangers* zeroed-in on the youngest member of the family, while using a variety of tactics to try to get the rest of us out of the way. To make matters worse, I had no idea how to explain such situations to a child, so admittedly I didn't try; in one instance, though, I addressed the issue with "When some middle-ager starts buddying-up to kids, it's never for a good reason," but unfortunately my caution was ignored.

WHY THE PROGRAMS ARE DANGEROUS

A person who has had no experience or firsthand knowledge about 12-Step programs may find it very difficult to understand how or why the programs can be so dangerous. While the trend of courts ordering dangerous criminals to become involved with the programs certainly makes it worse, it is not the only reason. When it comes to predators who are seeking human beings to harm or take advantage of in various ways, there are reasons a 12-Step program is the ideal setting-- and the reasons all revolve around *vulnerability.*

First, whether a person initially approaches a 12-Step program on his own, or because he has been influenced or pressured to do so, you can assume he has something in common with other newcomers: most, or nearly all, who walk into their first 12-Step meeting are there because their alcohol, drug, or other problem is serious enough to make it necessary. As the person is not likely to be in the best physical, mental, or emotional health, he is also in no position to make sound judgments-- including looking out for his own best interests. A person in such a position is likely to trust whomever "seems" or "appears" trustworthy, to take people at their word without questioning or investigating, and other general characteristics that mark one as vulnerable. An NRA can be nothing more than a vulture, looking at such a person as prey-- an easy target.

A second category of prey: young people. Children, teenagers, and even young adults can be vulnerable to predators for no reason other than their age and lack of experience.

There are individuals whose backgrounds and upbringing primed him or her to harm others. Although there have been many 'creepy' facets of NRA's, this, in my opinion, was amongst the creepiest: NRA's who had specific traits that translated, to them, as a symbol of Authority. Age and gender were two common examples. Throughout the years I encountered numerous NRA's who fully believed they could intimidate me, push me around, or in various other ways "have the upper hand," simply because they were older, larger, male, or some other characteristic that they thought was important. It was yet another example of how my refusal to "buy into their ways" irritated, angered, and even enraged NRA's.

Yet I have also seen many who *did* comply-- as well as the consequences. They simply did not understand that individuals in the programs not only had no authority-- but that they had no authority over *other people.*

All of these categories have one point in common: NRA's get away with taking advantage of others because they do not see others as their equals-- or, in some instances, as their betters. And this is one point that makes the programs a very dangerous place.

There is another category of why the programs are dangerous. Oddly enough, the two most well-known programs disagree on the issue. If you read literature from one program, you will see 'recovery' includes regaining 'the full range of emotions.' However, the other program-- the one on which all 12-Step programs were based-- says something entirely different. And, it is from his particular program that manipulators and other wrongdoers take their cue. They will tell you there is no such thing as appropriately expressing emotions-- and that you should not even have them.

Although the subject is addressed further in the References section, the main topic is *anger.* The most important point about this topic is you may find a wide variety of different approaches. First, in the original piece of literature, the NRA who claimed responsibility for writing the literature stated that anger is essentially a death-sentence if a person is an alcoholic. He claimed any degree of anger, regardless of how justified, will, without any doubt, cause an alcoholic to *drink.* As I am not an alcoholic, I obviously do not have any personal knowledge on that aspect of the issue; however, the more you read in that particular book, the more you can see how manipulative his viewpoints really were. As one example, his comments that married women should simply 'forgive and forget' their husbands' infidelities-- that they have no more place being angry about adultery than the husbands who actually committed the adulteries.

The catch, though, is neither I nor any other former members I have known were ever 'treated' to this NRA's comments about anger causing relapses. Instead, while I never heard it personally, many others who successfully left the programs related they were told 'anger is not spiritual.' In contrast, the manipulations I was told was anger is a sign of 'multiple-personality disorder, and triggers from the past.'

What places this subject in the category of danger is all of these approaches have something in common: the purpose is to shut you down- and shut you up. Regardless of what you are angry about, you are not supposed to feel it, and not supposed to express it. And this approach is *very* dangerous.

WHERE DO 'SEX ADDICTS' REALLY COME FROM?

Many people believe sex addiction and sex-related crimes generally stem from one source: childhood sexual abuse. While there may be individuals in this category, there are other factors that are more relevant.

It should not be a surprise to find there are countless numbers of individuals in Alcoholics Anonymous and Narcotics Anonymous who are 'sex addicts.' It bears noting that they can be either male or female. First, "addiction" itself is about compulsion and obsession-- one's needs, or self-perceived needs, are the utmost priority. Second, characteristics such as self-control and appropriateness are generally unknown concepts amongst the NRA population. However, a third factor is equally relevant: the inability to acknowledge another human being as a human being with feelings, free will, personal dignity, and rights.

Regarding this third factor, the lifestyle of "the wrong kind of environment" can set the stage for sex addiction. Specifically, when youngsters-- both male and female-- are encouraged to view sexual relations as a matter of personal gratification and status, there you have the foundation for sex addiction. And, in such environments, it usually starts very young.

While high schoolers in a locker room may boast-- with most boasting based on less-than-facts-- it is something altogether different when a situation involves NRA's who are middle-aged or even well past middle-age. Lacking the ability to connect with a fellow human being on a mutual human level, it is about "scoring," "bedding," or "getting it." The fascination with pornography also shows the inability to connect with another human being. But whether the situation involves porn or sexual relations, it is all about believing a human being exists to meet the addict's needs.

In these kinds of environments, individuals "have sex" in public places, "have sex" in front of other people-- verifying that they are nothing but animals. In addition, during the years I have been in this area, six males-- in a variety of age ranges-- have exposed themselves in my presence. By state law, this could have earned each and every one of them a place on the state's Sex Offender registry.

The younger people are when they "become sexually active," the more risk there is of developing sex addiction. It is no wonder that generations from the lowest-class origins not only have this problem more often than not, but think there is nothing wrong with it. In such environments, kids start drinking alcohol, using illegal drugs, and having sex, often before they are even teenagers. In some backgrounds, fathers go as far as to take their young sons to prostitutes; the message this gives: *'this is the place and purpose of women-- to satisfy your needs, without feelings, rights, or dignities of their own.'*

Sex addicts cannot develop, much less maintain, solid healthy bonds. They do not even know the difference between attraction, love, and "puppy-crushes." I have known individuals-- both male and female-- who reported that they had had sexual relations with more than two hundred people. None of these NRA's thought there was anything wrong with, or even unusual about, this kind of behavior. To further the insanity of sex addiction, one of these NRA's referred to his sexual behavior as 'relationships'-- although most involved one-night-stands with women whose names he did not even know.

In addition, there is a very fine line between "sex addicts" and "sex offenders." Believing other human beings' bodies exist for their gratification, the only actual difference is the sex offender has dismissed his chosen target's refusal to consent. A sex addict has the viewpoint that whatever he wants is his-- and if it is not given willingly, he will take it.

There are a couple of other subjects related to this particular topic. First, you may be familiar with the saying "He thinks he's God's gift to women." Not only is this common in the programs, it covers both genders, and NRA's of all ages. It is yet another way in which NRA's have an extremely unrealistic self-image.

Second, you will not hear one of these individuals saying he or she "is interested in" a person, or that he or she "likes" a person; the emphasis is on the word *"attraction"*-- as if they are nothing more than animals sniffing out another animal.

Third, if the entire subject is not gross enough, the sense of entitlement is what makes it dangerous. They fully believe the person on the receiving end of their 'attention' should not say no, and has no right to say no.

Obviously, there are repercussions to deeming perversion an 'addiction,' whether it is an accurate assessment or not. First, the general consensus is an *addiction* consists of *obsession and compulsion*-- an individual with an addiction does not have control over his behaviors. Second, individuals with active addictions are in denial that there is anything wrong with their behaviors, blame others when there are consequences to their behaviors, and believe 'everybody' is like themselves.

It can be messy enough when the addiction involves a mind-altering substance. Drunk-driving accidents and domestic violence are some common examples. However, other than pornography, *every* act of a so-called sex addict directly harms *another human being.* If a so-called sex addict cannot get what he wants through free will consent, he will take it *without*

102

consent. Regardless of one's viewpoint on alcohol and drug addictions, allowing sex addicts to walk free places human beings in danger and undermines the very quality of life. Individuals who cannot control their 'urges' should not be in the general population.

One incident should make part of this problem crystal clear. A male in his fifties made the remark: *"When a girl says 'no,' she really means 'yes'... or she at least means 'maybe.'"* While the individual did not appear to be particularly dangerous, it was as if he were speaking for this entire category-- the belief that girls and women are not full human beings with rights and free will, and that girls and women are essentially "up for grabs."

From my unfortunate encounters with this segment of the population, what is also crystal clear is that they are misogynists. I have heard such individuals refer to the girls and women in their pasts in such terms as "They were all psychos," "I just thought of them all as whores," and similar remarks. It is not a reflection on their 'bad choices'-- it is a reflection on the way they view the female gender. And, similar to those who are addicted to mind-altering substances, any consequences to their behavior results in blaming others-- whether it is rape or another form of sexual assault or violence, they blame the women for their own behaviors.

Consequently, they do not realize other people-- in fact, most other people-- have morals. They do not realize other people-- most other people-- do not run on wrongful motives. During the period of time I had the misfortune of encountering such individuals, I was 'treated' to a variety of examples. Not only were my morality and motives attacked, so were the morality and motives of virtually everyone I knew. Initially-- and for a long time-- I made the mistake of assuming they were nothing more than 'control-freaks.' Prior to becoming involved with 12-Step programs, I had no experience or knowledge with either subject-- I did not know any "control-freaks," and I certainly did not know any "sex addicts." However, the fact eventually kicked in that the common theme of addicts being that everybody is like themselves also held true for these perverts:

their motives and behaviors are on the animal level, so they assert the same holds true for everybody. Because of this, individuals who had no business being in or near my life in the first place leveled unfounded attacks against me, and against other people.

As only one example, one of these individuals pounced on my habit of often visiting a local church to speak with the priests about various concerns and questions. As the older priest of the parish often gave me good advice, and gave me some books, the individual accused me of having sexual motives toward the priest-- who appeared to be around eighty years of age. *"You're only going there because you want to f* him!"* was what I was told. As a second example, I was told that walking to the grocery store alone meant *"You want some guy out there to offer you money for your p*sy!"* Well, these perverts are everywhere; in another location, another one of these perverts accused me of having immoral activity with virtually every man or guy I knew. When I confronted him about his perverted beliefs and attitudes, and remarked that he certainly had a lot in common with the first individual, he didn't even know what I meant. Both of these pigs summed up what this segment of the population is really like: they believe everyone is like themselves. They seem to completely lack the ability to grasp that the majority of people are not obsessed with "doing it," "getting it," or using human beings for their own gratification.

The most relevant point, though, is the way this subject connects to the 12-Step programs. It is considered to be nothing more nor less than something a person must 'accept,' and if you do not, you will be accused of 'taking someone else's inventory.' In other words, whether a perversion is directed at you or only in general, you're not supposed to say it is *wrong*.

Think about that very clearly: whether something is simply disgusting, or whether you are actually on the receiving-end of it, *you are not supposed to say it is wrong.*

There have been numerous examples of this type of behavior and this type of approach. And, as I have already stated, while numerous they were, my only encounters with 'sex addicts' were within the 12-Step programs. Not only are there additional 'programs' for them, both A.A. and N.A. are filled with them-- both court-ordered criminals, and those who are there by 'choice.'

The very first NRA I encountered who was in this category was the individual I referred to early in the book as 'Bear.' An obese guy in his late forties, Bear claimed to be hooked on hardcore pornography, and popping out with offensive remarks for shock-value. Claiming that any type of negative reaction constituted 'taking his inventory,' he delighted in approaching women whom he did not know, making comments such as "I want to give you a French-kiss on your love-nest." Is this really something people must simply 'accept'?!

Another example involved an NRA who was younger than one of my own kids. This individual showed up at my door one afternoon, asking to use my phone. As the only phone I had at the time was a landline, he proceeded to walk into my apartment to make the phone call. I sat waiting for him to finish the call and leave, but instead he ran over to where I was sitting, yanked out his 'privates,' and exclaimed "So, what do you think of this?" True to NRA form, when I told him that kind of behavior was not o.k., and to get out of my apartment, he did not seem to realize I was serious. Instead, he plopped down onto my couch and began to handle his privates. My only recourse was to physically throw him out of the apartment. "But I love f* older women!" he kept saying.

These two examples of many bring to mind something I read on a forum long ago. A woman said a guy had approached her with the line "I've had sex with one hundred women- would you like to be number one hundred and one?" While she had turned to the forum in hope of finding some support, the first reply she received was "How dare you try to impose your morality on other people!" I was absolutely stunned-- for someone to say that kind of behavior is not o.k. was 'imposing her morality' on someone?! In other words, those of us who do have morals are expected to allow and condone any and all types of behaviors, and never even say it is wrong. So-- where exactly are *our* rights?! From disgusting remarks and behaviors to actual assaults, we're simply supposed to tolerate it? *Bullsh*t.*

JUDGMENT

This topic is so troublesome that it deserves its own chapter. You may have heard remarks about "judging others," "inventories," and "acceptance." From my experience, the way these terms are often used are in no way related to what the Programs themselves teach. Although I have seen countless people sucked into the misuse of these terms, the reason it is especially bothersome to me is it is the #1 reason for my own "downfall."

The general idea is if a person is experiencing the repercussions of drug or alcohol abuse, there is much he needs to do in order to recover. The general idea is drug addiction and alcoholism are serious enough to make focusing on one's own recovery the priority.

However, you may find newcomers and oldtimers alike who fail to grasp this, even though it is one of the most basic concepts taught by the Programs. Whether a person is still drinking or using drugs, or whether his life consists of decades' worth of "wreckage," he may be all-too-tempted to set his problems aside in favor of placing his focus on "others." The point: as long as he can put his time and efforts into picking other people apart, he does not need to deal with everything that is wrong with himself and his own life.

With that common situation in mind, it should not be difficult to understand how those terms can be misused. My mistake, which resulted in horrendous consequences, was even though a Program member who was serious about recovery explained all of this in the past, both his comments and the materials he advised me to read did not accompany me when I relocated to different areas. In short, I was not thinking about what he said, or what the literature said. If I had, so many disasters, mistakes, and misery never would have happened.

An example that sums it up: one individual, who claimed to belong to such a wide variety of Programs that it was like an alphabet-soup after his name, "shared" about his history; he followed all of this information with 'but you probably did most of those same things, too!' And that, there, is the problem: NRA's who misuse Program terminology to claim no one can 'judge' them, no one can 'take their inventory,' or that others must be 100% in-tune with 'acceptance,' are not looking for 'acceptance' at all. Instead, they are demanding other people condone their actions and behaviors. You are not only supposed to say that nothing is 'wrong,' but uphold the notion that you are not only no better than them, but no different from them. Read that last part carefully: *you are no different from them.*

You can continue by looking at it from both angles. First, when individuals who have committed atrocious acts are allowed to believe everyone is like themselves, they have no incentive to either acknowledge their wrongs, nor to change. However, the other angle can be more destructive: what position do you think you are in when individuals who have committed atrocious acts believe you are like themselves?

Not only does this misuse of terminology allow them to cling to the belief that you condone such behavior, but that you yourself have participated in such behaviors. It is one of the most destructive ways in which NRA's do not take 'rigorous honesty' seriously.

No, the Programs do not say you must put your "seal of approval" on horrible behavior; the Programs do not say you must allow those who have done horrible things to believe you, also, have done them, in order to not 'offend' them; and the Programs do not say you must allow those who continue their horrible behaviors into your life. What the Programs do say is that everyone deserves a chance for "a new way of life."

Judgment vs. Acceptance can take another dangerous turn. It is a topic on which I made serious mistakes-- and resulted in serious consequences.

I can illustrate the problem in terms of the way it was addressed in two 12-Step areas. In the first, groups held parties for various holidays, including a nice range of foods and treats prepared or contributed by members. These parties were not limited to participants in the program-- members were encouraged to bring their families to the parties.

In the second, youngsters from teenagers to little children were often present during meetings. Some of the kids took seats at the table; while there was a playroom, complete with toys and books for younger children, they would often wander around the meeting room while the meeting was in progress, talking to program members, showing their toys and other objects to the people they met.

The problem: when an adult is involved with a 12-Step program, complete with the "teaching" that you cannot "judge" others, and must "accept" others, kids of all ages can receive an entirely wrong message. If adults have trouble with it, consider the impact on kids: whether your kids are present with you in a meeting, attending a 12-Step party, and to whatever degree you interact with or associate with 12-Step program members, kids receive the message that all of these people are your true friends-- and, thus, safe and good people.

To compound the problem, while you may find there are kids of all ages who are naturally hesitant, the majority are not-- most kids have the natural belief that people in general are "good," and if they see such people in your own environment it only reinforces this belief. In other words, they will naturally trust individuals whom they should not trust-- thus leaving themselves and you open to a wide range of serious complications.

Perhaps there are people in 12-Step program who are indeed your true friends. However, the average youngster cannot differentiate between who your "friend" is and who he or she should stay away from. As for the latter, you *will* find NRA's who take full advantage of kids' lack of discernment for their own wrongful purposes.

Kids of any age should not be exposed to murderers, wife-beaters, child molesters, rapists, drug dealers, etc.-- and this means keeping kids out of the 12-Step environment, and keeping NRA's out of *yours.*

JUDGMENT: PART TWO

It's a topic that seems to be getting more and more popular; and, in general, is going in the wrong direction. Although it can affect anybody, it's most upsetting when kids are drawn into this "new approach." It's one more example of how the former generations were better off-- because they applied basic common sense.

I'm sure there are plenty of people these days who, if hearing about some of their approaches, would bristle "That's *judging*! That's *wrong*!" However, while I didn't think much about it in the past, I believe their approaches were absolutely right.

One incident from my early years involved a couple who lived in a nearby town. Upon questioning some of the older generation, I received the reply: "We don't associate with Mr. and Mrs. D., because they *drink*." What was meant by this was the couple not only engaged in out-of-control drinking themselves, but also went out of their way to push alcohol on others-- including kids. Because of this, many locals had the viewpoint that they were not people to associate with.

Another incident involved a woman who was commenting about one of her coworkers. The coworker had what the woman considered to be an immoral lifestyle. The woman's comment: "I am always courteous to her at work, but I would never invite her to my home for dinner with my family."

The older generation had the ability to draw the line-- it is one thing to be civil and courteous to everyone, but that did not mean "inviting" people into their lives.

Decades down the line, I encountered an entirely different approach. Based on "you cannot judge others," it was like that "line" vanished.

The first thing I learned was an old saying is far too accurate: *You are judged by the company you keep.* The people you associate with, and the places where you spend your time, result in the belief that you are like those people and those places. Even if you have not been guilty of any wrongdoing, it is a matter of "guilt by association." What I learned was exactly how damaging and destructive an undeserved bad reputation can be.

The first individual from whom I heard the "you cannot judge others" approach had a wide variety of behaviors that would normally have put him in the category of "people to not associate with." The most serious was he had been involved in a murder-- of his own child. "But nobody can judge me!" he insisted. While he never expressed any regret for his behavior, he simply claimed no one could judge him.

The second example was one of the many instances of "guilt by association." An NRA reeled off a long string of behaviors and actions, some of which were serious crimes. While I was creeped-out hearing this information, it paled in comparison to what came next-- he followed his list by shrugging and saying: "Oh, but I'm sure you probably did most of those same things, too." Although I had not done *any* of those things, and neither had anyone I'd known before, it was a matter of "guilt by association."

Often another factor comes into the picture. Throughout my growing-up years and early adult life, the viewpoint was you do not *insult* people. This was a common-sense approach, because everyone knew what that word meant. However, it has been replaced by the word "*offend;*" and the problem with this is individuals can claim to be "offended" by whatever they choose. What it comes down to in programs is it "offends" people if you tell the truth about yourself.

So, who exactly benefits from "you cannot judge others"? Granted, human beings can make mistakes-- sometimes very serious mistakes-- but it is what they do afterward that matters. The NRA's I have known were never in the mind-state "I did something wrong... I will make up for it... and I will not do it again;" they were in the mind-state "Everyone must condone this behavior-- and act as if they too have done these things."

The older generations would have thought I had "rocks in my head" over the way I was sucked into all of this. However, neither that nor the destruction it caused in my own life are as anger-inspiring or as heartbreaking as the effects it has had on my family. It is very difficult-- nearly impossible-- to encourage young people to make and apply sound judgments when you have not done so yourself.

The older generation's approach was better, and right: be civil and decent to everybody-- unless they give you reason not to-- but that does not mean taking them on as friends or associates. During the period of time that I was sucked into the "you cannot judge others" mentality, I associated with everything from drug dealers to prostitutes to murderers and virtually everything in between-- and, despite no wrongdoing on my own part, I am still suffering the consequences for it.

"RATIONALIZE AND JUSTIFY"

As much as I dislike this type of terminology, no discussion of 12-Step Programs would be complete without bringing up 'rationalizing and justifying.' In fact, the topic is addressed in Program literature, as it is one of those topics that make the NRA "tick."

As the literature says, drug addiction and alcoholism affects every area of the person's life. So does rationalizing and justifying. You can start with how it is connected to drug and alcohol abuse itself. *How does an individual rationalize and justify behavior that can endanger his own life and the lives of others, and, in some cases, is against the law?*

Some common rationalizing and justifying of drug and alcohol abuse: "The laws are wrong, the doctors are wrong, the experts are wrong-- *everyone is wrong except me;*" "*Because I want to;*" and, the ever-present theme of the perpetually screwed-up: "*Nobody can tell me what to do!*"

Next, move on to consequences and potential consequences of drug and alcohol abuse. From domestic violence and vehicular accidents to a wide range of other consequences, the individual who rationalizes and justifies his behavior will, each and every time his behavior results in consequences, blame it on someone else other than himself, and something else other than his drug and alcohol use.

The catch: rationalizing and justifying does not go away even if one becomes "clean and/or sober." NRA's who have made a strong foundation of their destructive attitudes when it came to drug and alcohol abuse will continue to apply it to every area of their lives.

While normal people realize "Because I want to" and "Nobody can tell me what to do" are simply not valid approaches in real life, the NRA's who never recover never grasp this fact. NRA's who fully believe "the end justifies the means," and cannot grasp that this approach is sick, destructive, and wrong, really have no business being in the free world where innocent people end up paying for their actions.

Unfortunately, this topic is only one example of how 12-Step Programs are often misused. They do not acknowledge rationalizing and justifying as shortcomings that need to be "removed," because they are amongst "others" who are doing exactly the same thing.

"GAMES" AND DANGERS

My first encounter with the concept known as "drug court" came in the form of an eighteen-year-old kid who rushed up to me as I was approaching a public water fountain one day. *'No, no- don't drink the water!'* He continued, telling me that if I were thirsty I should buy some Koolaid, but to absolutely not drink the water. Before I had the chance to respond, he seemed to realize I did not understand what he was talking about, so he explained: *"If you drink water, They will believe you're trying to flush drugs out of your body!"*

While neither 'They' nor 'drugs' had anything to do with me, this first encounter showed that even very young people easily and quickly learn how to 'beat the system.' After that particular encounter, I met up with other young people who were involved with drug court; what they all had in common was the viewpoint that they 'got away with' something.

The first point: although these young kids were involved with drug court due to relatively minor offenses, neither beating the system nor getting away with something should have been what they learned from the experience. The second point: it has been brought to my attention that throughout the United States, drug court is not limited to individuals who have committed minor offenses; instead, it is offered as a condition of probation or parole to hardcore criminals-- many of whom have committed violent crimes-against-persons. Some of these individuals have gone on to commit additional violent crimes-against-persons-- including murder-- against 12-Step program members who had no idea about their criminal histories.

The first problem: average people who enter 12-Step meetings are generally unaware of this-- until something happens. The second problem: when young people have the viewpoint that they got away with something and can beat the system, naturally it is much worse when it applies to hardened criminals

One individual related that his counselor had asked his group: "If you 'work your program,' are you still a criminal?" Although the NRA related that some people had said yes and others said no, he could not grasp the lose/lose 'game' for what it was-- there was no "right" answer.

There are those who commit crimes who can turn themselves and their lives around-- but 'sentencing' criminals to 12-Step programs is definitely not the way to accomplish it.

"PHONY RELATIVES"

When I first heard this term, I didn't know what to make of it. As the term was used, "phony relatives" did not mean "dishonest family members"-- it meant individuals who were not actually family members at all. I have seen it is very common amongst the NRA population-- and it is never positive.

First, there are those who refer to the programs as their "real family," or their "true family." It does not take a lot to understand the position this leaves their blood-relatives in-- it's as if they count for nothing. Whether an individual has parents, children, a spouse, siblings-- these people do not matter to an NRA.

Second, there is the element of dishonesty. Individuals use the terms "husband" or "wife" to refer to people they are simply living with; "stepson" or "stepdaughter" when they are not married to the youngsters' actual parents.

Third, the term 'family' is sometimes used in a Mansonlike manner-- covering the other NRA's one is living with. One example involved a teenager who exclaimed "I would never do anything my family disapproves of!" Initially, I thought he was referring to his parents, or possibly his siblings. He was not. Instead, he was talking about the group of young drug addicts with whom he was living.

The bottom line: families who have invested years or decades of love, care, guidance, etc., are often shut out of the picture altogether when individuals who have no legitimate role attempt to claim one by using this type of vocabulary. The programs do not teach members to lie about their relationships-- or lack thereof-- nor do they teach members to dismiss their own families. It is yet another example of how NRA's elect to run on self-will instead.

A common occurrence I have seen: many who claim "phony relatives" are those who did such a job of alienating their true families that their true families want little or nothing to do with them. However, if they were actually working on recovery, they would be focusing on making amends to their true families, rather than looking elsewhere.

We should also look at the implications of "phony relatives" on the NRA's actual families. As one example, the numerous males who stated they did not even know how many children they had. The "lifestyle" was such as to use and discard women (or girls), that in addition to children they abandoned, they assumed there were quantities of women (or girls) whom they had impregnated, yet had "gone on their merry way" before knowing whether or not a child existed.

The self-centered lack of responsibility and lack of care for one's own children is not limited to males in the programs. Various women claimed they were "glad" their children had been taken away from them by the courts-- because the day-to-day care of youngsters was something they considered burdensome, and something that could interfere with their lifestyle.

Many youngsters are not removed, however. In recent years, there have been many stories in the news about children and infants ending up dead or permanently disabled because their parents are on drugs. Unfortunately, instead of acknowledging such individuals as unfit to provide everyday care for youngsters, situations are often overlooked until a tragedy occurs.

Other situations involve biological parents who, if asked about their children, shrug it off as "They're being well taken care of." This means "They are being taken care of *by someone else*." Whether the "someone else" is a foster care program or a relative, it is a matter of the NRA extending their irresponsibility to their own children.

When it comes to families in general and children specifically, I take the hardline approach: Step up to the plate and meet your responsibilities; no one has the right to dismiss their real families in favor of substitutes; and individuals who place no priority on their own children are not fit to be parents.

IT'S NOT ABOUT THE WHEELS

You can pick any topic-- virtually any topic that exists-- and it would be wise to assume the NRA population has an entirely different way of looking at it than the rest of us.

My first experience with one particular topic began when I happened to meet up with a woman who was in her early thirties; she was driving along, and stopped to greet me. As she was a pleasant woman, intelligent, and easy to get along with, I was surprised when she offered me a ride but told other people who were nearby that they would have to walk wherever they were going. As her car was large enough to hold a number of people, I was curious and asked her the reason. "I can't tote guys in my car," she replied. Much later, I learned some NRA's who enjoyed making trouble for anyone whenever possible had been portraying her as immoral-- simply because she had given rides home to people she knew.

It goes beyond the "men help men, women help women" concept. On another occasion, I opened the door to see sprinkles had turned into a raging thunderstorm; the storm was so powerful that if I had attempted to walk to my destination, I would have been soaked before I walked a few feet. Noticing a middle-aged woman with whom I had been on good terms-- or so I thought-- I approached her and asked if she could drop me off. I was stunned when she replied: "No, I have my kids in the car-- you understand, don't you?" The fact was I did *not* understand-- not at the time, and not now when I think back on it; the woman had a relatively large vehicle, and often gave rides to other people whenever they asked. Yet she refused to do this for me, and pointed around the room at other people, telling me to ask one of them instead.

Now, in the real world, there are many people who own vehicles, and many who do not. To ask someone who is driving in the same direction you are going should not be considered an imposition-- or anything else. However, the world of NRA's is not the real world-- nor do they see it this way. Not only do they consider it a matter of imposing, the way their minds work they attach something immoral to it. One incident did not directly involve me, but a woman who had accepted a ride home from a much older NRA; when they arrived at her home, she was disgusted and upset because the guy asked for 'a kiss' in return for the ride.

An incident that did involve me consisted of an NRA making some intrusive, snide remarks about me 'dating' an individual who attended 12-Step meetings. What the NRA was referring to was the individual had offered me a ride home when I was walking home one winter night. Although there was nothing personal whatsoever about the incident, the NRA insisted that the person driving me a few blocks amounted to 'dating.'

In another instance, my mistake of accepting a ride from someone I did not know resulted in being told I was 'in a relationship' with the NRA, despite my clearly stating I had no interest in anything of a personal nature.

So what it comes down to is something as basic as not owning a vehicle can put a person in harm's way. Whether you know someone or you do not, simply requesting or accepting a ride can result in everything from being taken advantage of to having your reputation destroyed. Only in the warped minds of NRA's can something the real world takes as nothing more nor less than a simple courtesy be portrayed as something entirely different.

"TOBACCO ROAD"

You can pick any topic, and the approach NRA's take to the topic is so far out of bounds that it seems as if they are from a different world. One subject, which created confusion and difficulties time and time again, was cigarette smoking. In the real world, prior to Programs, my experiences involved people who smoked cigarettes and people who did not; and, for the most part, people in both categories considered the subject to be one's own personal business. Not so in the Programs-- where *nothing* is one's own personal business.

In the Programs, NRA's were in entirely different categories. One category, which never failed to irk me, consisted of NRA's who were former smokers. With the nearly-universal approach "I quit- so so can you!" their histories spoke for themselves: NRA's whose systems were so screwed-up from years or decades of drug and alcohol abuse that giving up tobacco was really no big deal. However, I also encountered NRA's for whom giving up tobacco required antidepressants and other psychiatric medications.

However, the second category was even more mindboggling: NRA's who did not want me to stop smoking, nor to even cut down on my smoking. My first experience with this oddity involved a woman who essentially dragged me to my first N.A. meeting. While the woman claimed "double-digit" time in a variety of 12-Step programs, and even "sponsored" a large number of women, she virtually ordered me to continue smoking cigarettes.

It took a long time for me to understand the reason for her ridiculous approach: as some of the 12-Step literature states that trying to give up cigarettes when one is trying to *become* clean and sober can result in a relapse-- returning to drug or alcohol abuse-- this was the framework she was attempting to present. Although I did not have any drug or alcohol problems, she wanted people to have the impression that I was such a 'hopeless, helpless Addict' that I would use mind-altering substances if I gave up cigarettes.

During the period of time I was involved with N.A. and A.A., quite a few other people also urged me to smoke cigarettes-- although I do not necessarily think they had any wrongful motives. It was simply another example of being in the wrong place, and people assuming I had the problems they had. On numerous occasions, people badgered me to smoke a cigarette when I really did not want one, and light up a cigarette in places or situations where it was inappropriate. Various people told me I *must* smoke around nonsmokers, in restaurants where people were eating, and so forth.

However, there were also incidents that showed any slice of life that average people considered unimportant can take on an entirely different meaning when it's in the hands of an NRA. One incident stands out in my mind: after his girlfriend had ordered me to not give up smoking, one NRA jumped on my compliance as if it had some kind of immoral connotations. Noting that at her insistence I occasionally left the meeting and stepped outside for a cigarette, the NRA shot me a look and said: "When you go outside to smoke your cigarettes, *I smell your game.*"

While all I could pick up from that statement was the NRA was accusing me of some kind of wrongdoing, it was his vocabulary that creeped me out the most. My initial reaction was *who the h*ll talks like that?!*

The point, though: nothing average is average, and nothing is the way it is, when NRA's spin their own warped interpretations on it. Even something as basic as smoking a cigarette is held up as suspicious. I later found the NRA was accusing me of 'soliciting for prostitution' when I was doing nothing more than standing outside smoking a cigarette.

HOLIDAYS

The last holiday I actually celebrated or fully observed was Christmas, 1997. As someone for whom holidays were always noteworthy occasions, even that statement is unusual. In 1997 and before, wherever we happened to be and however many people our family unit consisted of, holidays mattered.

1998 brought changes-- NRA's in programs who were clueless as to what holidays were all about, and clueless about appropriate ways of observing them. It included those who expected me to stay out of the way while they "ran the show." From being pushed to the sidelines that first year to holidays consisting of going to the movies and playing Frisbee, holidays lost their meaning. On a personal note, when the engraved ornaments I'd purchased for each member of my family, and even our Christmas stockings, were stolen, my heart was unable to get

in the spirit anymore. For years I went through the motions--
and then ceased even doing that.

Changes? Holidays went from family, relatives, and
friends, to strangers and unwelcome intruders. Holidays went
from normal ways of celebrating to approaches that were
definitely abnormal. One in particular makes the abnormalcy
quite clear.

An NRA insisted I sign my name on his Christmas cards.
While the request was bothersome enough, it went beyond
expecting me to present myself in a role that was not mine. The
fact that he had packages of cards that were preprinted with his
name was not unusual in itself. What was unusual was they were
also preprinted with a 'recovery' slogan: "Still clean and sober
after all these years!" As is often the case with NRA's, situations
that creeped me out overlapped with other situations that creeped
me out as much, if not more. I was bothered enough by signing
my name on his cards, but it paled in comparison to signing it
under a 'recovery' slogan, as if "clean and sober" had something
to do with me.

I didn't think about it at the time, but it was the consistent
emphasis on 'recovery' and 'programs' that suffocates NRA's
entire lives. This NRA, for example, claimed to have been free
from drugs and alcohol for nearly a decade, yet felt the need to
use something as average, basic, and normal as Christmas cards
to advertise it. And, drawing me even further into the mess of
12-Step programs, my saying I objected to signing my name to
this brought the response "You don't care about my recovery!"

I had never observed New Year's Eve, as I'd never
considered it an important occasion. One year, I was approached
by a program friend who told me every time she tried to get
assistance with holiday parties, no one was willing to help. She
said most people made excuses, while others offered to help but
never followed through. For this reason, I agreed to assist with
the New Year's Eve party.

I showed up early, my friend surprised to see I'd followed
through as I'd said I would. I helped her set up chairs,
decorations, and plates for the refreshments. One of her other

friends had passed out flyers, and I read one that was on the table: *"Bring in the new millennium in recovery!"* was what it said. Admittedly, I didn't pay much attention to it-- the heading on the flyer making it clear I did not belong in that environment. Later, my confusion rose when one of the guest speakers stood at the front of the room, talking about someone he knew: "He died an addict's death!" While I was shocked by his words, I was still one hundred percent clueless.

Ever since my late teens, Thanksgiving was always the high point of my entire year. The others were always important, too-- everyone's birthdays, Mother's Day, Christmas, Hanukkah. They have not really existed for many years. The numerous times I tried to "resurrect" holidays, nothing I did made a difference.

IT STARTED WITH VANILLA

If you do something you really don't want to do, or refrain from doing something you do want to do, either because it's "the right thing" or because you are placing someone or something else as a higher priority, it can be positive-- *because* it is of your own free will. However, it is much different when your actions or lack of actions are due to force, undue influence, or the concern of what would happen if you were to follow your own free will instead.

The NRA population who have made no progress with recovery do not understand the basic concepts of "limits and boundaries." They will either begin to impose on you inch-by-inch, or by one massive "takeover."

It started with vanilla. I've cooked and baked ever since I was a child, and vanilla was a product I often used. As was the case with countless other subjects, it was never an issue until I became involved with NRA's in 12-Step programs. It was one of the inch-by-inch examples. Because of this, it did not seem significant.

One particular NRA, claiming to be a clean-and-sober addict/alcoholic, told me I must stop buying genuine vanilla, and buy artificial vanilla flavoring instead. It was my first experience in catering to the NRA population. At the time, though, it did not seem important-- it didn't taste any different in food, and I could buy a larger bottle at a lower cost. However, it was the first example of NRA's taking over-- eventually to the point that there was not much left of 'me' or 'my life' at all.

Whether it is something that seems minor, or something that is clearly major, for an adult to be told 'others' will determine your way of life-- what you can and cannot wear, what cosmetics you can and cannot use, who you can and cannot associate with, etc. etc. etc.-- is degrading and dehumanizing. It is a matter of taking away your rights, and your right to free will. It is a violation of your rights as a human being. When 'others' come to your home and refuse to leave, or barge into your home when they've been told they are not welcome, it violates your rights in your own home. When 'others' put their hands on you against your will, they are violating your rights over your own body-- and are also committing a crime.

My time was not my own, either. I lost any true sense of the words 'my' and 'can.' Nothing was *mine* anymore.

What are the repercussions of asserting your own free will-- including the right to say 'no'? You are told there is 'something wrong with' you. In the twisted minds of "unreformed" NRA's, the only "will" that matters is their own.

Another early experience may illustrate how even a 'massive takeover' may not be noticeable until long after the incident occurs.

In this particular incident, an NRA whom I barely knew was talking to his sister about me. He said: "She's not an alcoholic-- but she gave up drinking entirely *for my sake.*"

I was a little frazzled by witnessing this exchange-- mainly because, as I had not had a drink in approximately eleven years, it obviously had nothing to do with 'the sake' of someone I'd just met.

However, as I was focusing on the idiocy of his remark, there was something even more important about the entire situation that I did not realize for a long time-- in fact, not until I had many more experiences. Although the experiences covered a wide range of topics-- and virtually *every* topic in existence-- what it came down to was the degree to which NRA's insist and demand others *"cater" to* them.

Similar to the vanilla, I did not think it was a big deal-- not at the time, anyway. As having a drink was never very important to me, "not drinking" was something I simply shrugged off without a thought. The catch: it does not matter whether something is important to you or not-- NRA's will expect you to *comply* with their wishes.

So what it comes down to is: how much are you willing to give up, sacrifice, do without, change, etc., simply 'for their sake'-- or, more to the point, perhaps you should not be willing to give up, sacrifice, do without, change, etc., *anything.* And what it *really* comes down to is it is yet another creepy similarity between non-recovered addicts and alcoholics in 12-Step programs and the experiences of battered women in domestic-abuse situations. Using "pop-psych" terminology, it's "all about *Control."*

I really did not think changing to artificial vanilla flavoring was a big deal. However, it was only my first encounter with individuals who cannot grasp that their wishes are not meant to supersede other people's personal wishes or other people's rights.

Whether it's inch-by-inch or a massive takeover, the entire point is NRA's do not acknowledge the existence of other people's right to free will-- or other people's rights at all. If you assert yourself, they will haul out the "programese" and a wide range of other attacks; the point is you are never supposed to say 'no,' never supposed to stand your ground, but simply allow them to have their own way.

I believe I can safely assume most people would not think this is o.k. One example of many: an NRA who was a few years younger than myself, and whom I intensely disliked, *literally crawled* onto me, stating in a bold tone: "I'm gonna take you to a motel- and I won't take no for an answer!" This is the type of common garbage I encountered in 12-Step programs; and I am sure I am not unique in saying *it is not o.k. at all.*

In another instance, there was a situation that left me feeling amazingly exhilarated-- simply because it was something that had been absent from my life for such a long time. One day I went into my kitchen, made a sandwich, and ate it, and then I went into the living room and read a book. It was such an amazing experience that I read a second book. Now, for anyone whose life has not been beaten into the ground by NRA's, none of this would sound exceptional. For me, though, it was-- because it was the first time in a very long time that I was free from NRA's, and had enough freedom and privacy in my own home to eat a sandwich and read a book without any intrusions from unwelcome outsiders.

The most important point: in the real world, it is an individual's place as a human being to set the limits and boundaries in and for his or her own life-- what is and is not acceptable. However, this logic goes out the window when one is dealing with an NRA. An NRA, instead, fully believes it is his right to draw the lines on other people's lives-- and move that line whenever and however he sees fit.

LIMITS & BOUNDARIES

Years ago, a program friend talked about "Limits and Boundaries." While my friend was much younger than myself, she was a married woman with two children. She was saying she was learning about this topic, and needed to learn more. While I'd never heard that particular term before, what struck me as odd was an adult saying it was something she needed to learn.

For most average people, it's a part of the socialization process of early childhood. A child who, for example, lives with his or her parents and siblings, learns early what is "his," what is "someone else's," and what is "everybody's." Under normal circumstances, this knowledge and behavior carries over into the child's school, community, and into later life. Unfortunately, there are individuals who did not learn any of this when they were children-- nor at any other time.

Similarly, there is a concept sometimes referred to as *"PPP-- Public, Personal, and Private."* Public essentially covers everything that is fully open. As an example, when most people are working at their jobs, anyone from coworkers to the general public can see this, know this, and be there freely. Personal is limited to a select few-- as an example, your home is your personal domain, and it is not "open to the public." In contrast, a person's private 'world' is theirs and theirs alone-- such as your relationship with your God, and your thoughts. While access to your Personal world is "by invitation only," it takes very special circumstances to allow anyone "entrance" to your Private world. And both need to be *voluntary.*

What happens when individuals have never learned about limits and boundaries-- and fully believe that whatever is "yours" is not *really* yours? One NRA came up with a very accurate term: *intrusion.* Intrusion can take many forms. It can take the form of getting into your personal world without your consent, and it can take the form of getting into your private world without your consent. While a person's home, family, and other aspects of his personal life are not open to the public, his individual privacy is not, either.

Most average people who are past young adulthood can relate: what are things that are going on in your mind today-- your worries, your dreams, your concerns? what are things in the past that are "over and done with," and the past is where you reasonably expect them to stay? are there any good memories that are best left alone, or bad memories that are also best left alone? *And-- what if someone used underhanded means to get ahold of it all, and turned your personal and private worlds into a public spectacle?*

A term used to describe it is *psychological rape.* Every person needs and deserves his or her own privacy. When this privacy is violated, it shows a person's mind can be violated in a way not much different from the body being violated-- and it is equally destructive. It is like you no longer have what rightfully belongs to you and you alone.

With no experience with this in the past, either, my initial thought was a statement I recalled from my younger days: "I won't dignify that with an answer." In other words, individuals do not 'deserve' the truth when they are not legitimately entitled to it. Or-- 'don't ask questions that are none of your business, if you really expect a truthful answer.'

Translating an old Yiddish saying into English, it is like someone has crawled into your very bones-- it is like being laid open and bleeding in the middle of the street for passersby to gawk at. In addition to all of the other negativity, it leaves you feeling as if there is nothing left of yourself.

Whatever is in your mind or your past, it does not need to be extreme or bad or even important; the point is it is *yours*-- it is not there to be put on public display. Whether it is good or bad or neutral, your privacy is your *right.*

NORMALCY

If there is one subject that causes many NRA's to bristle, it's "normalcy." I've heard such remarks as: "Don't ever use that word-- say 'average' if you must, but never ever say 'normal'!" "There is no such thing as normal!" "I haven't been normal since the day I was born!" "We don't have what it takes to be normal!" "I don't want to be normal!" "I'm not normal- and everybody knows it!"

The last NRA quoted was the perfect example of the problem. An overweight middle-ager, he habitually trotted around town in purple "hot-pants," fishnet tank-tops, and quantities of huge dangling earrings. My reply was that what 'everybody knows' was largely based on the way he presented himself. And that is essentially the case with those who either claim they are not normal, or that normal does not even exist: whether in appearance or behavior, their personal choice is to be *Abnormal*. Whether they follow this by demanding to be 'accepted as they are,' or use it as an excuse, or use it to blame others, the bottom line is it is a matter of personal choice. After all, like the individual with the hot-pants, no one is forcing these individuals to behave as outlandishly as they possibly can-- and, if you were to confront someone directly, you would surely hear it explained as "because I want to!" or a similar variation.

     Abnormal extends to behavior, too. One way abnormal behavior is approached is often by "making up a name for it," as if this somehow validates it. One person said they felt the need to "always know what other people are thinking"-- and called this being 'detail-oriented.' Another used the term 'analytical mind' to cover picking apart other people's every action. Another: 'the way my brain is wired.' Another could not watch a television show or movie without picking out every single actor and actress, and then trying to come up with every single movie or t.v. show the actresses and actors had appeared in.

     Another indication of abnormalcy is viewing everyone as themselves. They cannot grasp that the majority of the population can do or like or enjoy anything without being 'addicted' to it, as in their minds, 'everybody' has the compulsions and obsessions as themselves.

     Yet another hallmark of abnormalcy in the NRA is what can be called "making mountains out of molehills," or "blowing everything out of proportion." With this type of exaggeration, everything appears more extreme and more significant than it really is. Nothing is small or minor to those who are still "living in their disease."

     Individuals who have not made any real progress in recovery also show their status as Abnormal by the inability to recognize what is and is not an appropriate topic of conversation, and what is and is not appropriate interactions with other people. They do not recognize normal boundaries.

These are some of the most common examples. The fact, though, is 'not normal' is a personal choice-- and an excuse to continue going the wrong way in life.

A personal choice? yes, without a doubt. One NRA, for example, related about a wedding he had attended: *"It was an N.A. wedding."* Upon meeting more and more people, I have learned this abnormal approach to an otherwise normal situation is not uncommon-- even something as basic as a wedding can be focused on *The Program.* As one bystander accurately remarked: *"They define themselves by their problems."*

Counterproductive, for sure. Another NRA, speaking of his own upcoming wedding, said he planned to wear a dress, and the woman would wear a tuxedo. "We want to be *different!"* was his explanation. And that does say it all.

"DRUG-OF-CHOICE"

One topic a 12-Step program warns about is the concept known as "drug-of-choice." Unfortunately, many disregard this warning, either intentionally or unintentionally. This can result in blocking recovery-- or never starting true recovery at all.

The drug-of-choice concept begins with the assumption that many or most addicts have favored one particular drug over other drugs, and some have even limited their use to that one particular drug. It is this "I used *this-* but not *that*" that undermines the entire process of recovery. One reason is many who take this approach feel their addiction is not as serious as someone else's addiction. Another reason is focusing on one drug as their problem leaves many open to using other drugs, believing only their "drug-of-choice" is a real problem.

You may hear individuals say they "only" abuse alcohol, marijuana, or prescription medication. A 12-Step program does not condone this viewpoint; instead, addicts are told they must not use any drugs that alter their minds or their moods. For someone with substance abuse issues, no drug that alters the mind or mood is safe-- not marijuana, alcohol, or prescription medications.

Within the programs, though, you can find many NRA's who do not pay any attention to any of this. You will find individuals who claim they are 'sober' because they engage in the "marijuana-maintenance program," drug addicts who choose Alcoholics Anonymous because 'the desire to stop drinking' does not address their illegal drug use, those who claim to be clean and/or sober while regularly using mind-altering psychiatric medications, and various other examples. It is a prime example of how NRA's can manipulate anything to suit themselves.

Drug-of-choice, though, was a topic that was addressed to me after my first 12-Step meeting. A young adult approached me and asked what my "drug-of-choice" was. As I didn't use *any* drugs, it was not an easy question to answer. If I had replied, truthfully, that I did not use drugs, the person may have asked or at least wondered "Then why are you in a Narcotics Anonymous meeting?!" Or, if it had been an oldtimer, complete with years of practice in manipulation, my truthful statement about not being a drug user probably would have brought the reaction 'You're in denial,' 'You're just not ready to see it yet,' or 'You're lying.' Because when it comes down to it, NRA's in 12-Step programs do not like, and do not want, the truth.

ADOLESCENCE IN PROGRESS

Adolescence is described as: "The period following the onset of puberty during which a young person develops from a child into an adult;" "the process of growing up;" "transitional stage;" and similar variations. In some regions, the absence of adolescence has existed for generations. It has been considered acceptable for individuals who, by age and level of maturity, are still children to either be granted or to take on adult-appropriate privileges and responsibilities. As the individuals do not go through this essential developmental stage, and experience it as it is intended, the result is individuals who have never truly "grown up."

I do not recall meeting any NRA who did not have that factor in common: both experiences which, in normal society, are reserved for adulthood, and experiences which most average people forgo entirely, were taken on when they were *children.* The additional common factors were parents who either "weren't there, or didn't care"-- neglecting their parental responsibility to provide solid foundations and guidance to their kids.

One point is drug and alcohol abuse. As most knowledgeable people are aware, the human brain is not fully developed until a human being is approximately twenty-seven years of age. What this means is while drug and alcohol abuse is unhealthy and harmful to anyone, it is especially unhealthy and harmful to youngsters. They are affected both physiologically and psychologically. The effects are neither changed nor reversed, even if a person later becomes "clean and/or sober." Yet, the majority of NRA's who have told their stories claimed they began using alcohol and/or drugs between five and thirteen years of age. Recent studies have concluded individuals who begin drinking before they are legally adult-aged have at least a forty-percent chance of becoming alcoholics. The dangerous, and potentially-deadly practice known as "binge-drinking" is also much more common in individuals who started drinking when they were minors.

A second point is the lifestyle, attitudes, and behaviors which often accompany drug and alcohol abuse. From seeing it as something they can "get away with" to the self-centeredness that is the hallmark of NRA's, the earlier youngsters begin engaging in these attitudes and behaviors, the less likely it is they will ever gain full recovery.

A third point in the absence of adolescence is the sexualization of youngsters. While in some places it is "allowed," in many it is actually encouraged. Parents and other adults who encourage youngsters to become "sexually active" likely do not even realize they are committing child abuse. Encouraging youngsters to become sexually active is known as "corruption." It prevents normal, healthy development, and it also prevents youngsters from developing solid values.

Youngsters who engage in early sexual activity do not develop a solid concept of "love," and cannot develop or maintain healthy relationships in their later lives. You will find those in the older generations living with one person after another. You will find those in the older generations speaking in terms that makes it clear they cannot differentiate between the "puppy-crushes" of young adolescence, lust, and actual love.

A normal part of adolescence is living in, and seeing only, the present. While adolescents do not normally envision their futures in general, this factor also leads to risk-taking behaviors. The bottom line is kids end up dead because parents and other influential adults fail to show boundaries as to what is and is not acceptable.

In areas where adolescence, as it is defined above, has not been acknowledged as an essential part of growing up, I have resided amongst flocks of individuals who have never grown up. It is like living amongst large numbers of twelve-year-olds in adult-sized bodies. Worse yet, the same patterns are being passed on to younger generations.

However, while true adolescents have only the present as their frame-of-reference, older NRA's live in the past-- *their* pasts. While they display the same risky behaviors and careless attitudes of youth, even their vocabulary reflects where they are at-- unable to realize that normal topics of conversation for adults do not revolve around their "childhoods" or their "teenage experiences." Both in terms of development and maturity, they never moved past their youth.

The ridiculous emphasis on their "age," coupled with attitudes and behaviors that do not reflect it, may seem to be a very odd contrast. Upon listening to many NRA's talk, however, the connection is not only clear but disturbing. While they did not mature and "outgrow" such behaviors, they have a different way of looking at it. They seem to actually believe that since risky behaviors have not killed them *yet,* they never *will* and never *can.* You will find NRA's in all adult age groups-- even "senior citizens"-- who fully believe they are immortal and invincible.

In true adolescence, it is primarily the responsibility of parents, and to a lesser degree other adults in influential positions, to lessen the risks to young people's lives with sensible rules and sensible guidance. Unfortunately, while many NRA's did not have this type of solid background, they continue without it; and, similar to the normal adolescent brain which is not fully developed, they continue to have the approach that nothing can "do them in."

PETER PANS

Of the many areas in which NRA's show themselves as "Peter Pans who never grew up," financial irresponsibility is amongst the most obvious. Totally unfamiliar with "the nature of addiction," I witnessed a few examples of this oddity before I knew what it was all about.

The first "Peter Pan" occasionally asked me to go to the bank for him, and to withdraw specific amounts of money for him-- $100, $200. I did so, with little thought about what such large sums of money could be for: wind chimes, board games, etc.-- building his "collections" at a hundred and two hundred dollar a pop.

I also had acquaintances who had a large family, a business, and pets-- a fondness for unusual, purebred animals. Frequently, their utilities were shut off because their earnings went on new pets rather than on paying their bills.

I've noticed this Peter Pan approach of irresponsibility covered NRA's in all financial situations-- from those who had very little, to sporadic, to plentiful-- and there was no difference.

The idea was "when I want something, I must have it, and I want it *now*"-- even when it means neglecting everyday obligations.

One guy drove up to one of his friends in a brand-new sports car. His friend looked, made a double-take, and crowed "See what recovery will get ya?!" He emphasized it, repeating happily "See what recovery will get ya?!" While the idea may be when someone stops using his money for drugs and alcohol he'll be able to afford nice things, that is rarely the issue. In this guy's situation, for example, he had no trouble forking over thousands of dollars as a down-payment on a new car, while continuing to expect a family member to provide him a place to live and other basic necessities.

In another instance, an individual left the utilities turned off in his home-- instead of paying the bills, he bought a new car, and ate at restaurants every day.

Another aspect of the Peter Pan view of money is you will not find one who spends anything on anyone else, without expecting something in return. Peter Pans, regardless of their financial situation, spend on themselves. If they do purchase a gift for someone else, it is either a matter of wanting to look important, or to say you owe them something in return. Financial responsibility is not a part of "the nature of addiction." Neither is generosity-- unless it is fake generosity with strings attached. I have even known a number of women in the Programs who had to buy their own engagement rings and wedding rings. And I, personally, experienced incidents in which NRA's believed they could "buy or bribe" me with gifts.

Normal people learn differently about both at a relatively young age-- obligations come before enjoyments, and giving with no strings attached is a good thing. The absence of these "lessons" is yet another way NRA's stay stuck in the childhood viewpoint of "It is all about yourself."

In contrast, the Peter Pans of the NRA population do not want anything to be 'about You'-- that is, anyone other than themselves. An accurate way of looking at it is like the most horrible toddlers in adult-sized bodies. *You* do not exist-- not your rights, feelings, needs, or personhood. If there is a Peter Pan

NRA in or around your life, *everything will and must* revolve around *him.*

If you dare to express or assert yourself, you are likely to be accused of being selfish and self-centered. If you need a doctor when you are ill, do not want to become involved with someone, or virtually any other example, you may hear the asinine remark: "It's *all about You!"* Because, in the world of Peter Pans, *You* essentially do not exist.

One 12-Step programs states that it is believed addiction-- or at least the potential for addiction-- is present in an individual long before the individual ever puts a mind-altering substance into his or her system. While various topics in this book do seem to point in this direction, one is the Peter Pan focus on money and possessions.

One example came a very long time ago. A girl, who was not yet a teenager, could not show new clothing items to other people without bragging about how much they cost. Instead of saying 'Look at my nice new shoes,' she would say 'Look at my $100- (brand name) shoes!' Upon encountering the girl decades later, I learned she had not only become addicted to drugs and alcohol, but had also become the quintessential "shopaholic"-- unable to control her spending, usually for items she did not need. Her entire room and closet were filled to the overflowing with these items-- including hundreds of pairs of shoes.

However, as time passed and I met more and more NRA's, something else became clear: many of these NRA's place the entire value of a human being on what a person owns, and how much money a person has. They consider ownership to be the sole determining factor in the value and worth of a human being.

INAPPROPRIATENESS

The very first time I noticed inappropriateness was the first birthday I had after becoming involved with the NRA population. I was told it would be nice for me to have a birthday party, and, as I had not had one since I was in the fifth grade, I agreed. Everything about it was inappropriate-- the setting: the playground area of a local park; the gift I was given was something I had no use for, but something the giver had wanted for himself; my birthday cake: appearing to be from a grocery store bakery, the cake was decorated with a number of colorful plastic rings shaped like Mickey Mouse. A playground party, a useless gift, and a Disney cake-- for someone who was nearly middle-aged.

In the fourteen years since then, one fact has stood clear for countless numbers of NRA's I have known: even those who are middle-aged and older lack the ability to relate to normal adults. As they stunted their own emotional and developmental growth with drugs and alcohol abuse long before they became adults, they never truly "grew up" at all. They act like adolescents, have the mindsets of adolescents, and prefer the company of youngsters.

From the perspective of an adult-- a "grown-up"-- it is something that was mindboggling from the beginning, and has never stopped being mindboggling. Behavior that one would normally expect from an average young teen is consistent in NRA's from middle-aged and older. While being "youthful" or "young-at-heart" can be a positive, healthy attribute, this is not the case with the NRA population-- they simply never grew up at all.

THE ELEMENT OF CHOICE

The programs advise people to think about their *last* drink or drug, rather than their first drink or drug. There is a sensible reason for this: to help people who want to recover keep in mind the state they and their lives were in when they reached the rock-bottom point of giving up drugs or alcohol. If an alcoholic or addict focuses on his initial experiences with drugs or alcohol, he's more tempted to attach something positive to drinking and using.

Unfortunately, the NRA's I have known ignored this advice, focusing instead on what they felt were *positive* aspects of drug and alcohol abuse-- "having a good time," "good mellow memories," etc. Logically, the need to change is not very strong whenever those who claim years or decades "clean and sober" look back on drug and alcohol abuse and everything that went with it, and see it as "good," claiming there was 'nothing wrong' with it.

However, there is an additional point I do not recall seeing in the literature: of all the NRA's who related their stories, not a single one ever expressed that anyone had *forced* them to begin using drugs or alcohol-- it was a matter of "personal choice." While no one "chooses" to become an alcoholic or a drug addict, and the "disease" proves to be stronger than they are, beginning on that path in the first place was their own decision. Furthermore, as one of the hallmarks of addiction that shows itself in every area of their lives, all the NRA's who elaborated on the subject made it clear they started drinking and using drugs "because they could get away with it."

These two points can be summed up in the popular Program saying: "It was your best thinking that got you here." This does not necessarily mean a person was smart to join a program-- it means their warped ways of thinking came to be why they needed a "Program" in the first place. The view that life is about getting away with something is one of the largest parts of it.

Other common terms are "self-will" and "self-will run riot." While there are certainly those who put their honest efforts into true recovery, from what I have seen they are in the minority. The others continue to run on warped thinking and self-will-- and heaven help anyone who gets in their way. They do not want to hear there is anything wrong with their behavior-- just as they did not want to hear there was anything wrong with illegal drug use, abuse of legal medications, underaged drinking, or alcohol abuse.

"COULD IT BE THE DRUGS?"

When it comes to a person's past and present life problems, attitudes and behaviors and lifestyle, the Programs say one of the first steps toward true recovery is to ask oneself "Could it be the drugs?" Unfortunately, you will find many NRA "oldtimers" who have not yet reached that point.

Also unfortunately, there are too many medical and mental health "professionals" who are not familiar with the nature of addiction. You simply would not believe the huge numbers of people who are "on meds;" and I have also known a few people who have been in mental hospitals. One person in the latter category who freely shared his story was fortunate to eventually encounter a doctor who realized it was, indeed, "the drugs." The person did not have any "mental illnesses"-- all of the problems he was experiencing were the results of his drug addiction.

Many are not as fortunate-- they do not get the help they need. Whether they spend time in hospitals, go through the rest of their life medicated, or dance along denial road believing there is really nothing wrong with them, like the saying goes "when nothing changes, nothing changes."

Long ago, a friend accurately described one result of drug and alcohol abuse as "dulled emotions." Similar to an old article about a popular celebrity, a person can "deaden" his entire system. In psychology, it is known as "affect"-- a person may be able to realize his emotions are present, yet not be able to fully understand or feel them.

The friend went on to say in the absence of full emotions, all that is left are fear and rage. He added fear and rage are not actually emotions, but "primal instincts." Human beings are reduced to an animal level.

True recovery includes being able to experience the full range of normal emotions. While this involves both feeling and appropriately expressing, many do not get that far.

Recovering the full range of normal emotions requires change. One part involves examining past and present life problems, attitudes, behaviors, and lifestyle. A person will get nowhere if he continues to assert his attitudes and behaviors and lifestyle are "normal," or if he continues to assert that his past and present life problems were all someone else's fault.

One of the most significant facts-- which, unfortunately, I did not know for many years-- is drug and/or alcohol abuse are merely symptoms of a much larger problem. Getting "clean & sober" is an important step-- but it is only one step. Abstinence does not amount to recovery-- nor does "belonging" to a Program, or attending Meetings.

Logically, drug and alcohol abuse affects one's entire physiological system; this includes one's brain. The so-called lifestyle that often accompanies addiction worsens the problems. If a person wants true recovery, there is much he must do to accomplish it. Many do not take those steps.

Why not? From what I have seen, it is less about fear or ignorance than it is about being led in the wrong direction by "Oldtimers" who have an ax to grind and ulterior motives. These are the individuals who, despite their own addictions, remark that becoming an addict is all about "choice;" the individuals who encourage young people to experiment with drugs and alcohol; the individuals who try to gain the upper-hand over others for wrongful reasons.

A Program cautions addicts and alcoholics to be on the alert to "Could it be the drugs?" Yet many persist in fishing high and low for some other reason, *any* other reason, for their predicaments. As one might expect from someone at rock-bottom in active addiction, they persist in pointing fingers of blame-- at people and situations in the past, people and situations in the present-- as ready excuses for their mental states and their behaviors. Someone else and something else must be blamed-- because they do not see their alcohol or drug addictions as the cause.

If you read the main literature of these 12-Step programs, the references you will see to "the past" involve "seeing it for what it was, dealing with it, and moving ahead." The programs do not provide addicts/alcoholics with an "easy out" by blaming "bad childhoods, bad parents, etc."-- instead, from the very beginning they inform addicts/alcoholics that their addictions are the cause. The only real recovery lies in a new way of life. This does not mean only getting clean and sober-- it means radical changes in every area of their lives.

CHANGE

One topic you may hear from individuals involved in 12-Step programs is "*Change*." Unfortunately, it is a topic many misuse-- either due to misunderstanding, or intentionally.

A person I met many years ago had a solid grasp of the concept, and discussed it with me. He said change, as it pertains to recovery, is similar to the change one experiences in a religious conversion-- an entirely different outlook and an entirely different way of life than one had before. Similar to the way a true religious conversion is intended to result in a transformation of the person and the person's life, true recovery results in such a transformation. While part of this is addressed in Step 12's "spiritual awakening," earlier Steps are also about change: the desire for shortcomings to be removed, making amends, and so forth.

Many NRA's do not "get it." Some are so insistent on continuing their old way of life-- with or without the alcohol or drugs-- that they attempt to reinvent their own program's definitions. Some take it to mean never being satisfied-- and continue to live in chaos. Others, however, take it as an opportunity to change other people to suit themselves. When you hear "you're not willing to *change!*" what the speaker is actually saying is he believes you must accommodate him. It is a prime example of what some would call a "control-freak."

In addition to what my old acquaintance explained about "conversion," the programs are also clear on these other aspects of the subject. Program members are cautioned to not meddle in other people's business or lives, to "clean their own houses" instead of looking at other people's, and that the only "changes" they should be attempting are changes to themselves.

One middle-aged woman stated her point of view, and she could have been speaking for the majority of NRA's: *"We're not in these programs because of what fine people we are,"* she said.

The catch: whether an individual has alcohol or drug problems, there is rarely anything standing in the way of them *becoming "fine people."* The only reason they do not: because they choose not to.

CHANGES

During my involvement with 12-Step programs, there have been many changes-- and none were positive changes. One change that was particularly distressing was something I noticed as soon as I began interacting with 12-Step program members. The best and most accurate way of explaining it is prior to Programs, *people believed in me.* After I became involved with the Programs, that was no longer the case.

While the fact that I had always been a decent human being with integrity was part of it, it went beyond that; upon sliding into the quicksand of Programs, I was immediately seen as *defective* and *useless.* This misconception covered both my own life and matters of relating to other people.

140

Prior to Programs, most people who had been in my everyday life throughout the years saw me as someone who was intelligent, stable, compassionate, and had much to offer. One viewpoint specifically, coming from individuals as diverse as a much-older cousin and a teenage step-nephew, was since I had such a solid understanding and good rapport with people, that I should put my talents to use by going on to school for a career in a 'helping' field. The viewpoint that I could always be counted on to be rational, have sound judgment, and offer useful advice, went as far back as my high school years. Even friends brought their personal problems to me, as if I were the local "Dear Abby." And, throughout the years, in a variety of different locations, and amongst a variety of different people, the viewpoint that I had what it took to help others did not change.

It only changed when I became involved with 12-Step programs.

Logically, if you look for answers in the wrong places, you will find the wrong answers. When I became involved with the programs, few people had any interest in who I really was, or the kind of person I was. Instead, they were content to 'measure' me by 'their own yardsticks'-- tagging me defective and useless.

One of the many oddities I encountered in the programs was the NRA viewpoint that there are two categories of people: they asserted that everyone outside the Program was 'in denial,' and everyone who belonged to the Program was too messed up to do or accomplish anything. In other words, NRA's do not believe the Program's statement *"Life on life's terms"* is based on reality.

So, in a relatively short period of time, I went from a fully-functioning adult to consistently hearing I must be in either one or the other of those categories. And not only me, but everyone else as well.

RESENTMENTS

When I was eight years old, we had a visit from a nine-year-old girl who lived in a different state; her father and my uncle had been Army buddies. The girl saw one of my toys, and asked if I would give it to her. This resulted in an ongoing exchange of my saying she could play with the toy but not take it home, and her pressing me to give it to her. Eventually, she took the toy and twisted it in her hands until it was ruined. Smugly, she remarked that the toy wasn't any good anymore, and smirked "You don't want it *now*, do you?"

Normal people are capable of appreciating something of someone else's, and appreciating the fact that it is indeed someone else's. Even a child who likes a friend's toy may ask to borrow it, or pester his parents to get one for him. Individuals who are abnormal, though, have an entirely different angle: if they want something that is someone else's, they will either take it or destroy it. It brings to mind a long-ago news story about some Junior High girls who threw acid in their friend's face because they were so jealous and resentful of how nice she looked with her new hairstyle.

From what I have experienced, there's no topic that causes resentments in the NRA population as much as the topic of *Family*. Whether it's a matter of one's family-of-origin or the family one has built in one's adult life, what they did not have, they resent other people having.

When it comes to the latter, I have seen a number of different categories. There are those who literally abandoned their own children; those who placed their 'lifestyle' above their children; those who abused or neglected their children, or both; those who had their kids taken away; and those who never had any in the first place. I've also known individuals who claimed they did not even know how many children they had. In every category, "family" was not their priority. Consequently, numerous individuals have had extreme resentments over the fact that throughout my entire adult life, my kids have been my priority. The havoc they have wreaked has gone way beyond outrageous. Similar to the nine-year-old girl, it has been like the Program saying "If you want what we've got, and are willing to go to any lengths to get it," the approach has been to try to take it or destroy it.

Background differences have also resulted in resentments. During my growing up years, I had the stable influences of my father and aunt. Throughout the majority of my childhood I lived in a 25-room house, and never lacked for anything. During those years, my father was in between his two main jobs, yet he always worked and supported his family. Despite my mother's oddities, there was always a clean house and food on the table. If these-- what one person referred to as 'advantages'-- weren't enough, I was taken care of when I was ill, listened to when I had something to say, and my childhood did not include anybody beating up on me. Any of these factors individually or combined has resulted in seething resentments from the NRA population.

Both subjects are covered as "what they did not have, they resent others having." However, there is one huge difference between the two categories: while a person's childhood was essentially out his hands, what a person does in and with his adult life usually has much to do with his own personal choices. In other words, NRA's who abandoned their kids, didn't have any, 'partied' their way through their kids' childhoods, etc., did so because that was what they *wanted* to do.

One NRA went as far as to admit how much he resented the good relationships and bonds between my kids and myself-- most are not that honest. They simply take out their own wrongs and failures on someone who did not commit those wrongs and failures. Before my first child was born, I decided I was going to be a good parent-- and I've put every possible effort into doing so. The fact is the chaos, upheaval, and negativities only began when resentful NRA's began running roughshod over our lives.

Resentments is a topic covered in great detail in the 12-Step Programs-- because it is amongst the most destructive elements in an alcoholic/addict's life. A person who has been successful with his or her recovery does not use Resentments to harm others. "Winners" appreciate that what is someone else's actually is someone else's, and if he or she wants something similar for himself or herself, they earn it or build it for themselves.

THEY HAVE ONLY ONE ANSWER

Not only from my own experiences, but experiences from many other former program members, also, brought psychological manipulations to the top of the list of the goings-on in the programs. One form of manipulation which many others have commented about is the NRA response to not getting their own way. If a person refuses to go along with something he or she does not wish to go along with, the NRA will not simply take no for an answer-- instead, he will claim there is something wrong with the person.

A brief, minor situation I experienced can illustrate this point. Many years ago, tired and with a little free time while waiting for my bus, I happened to go into the office of an apartment building where I had previously lived. The managers who had worked there when I lived there had moved away, and the office was being tended to by a temporary assistant. I was invited to sit at the table to wait for my bus to arrive. During my wait, the temporary manager chatted about nothing in particular, and there was only one oddity: upon noticing there was an ashtray on the table, I took a pack of cigarettes from my purse and started to light one. The temporary manager barked loudly in my face: "Do not *ever* light a cigarette in my presence!" Taken aback, I started to put my cigarette back into the package-- and he immediately began laughing, turning on his own cigarette lighter and extending it toward me.

Other than that idiotic demonstration, there was nothing unusual; he simply chatted pleasantly about the neighborhood and similar trivial topics. However, when it was time for me to leave, he changed his approach. He said I should skip taking my bus, take one the next day instead, and go out for a "nice dinner" with him, and then accompany him back to his apartment for the night.

Making my way to the door, I politely refused. Like any NRA, he did not take a simple no for an answer. Instead, he did a dismissing motion with his arm, and sneered: "Oh, you're crazy anyway."

This relatively minor, yet rattling, experience sums up NRA's approach to being turned down or told 'no.' You are allegedly not a human being with the right of free will-- you are simply 'crazy' if you do not go along with what they want. In some instances it is nothing more than a one-time dismissal; in others, asserting your right to say no brings on full-fledged attacks, character-assassinations, and damage to your reputation.

In other words, NRA's believe they are entitled to whatever they want-- and, one way or another, will put you in a negative position if they do not get it. You may find yourself defending yourself when you should not need to do so-- or you may find the NRA has taken it as far as to damage your reputation. In the world of non-recovered alcoholics/addicts, other people do not have rights-- including the right of free will.

COWARDICE

I see nearly every topic in existence differently than "the NRA population." One topic in particular, which has surfaced time and time again, is the way they see deception and underhandedness.

Individuals who seek to wrong or harm others do so in a sneaky manner-- not only the 13th-steppers I've had the misfortune of knowing along the way, but others as well. Their approach is "*Say/do behind a person's back so the person does not have the chance to defend herself-- and by the time she finds out what's going on, it will be too late.*"

I have noticed those who use this approach see themselves as "clever." That's the word that came to mind when I began to think about it-- not clever in terms of smart, but they feel they are "*getting away with*" something; they feel they are *"putting something over on"* someone-- like a sneaky child who does wrong, and is clever enough to not get caught.

I have actually seen instances in which NRA's seemed to get as much, or even more, from this "game" than they did from its results. Lying about a person behind the person's back, participating in wrongful behaviors, etc., is like tittering with childish glee over "getting away with" something.

I see it much differently: I see those who resort to sneakiness and underhandedness as *Cowards*-- for only cowards resort to sneaking around to get what they want.

To complicate matters, many are also what the older generation would have called "two-faced;" "phony" is another accurate term-- the way they treat you to your face is much different from what they are saying about you behind your back.

In my opinion, anyone who cannot be upfront is a gutless coward-- yet they see themselves as clever little children.

Some cowards also demonstrate the same kind of cowardice as schoolyard bullies. The only way they can interact with others is by force or with threats. You may be surprised at how many adult-aged NRA's cannot face others without the "backup" of their associates, weapons, size, or whatever else they need to have on their side because they are nothing more than cowardly little children.

When it comes to NRA's, though, nothing is simple. While I was not familiar with any of these approaches, there was an additional factor I was also not familiar with. Amongst normal people, wrongdoing is automatically highlighted by a person's conscience-- he or she feels bad about what he or she has done. However, the most warped NRA's do not stop at "tittering with childish glee," but go further to express scorn and contempt for the individuals they have harmed. One NRA, for example, smirked that a woman was "a stupid bitch who doesn't have a clue." While that and similar examples made my skin crawl, I later learned contempt and scorn for one's victims is yet another hallmark of a sociopath: whatever the wrongdoing consists of, a sociopath believes the victim 'deserves' it because the victim is 'stupid.'

SANITY

If you look at the Twelve Steps, one of the first things you may see is the reference to *'sanity.'* The viewpoint, which appears to be completely accurate, is drug and alcohol abuse interferes with 'sane' attitudes, beliefs, and behaviors, and puts attitudes, beliefs, and behaviors that are 'not sane' in their place. On this particular side of the topic, a large percentage of recovery is about changing those attitudes, beliefs, and behaviors from 'not sane' to 'sane.' The Programs add that it is not only about "the Program"-- one must also apply these principles to everyday life. It is not impossible, for I have known many individuals who had had drug and/or alcohol problems who successfully accomplished it. They are, without a doubt, "Winners."

There is another, equally valid, side to this topic. While you may see it to some degree in general, it is especially clear when it comes to "13th-Stepping." As I have discussed in the section on 13th-Stepping, NRA's who engage in this kind of behavior not only have years or decades of active drinking or using, they also have years or decades of "Programs." It is, as a friend said, a matter of *"some stay sick, and others get worse."* Some of the literature even addresses the issue: individuals whose primary purpose in 12-Step programs is to use what they learn in the programs to continue wrongful behaviors and harming others, rather than to make progress with recovery.

Speaking only from my own experiences, 13th-Steppers-- at least those I've encountered-- are not 'insane;' not by the commonly-accepted definitions, anyway. The commonly-accepted definitions of 'insane' are a) the individual lacks the ability to recognize the wrongfulness of his or her actions, and/or b) lacks the ability to refrain from those actions.

In contrast, the 13th-Steppers know exactly what they are doing-- *and* that their actions are wrong. Each of the examples I describe involved NRA's who went out of their way to hide what they were doing-- *so they would get the results they wanted without getting caught.*

THIRTEEN

Throughout my life, I had a well-deserved good reputation. This changed when I became involved in 12-Step programs. On the minor end of the scale-- although it was far from minor-- individuals took their negative characteristics and placed them on me. In many cases, it was nothing more than an honest mistake on their part. However, on the most serious end of the scale have been those who, despite knowing the facts, lied for their own personal gain. These acts of defamation destroyed my reputation, and, with it, both my credibility and interactions with others.

The fact is NRA's who engaged in defamation did so for that precise purpose-- there is no surer, easier way for wrongdoers to "get away with" something than to destroy a person's reputation and credibility.

During the last few years, especially, whenever I happen to meet up with individuals whom I'd met briefly in the past, or never set eyes on before, they look at me with disgust. Depending on the particular individual and situation, the approach toward me is of someone they do not wish to associate with, someone to take advantage of, or someone to pity.

It can be summed up quite accurately in that old childhood taunt: "Liar, Liar, pants-on-fire." In each instance, wrongdoers had no conscience about how their lies and underhandedness affected other people; there has been no extreme too great, when it was for the purpose of getting away with something-- and getting something they wanted, at someone else's expense.

In three different instances, I became a target for what is sometimes called "13th-Stepping." In the broadest sense of the term, 13th-Stepping is about taking advantage of and exploiting someone who is vulnerable. In each instance, there were two reasons I was vulnerable enough to be "chosen" as a target: first, as I had no substance-dependency issues, I knew nothing about "the nature of addiction;" and second, I was new to areas where I did not know anyone and no one knew me.

The first and third incidents involved individuals; the second incident involved a male-and-female team. In each situation, there were clear patterns in what I experienced:

A 12-Step Program states "the nature of addiction" often includes "*manipulating people and manipulating situations.*" To *manipulate* is defined as being "shrewd and devious"-- dishonest, underhanded, and sneaky. Although 13th-Stepping may vary, this is what I experienced in three different locations. Using the term 13th-Stepping in its broadest sense-- to target and exploit a person-- each situation could easily be described in program terms: *"If you want what we've got- and are willing to go to any lengths to get it."* Although my experiences were by no means uncommon, all of the situations involved a number of very clear patterns:

1. In each situation, my vulnerability to 13th-Steppers had nothing to do with drugs or alcohol; I was vulnerable because I was new to each area, didn't know my way around, and didn't know anyone. This factor resulted in a) having no one to turn to for help; and b) locals who did not know me were easily convinced of whatever the NRA's wanted them to believe.

2. In each situation, the NRA's lied to people about how they knew me, and how they had come to be in my life. While in each situation the NRA's were total strangers whom I had never even met before, the liars claiming otherwise led people to believe they had known me for a considerable period of time, that they had been on good personal terms with me, and therefore "knew all about" me.

The first liar claimed we had known each other a decade in the past; the second purported we had been close friends for a long time; the third claimed we were in a personal relationship. While all of these were lies, it led people to believe the NRA's knew what kind of person I was, and believe the liars had a legitimate place in my life.

3. In each situation, the NRA's told outrageous lies about me behind my back so I did not have the option of defending myself or refuting the lies. The slander involved such topics as claiming I had been in a drug rehabilitation facility, often wandered around drunk in public, was using illegal drugs, had mental illnesses, neglected my family, was a prostitute, was a drug dealer, was immoral, was abusive, committed harassment, and a variety of other accusations that contained not a shred of truth. Each lie was concocted by the 13th-Steppers to portray me as someone who could not be believed or trusted. People thought the worst of me because they didn't know me and I was not there to defend myself.

And, as anyone who is familiar with abusers knows, the surest way of getting what they want and getting away with it is to discredit the person-- if they can get people to believe you're a bad person and/or there is something wrong with you, no one will listen to you if you do reach out for help. Attempting to silence victims with character-assassinations about "abusiveness," immorality, and lack of mental stability, not only helps 13th-Steppers get away with their behavior, but is the hallmark of *most* abusive situations.

4. In each situation, they tried to break me down by what some referred to as a "hostage situation." They attempted to *control* where I went, what I did, and with whom I associated. (Keep in mind these were individuals whom I had just met.) The purpose of this type of situation: so I could not go to anyone for help, and so they could continue spreading damaging slander.

5. In each situation, the 13th-Steppers further attempted to break me with verbal attacks and bullying. This included such behaviors as intimidating me into remaining silent about the goings-on, threats of physical violence and other extreme consequences, actual assault, and various other behaviors designed to threaten and intimidate me.

6. Each situation involved 13th-Steppers who claimed to have diagnosed but untreated mental illnesses, histories of drug and alcohol abuse, histories of abuse against women and/or children, criminal backgrounds (three of the four were convicted felons, one of whom was a murderer).

And, common to 13th-Stepping, all four of the individuals claimed "double-digit" clean/sober time in 12-Step programs. This, I suppose, is what's meant by "Some stay sick, and some get even worse."

So, in each of these situations, upon landing in new areas where I didn't know anyone, 13th-Steppers had chosen me as a target for precisely that reason. They could be accurately described as predators and perpetrators-- not as individuals who 'worked a program.'

The difference, however, was in their M.O.:

In the first instance, I had no idea about any of the goings-on until it was all over-- I was then given a long letter written by the individual, in which he admitted everything. It was essentially a matter of 'Ha ha, look what I got away with.'

In the second instance, the two individuals evidently did not want me to ever know the facts, and assumed I never would find out. Eventually, I was given the facts by the authorities.

In the third instance, there was an even sicker aspect to the individual's approach and behavior: the NRA frequently approached me, informing me of what he *had* done, *was* doing, and was *going* to do-- always with a shrug and a smirk, challenging me with statements to the tune of 'Go ahead and tell people, go ahead and report me- nobody will believe you.'

So while the first two situations involved NRA's who were "shrewd, devious, dishonest, underhanded, and sneaky," simply deciding what they wanted and going after it, the third had the additional tack of "creating powerlessness" and daring me to try to do anything about it.

I will also add- similar to what Dr. Sandra Brown (an expert in the field) says about such individuals, those who have no conscience about the harm they cause others would also have no hesitation in using any means to silence a person permanently. They do not see human beings *as* human beings, but merely as an object and an inconvenience.

I believe it is also important to note an additional pattern: in each of these situations, there was not a single instance of 'hit or miss'-- each individual decided what they wanted, and systematically and methodically planned and carried out each tactic, behavior, and action that would result in reaching their goals- *and, equally important,* that would result in them not getting caught. And, true to form, none had any conscience about anything they did, nor about the consequences.

There are various viewpoints on how these kinds of situations can go on with such regularity. My point of view is while some individuals in programs may believe 13th-Steppers

152

are not that big of a deal, others are simply gutless cowards--
even if they know human beings are being harmed, they are
simply too chicken to speak up and say it is wrong, or to defend
people who are being harmed. And, as the saying goes, "If you're
not part of the solution, you're part of the problem."

You can use two references-- the literature of the 12-Step
programs, and the "12 Steps" themselves-- and you will see a
huge difference between the situations I experienced and what
these programs describe as "recovery." As a matter of fact,
something very important comes up near the beginning of
Stepwork-- look at the literature, or any other resource where it
can be found, and read the words of "Step 2." You can follow it
by reading about "moral inventories," "the exact nature of
wrongs," "removing shortcomings," and "making amends."
Evidently, none of these individuals "worked the Steps"-- and
you can go as far back as Step 2 to see how they never applied it
to their attitudes, beliefs, and behaviors. There is nothing
whatsoever that could be defined as "*sanity.*"

In each instance the 13th-Steppers wanted something
from me, and these are the tactics they used. An important point
to bear in mind is each and every one of the 13th-Steppers
claimed to have belonged to one or more 12-Step programs for a
decade or longer.

THIRTEETH-STEP: NUMBER ONE:
OUT OF THE FRYING PAN, INTO THE FIRE

When I boarded a bus at Chestnut Street in August, 1998,
I was not aware the bus's destination would be the first step in my
journey through Hell. Looking back, there were signs that
something was very wrong-- but, as this and other situations
illustrate, it is easy to miss signs when you have no idea what

they mean, because it is nothing like anything you have ever experienced before.

I didn't think it unusual to have "pen-pals," as it was something I'd done when I was much younger without any negative complications. In addition, the first individuals I communicated with were people with whom I had much in common, and they generally seemed like good people. So, when an NRA whom I will call "Paul" approached me, I didn't pay as much attention as I should have to what I believed were simple oddities on his part-- not realizing they were "danger signs," and not knowing numerous situations would later play themselves out again and again as symptoms of "the nature of addiction."

First, in psychobabble terms, he "played the victim." It was like what we normies would call "sob-stories," or what some in Programs call "being on the pity-pot." Because of the alleged "abuse" he'd suffered as a child, he claimed his "issues" were "fear of rejection and fear of abandonment." While he commented that he'd used and discarded countless numbers of women, and had abandoned his own wife and child, he claimed his only wish was to have people to consider his Family. He said if I'd agree to move there, I could have a good job with a reasonably good income, a nice home that I could 'decorate' however I chose, and I'd eventually be able to afford to move back to California.

At first, his "poor me" approach worked. As I'd never encountered anything like that before, I believed he was on the level. However, upon careful consideration of the situation, I had second thoughts-- perhaps it would not be a good idea to relocate to an unfamiliar area where I didn't know anyone. When I expressed my hesitation, his response was one I encountered numerous times since then: *my refusal to blindly go along with what he wanted meant, in his words, that I was "sick."*

I didn't know what to make of it, but when I brushed it off he used another tack: verbal bullying. Remarks of the kind I'd never heard in my life, such as "why don't you get your head out of your ass?!" Thinking it was nothing more than frustration or minor anger, I brushed that off, too.

If I'd known anything about the nature of NRA's, and how their perceptions are not based in reality, numerous comments should have been a red flag. One example was a remark about not believing I was actually single: "I know you're lying! I know you're married-- and the bastard is Abusing you!"

His next tack did me in: he said if I did not show up before the end of August, he would commit suicide. He said he even had a tombstone designed for this purpose. Believing someone's life was literally in my hands, I fell for it.

When I arrived, I found a much different situation than what I had been told. First, I found I was not going to get the job. He smirked that the woman in charge of hiring only hired people with certain qualifications, and they were qualifications which I did not have; and the 'nice home' was actually his fully-decorated apartment, in which I was not to touch anything. Second, I was forced into a phony "marriage" (which I later had annulled). Third, after the verbal and mental abuse escalated into physical, it was the first time in my life I'd ever needed to obtain a restraining order against anyone. Fourth, he stole virtually everything I owned. Fifth, not only was this NRA in a variety of 'programs,' so was virtually everyone he knew. As such, I was put in even worse positions by these individuals backing him up. One example was I found I had no legal right to live in the apartment-- my name had never been put on the lease.

Similar to the other 13th-Steppers, his focus was on *"abuse."* It was the first time anyone had ever asked "Who abused you- was it your Mom and Dad?" No one before had ever said anything like that. However, the NRA in question made it clear he was not talking about physical abuse or neglect, but sexual abuse. When I said nothing like that had ever happened, he took an approach that I'd describe as insidious-- he started asking me all kinds of questions, and when I happened to mention I'd had a minor medical issue when I was a young child that required prescription medication, he fell silent, got a weird look on his face, and, after asking me to describe the size, shape, and color of the pills, said in an odd tone that my parents had been 'lying' to me, that the medication was not for the medical condition, but that it was a powerful narcotic and they were 'drugging' me in order to 'abuse' me. (Years later, I found the drug he was insisting they'd given me was not even available in the United States at the time).

Next, he zeroed in on my much-older brother, and claimed he must have 'abused' me, also. He then got ahold of all my family pictures, tossed them in a wastebasket and set fire to them. He said 'You've gotta mark them all as Perpetrators.'

There were other similarities, too: he flat-out told me he was jealous of, and resentful of, the bond between myself and my adult-aged child. He said he also resented the fact that my youngest was a healthy, happy, boisterous kid who'd had a chance to live a normal childhood. He made a point of avoiding my adult-aged son as much as possible, while acting like my youngster's childhood playmate, and tried to turn her against me by giving her permission to do things that I'd told her she could not do. He also tried to ally her by giving her money.

However-- it was the entire scenario of deception that was the main issue; and, as usually happens with 13th-Steppers, I had no knowledge of any of it until it was too late for me to do anything about it:

Before I moved to that particular area, this NRA had told everyone he knew that he and I had had an affair years earlier when we were 'in a rehab together.' He said I popped up out of his past to inform him the brief affair had resulted in a child-- his biological child. As I didn't know about any of this, I was surprised when everyone in the area greeted and welcomed me so warmly.

The truth: I had never met the guy before. We had never even lived in, or been in, the same states. And I have certainly never been in a "rehab"!

After the NRA got what he wanted (money from the IRS that he was not legitimately entitled to, quantities of food stamps that he was not legitimately entitled to, and emptying out my bank account), he told everyone that I'd been lying to him from the beginning, and had just then told him the child in question was not really his. As I didn't know about this, either, I didn't understand why everyone had suddenly turned cold and distant toward me. The reason was he convinced them that I was a liar, a schemer, and an opportunist.

The truth: obviously, since I'd never met the guy, I'd never said anything about the child being his.

In the interim, I was prevented from associating with people-- he didn't want to risk anyone learning the truth about his scams by "comparing notes" with me.

After he got everything he wanted, his tack was to get me out of the state as quickly as possible. His means to this end was he took all the money out of my bank account and took all of the food stamps, so my family and I had nothing to live on. As he said he would give me a very small amount of my money back if I left the state, I had no other options.

First, I tried to sell the typewriter my father had given to me to a local thrift shop so I could buy food; as he was a "regular" at the store, he'd told them to not buy anything from me because anything I might try to sell was actually "his."

Second, an acquaintance offered to let my family stay with her family until I could figure out what to do-- but he said he would keep all of my money if I did so. The acquaintance then offered to hold onto items we couldn't carry with us-- and later told me her "friends in the Program" advised her to sell all of our possessions and keep the money.

Third, the restraining order backfired-- I learned my name had never been put on the lease, and, because the landlords were "in the Program" they told me I had to leave so "Paul" could move back into the apartment.

Shortly before I left, one of his friends approached me and told me Paul said I'd 'just then informed him' that the child in question was not his. This was the first I heard of any of it. I didn't get the whole story until I was waiting to board the bus and was given a letter he had written, detailing his scam from beginning to end: it was "all about" claiming a "daughter," "wife," and "'stepson'" that were not actually his, and claiming we had been in the state much longer than we actually had been, so he could get a huge refund from the IRS and a large amount of food stamps that he was not entitled to. *"Because I deserve it"* was his rationalization.

Similar to the other 13th-Steppers, he believed he "deserved" what he had no right to; and similar to the other 13th-Steppers, he had no conscience about the consequences to my family and myself.

As the first NRA I had ever met in person, there was nothing whatsoever about the entire situation that I had ever encountered, experienced, or witnessed before. *Nothing whatsoever.* One example-- and the complications and confusion it caused-- came from one of the initial comments Paul had made: *"Half this town is in recovery- and the other half should be."* I was one-hundred-percent clueless about what he meant.

What I found: I had very little access to "average people;" instead, it was a matter of "NRA's on one side, and the Authorities who were trying to help me on the other." As I'd had no experience with either segment of the population, it was a confusing and difficult situation.

First, I learned the landlord was *"in the program."* This individual approached me, telling me if I did not drop the restraining order against Paul, I'd no longer have a place to live. He conveniently left out the fact that since he had never put my name on the lease, I'd have no place to live anyway.

In addition, whether he was aware of it or not, *I* had not requested the restraining order-- the police and Assistant District Attorney had initiated it. How this occurred: a police officer arrested him for committing a minor physical assault while trying to stop me from walking out of the apartment. This resulted in being "squashed in the middle" between Paul and his Program friends, and the Authorities. On one side, his friends were demanding I have the restraining order dropped, demanding I state that I 'over-reacted.' At the same time, the Authorities, who were obviously experienced with such issues, pressed me to keep the restraining order they'd initiated in place-- they clearly knew that even a minor incident was likely to escalate into something more serious, even though I myself was not aware of it.

And it turned out the Authorities were correct: Paul later claimed I'd "betrayed" him, and that he 'should have punched my lights out.' And, similar to all manipulative NRA's, he even tried to present himself as 'the good guy'-- saying he'd done me a favor by not lying to the police, because he could have lied and said *I* had physically attacked *him*. It was the first example where I learned experienced authorities are more knowledgeable about the underhanded and abusive ways of NRA's-- but it was only the first experience of its kind.

Second, a good-hearted but clueless individual who seemed to be new to the programs spoke to me as if he felt I was being foolish and unreasonable: urging me to jump at the chance to move to a different state, he exclaimed: "You have a *job* there! And a place to live!" This person expressed his opinion that anyone who was involved with a 12-Step program was clearly honest and trustworthy.

What it came down to was I had no options. Paul had taken all of my money and the food stamps so my family and I had nothing to live on, claiming he would give me a small amount of my money back *only* if I left the state immediately. In addition, he stole my lottery winnings. While buying lottery tickets was something I rarely indulged in, I purchased a ticket for one dollar, and won fifty dollars; and while neither my one-dollar investment nor the winnings belonged to him, he simply stole what I had won. At the time, I was not yet aware of the term *"financial predators"*-- nor the fact that these programs are full of them.

The most important point: Paul was my first in-person experience with an NRA who met a common factor of NRA's in general-- *they are not who or what they present themselves to be.*

Now, you can read this story and accurately conclude Paul was a liar, a manipulator, an opportunist, but there is even more to it: not only do NRA's with personal, wrongful motives attempt to "rewrite" other people's life histories, they also tend to rewrite their own.

Although I'd had no prior experience with such individuals or situations, as the saying goes, certain things "did not click," or "did not add up"-- that is, his attitudes and behaviors did not add up to the stories he had told. They did not add up to someone who had been severely abused and repeatedly sexually abused throughout his childhood and youth; they added up to someone who had severely damaged his own brain from decades of ingesting every drug imaginable.

There was an additional point that I did not pay much attention to at the time. As it should be clear that when situations are occurring that are so far from anything one has ever experienced, and one's entire focus is survival and the survival of loved ones, much can be overlooked that should not be overlooked.

The additional point: even after Paul got his own way-- obtained everything he was after-- there was an incident that should have caused great alarm. Not only did I find he still had a knife, but that it was strategically placed in a manner that could only have had one purpose. Between the location of the knife and various details about my living arrangement, there is absolutely no other conclusion than Paul's intent to stab me to death while I slept.

The situation clearly showed intent-- premeditation. Similar to other NRA's, the entire situation from the beginning was no more nor less than use human beings, and have no qualms about 'offing' them afterward.

Although I did take the knife to the police, I was too busy leaving the state to follow up on it.

NRA's treat their Programs as a cover or as a joke. They have no concern for 'recovery' or 'change.' One of the many examples involving Paul: one day he approached me with false contriteness, saying he had 'relapsed' the night before. While I did not know much about the programs at that time, one thing I did know was what A.A. and N.A. mean by that word is someone who has been 'clean and/or sober' has 'blown it' by drinking or using drugs. Upon pressing him, I found he was not talking about alcohol or drugs: "I relapsed on *potato chips,"* he said.

With all of his manipulations, deceit, and other lownesses, there was yet another purpose to his wish to portray me in roles that were not actually mine. As he had lost his privilege to drive anywhere in the United States, he asked me to write a letter to the state where he had initially lost his license-- to say what an honest, responsible, upstanding citizen he had become.

THIRTEENTH-STEP: NUMBER TWO:
CORRUPTION IN THE DEEP SOUTH

The next NRA I encountered wanted me to believe that not only I, but also every member of my family, were "drug addicts." As I've stated in this book, I have never had any interest in "mind-altering, mood altering substances;" however, this particular NRA insisted I was a 'drug addict.'

As she had nothing to go on, because there was nothing there, she put great effort into fishing for "some something." Upon hearing I'd had an allergic reaction to one normal dose of cold medication years before I met her, she'd pounced on this information with fervor-- claiming I was an 'addict' who had 'relapsed,' and if I were to 'go into denial' about it I'd 'end up with an eating disorder.' Furthermore, she insisted if a parent or sibling correctly used a prescription medication for a legitimate medical purpose, that meant 'they were all addicts, too.' Claiming double-digit time in Programs, she heard at every single meeting that an addict is someone whose life is controlled by drugs; but the facts did not interest her in the slightest.

If this was not enough, she went even further: as one of the NRA's who had claimed large numbers of sex partners, she met my disapproval by saying since I had never engaged in that kind of behavior I must be a 'lesbian in denial.' She added if I did not believe this, I 'had not made much progress in Recovery.'

The situation:

1. The woman, who had consistently presented herself and her boyfriend as a married couple, lured me and my kids to the area where they lived with the promise of a job and help finding an apartment. I arrived to find the job did not exist; and she informed me I must give all of my money to her son who lived next door, in order to be his "roommates."

2. The woman and her boyfriend immediately began trying to alienate my ten-year-old against me and my son. As examples, they gave her money, telling her she must keep it in their apartment or else 'your mother and brother will steal it from you.' They also told her 'don't listen to anything your mother and brother say-- we're the only ones who know what's best for you.' (Keep in mind these were individuals whom we had never met before).

3. When my son was sitting calmly at our computer, the woman's boyfriend barged in, ran over to him, and began choking him. He grabbed my son, slamming him into the back of his chair over and over again.

4. After those incidents, I rented a place a few blocks away and got a job as a Home Health Aide. I sent an email to the woman telling her I didn't want her or her boyfriend to have any contact with my child. (They responded to this by starting to file streams of false reports with Child Protective Services, although I didn't know it at the time.)

5. One morning when I was waiting for the school bus, the guy approached me and began threatening me with physical harm. I went to the police department and asked if I could obtain a restraining order to keep them away from my kids and myself. I was told I could not.

6. When I found my new landlady and her boyfriend were drug dealers, I felt the need to move. In one instance, a guy

who had been telling people he wanted to rent his trailer offered to let us stay there. He stole nearly everything my son owned, from his CD collection to his clothes; but although he admitted to the sheriff's deputy that he'd done it, the deputy told me nothing could be done about it. I later found this guy was a friend of the couple's, and he'd stolen from my son because they told him to.

7. My job hours were lengthening so I rarely saw anyone, but noticed many individuals in the program had begun treating me strangely-- women whom I'd thought were my friends would no longer associate with me, and refused my phone calls; numerous odd men began propositioning me. I later found the reason for this was the couple was telling people I'd been lying about having a job and was actually a prostitute. They said I "solicited for prostitution to pay rent and buy cigarettes." They also said I 'married some guy that I'd met over the internet.' These statements, naturally, were lies.

8. One day my youngster came home from school with a business card from a Child Protective Services social worker. When the worker came to the house, I found the couple had started the reports *the day after* I told them to stay away from my youngster. The social worker said CPS knew it was a scam, but after four months of being consistently harassed by the couple, they were required by law to investigate. The false allegations included claiming I never fed my child anything but 'Vienna Sausages and Cheez-Whiz,' that I habitually wandered around the city drunk, that I was often under the influence of 'some kind of drugs,' that I had 'some kind of mental illness.' Every one of those allegations was a lie.

As per the law, CPS investigated, including communications with staff at my child's school, my employer, my landlord, and even neighbors. She and I both underwent psychological evaluations, and she underwent an evaluation for sexual abuse. The conclusions were that there was nothing wrong with either of us, that she'd never been abused or neglected in any way, and that she was a "happy, well-adjusted child." In fact, they said the only thing unusual was a youngster who had just turned eleven years of age had "the intellect of an average twenty-four-year-old."

During this time, the woman continued to call CPS; the social worker said one message she left was "I'll keep torturing you and torturing you until you take that child away!" She said the woman's boyfriend started dropping into her office, too. One of the social workers also told me the woman claimed to have connections to one of the state's senators, and if CPS did not do what she wanted she would go to the senator to override CPS.

9. Two more incidents occurred: in one instance, the woman approached my child when she was alone, attempting to get her into her car; in another instance, the woman approached her and again gave her some money.

10. When they found CPS was not going to take my child, as there was no reason to do so, they tried another tactic: the woman had her sister, an attorney, draw up a petition for a restraining order, filled with nothing but lies. She claimed I'd been repeatedly harassing her by phone, had vandalized her son's car, hung around in their yard at early hours of the morning, and followed them around the city. A second CPS social worker came into the picture and became very upset when I showed her the petition. She said the couple wanted to get the adults in my family thrown in jail so they could have access to my child.

This social worker told me the couple had "such powerful connections" in the state that I could never win against them in court, and that the authorities would never protect my family from them. She also said the sister had somehow managed to choose one particular judge to preside on the case, and told me no parent ever stood a chance with this judge. She advised me the only thing I could do for my family's safety would be to leave the state immediately, and CPS bought us bus tickets to do so. I met an attorney, and he agreed with what she said; he added if I left the state, I'd forfeit the case and the couple would 'win.' He also said it would be a bad idea for me to go to court, because, in his words "You've already lost, because they have all the power."

There was, though, an additional factor connected to the NRA's requesting a restraining order without grounds: while my first visit to the police resulted in being brushed off, my second visit eventually netted results. The second officer I spoke with took my report to file criminal charges against the woman's boyfriend.

While I was not told whether or not the NRA was arrested on those charges, I was informed of a court date-- the NRA would have to appear in court to answer the charges I brought against him. However, *after* that particular court date was set, the NRA's petitioned for a restraining order, with *their* court date being set as shortly *before* the date the court had set on my behalf.

The results: as I was advised to relocate prior to the restraining order court date, it meant I was not present to go to court against the NRA for the criminal charges against him. And, because I was not present, he 'got off scott-free.'

11. After we settled in a different state, a longtime friend told me I should press charges against the couple. I contacted a victims' advocacy group, and the person I spoke with agreed with this. However, when I went back, and told them the names of the couple, they said they couldn't help me. Shortly after I arrived, someone from the Sheriff's office and a different social worker showed up at the door. I was informed the couple was now saying I was making my child go hungry (although she was sitting there eating dinner when they came to the door). This new social worker said there'd be another investigation, and that I'd also need to submit to drug testing. While I was offended at the thought that anyone would accuse me of using drugs, I took the test. However, the situation went way beyond offensive: upon informing me I would be submitting to a drug test later that day, the social worker told me that when I went out for lunch I must tell the cashier in the fast-food place to make sure the hamburger rolls did not contain sesame seeds. Outside sources netted the information that eating sesame seeds would result in a false-positive for marijuana. Not only did this incident dictate what I could and could not eat, it essentially branded me a 'drug addict'--

for no one other than a drug addict would make an issue of whether or not there were sesame seeds on hamburger rolls.

As the school term was beginning, we got on a bus and left again, so my youngster would be back in time for school. The social worker informed me she'd be conducting the investigation with my child's new school, and other people in the area.

All of these incidents were very wrong, and many were criminal actions. Not only had I relocated in good faith over a job offer, upon finding the job didn't exist I took the right steps to get a place to live and support my family with a legitimate job. I have always been good to my kids, and always provided for them. However, the situation was outrageous: as the woman had told me she'd lost their daughter before birth, they were sick enough to believe they could simply take mine-- and had no reservations about breaking the law, destroying my reputation, physically attacking my son, and putting us through the humiliation of "child abuse" investigations, in order to get what they wanted. The second social worker said the couple believed if they could get my child out of my custody, they could "adopt" her. In addition, after my family was out of the state, a friend informed me the couple had started using similar tactics on another young mother and her child. While I did not learn about the outcome of that particular situation, the couple was never held accountable for what they did to my family.

Where I'm from, the general idea is law-abiding people have nothing to fear-- and if people do find themselves in dangerous situations, they can count on the authorities to help and protect them. Unfortunately, I have learned in some areas this is not true-- as the social worker and lawyer told me, in some areas it is "all about power." In the area in question, a couple of NRA's had the "power" to run roughshod over our rights, attempt to tear my family apart; and, as is the case with the addict/alcoholic population who has no interest in recovery, got away with it.

166

To be completely fair and honest, those meetings-- which were the first 12-Step meetings I'd attended-- were filled with good, kind, decent people. That statement described the majority. The catch: regardless of age, gender, or the length of time they had belonged to *the program*, they were also *powerless*-- powerless to stand up against a couple of sick, twisted "oldtimers." Not only did they feel unable to "do the right thing," none warned me about what was going on behind my back.

This was why I not only did not understand many people treating me differently than they had before, but also did not understand comments that were said directly to me. As the the sick freaks portrayed me as "a low, desperate addict," one individual who believed their scam remarked "*They're only trying to help you!*"

Another oldtimer said: *"What they did to you was shitty-- just plain shitty!"* and another remarked: *"Everybody deserves a chance!"* Clearly even those who were on my side believed the garbage the couple was saying behind my back-- and I could not defend myself against the lies, because I was still not aware of it.

However-- one of the most asinine, outrageous remarks I heard was: "You should *pray* for them-- because they are *spiritually sick.*"

How did all of this occur with many people being aware of the situation even before I knew anything about it myself? There was much about this couple that was also unlike anything I had ever encountered, witnessed, or experienced. One example was the way they managed to "run roughshod" over every person they knew. In addition to their lying, underhandedness, and sneakiness, it was mindboggling the way they managed to dominate everyone.

The guy was a middle-aged ex-con who managed to terrorize nearly everyone-- including full-grown men-- by frequently reminding them how much "time" he had done in the state penitentiary. He did not stop at this, but included his personal viewpoint of being a 'saved Christian'-- telling people "Jesus" was his "shield," and that he could easily commit more murders and "Jesus" would protect him from ever being held accountable. On a number of occasions I witnessed grown men essentially cowering in front of this NRA's insane rantings.

His girlfriend was the quintessential definition of a "control-freak." This was a subject I also had no experience with before I became involved with 12-Step programs. The woman had no qualms about ordering people around, being arrogant and obnoxious, and being "manipulative, abusive, and deceptive."

One of many incidents comes to mind: when I happened to wander into a meeting one evening, the woman lit up like a Christmas tree. I was not aware the two of them had planned it, wanting the opportunity to tell some of their lies in front of me. At one point, she requested that everyone join her in a prayer; as the other people bowed their heads when she instructed them to do so, she shot a smug glance at me and said: *"Let's all pray for an addict's children."*

Perhaps I should have said something, but my thoughts were accumulating faster than my ability to speak. The stupid lying tramp was fully aware that I was not an 'addict,' that I was a good parent, and that my kids were both doing fine. My other thought was if she had concern for 'an addict's children,' she should have looked in her mirror-- and asked herself how *her* kids had fared, having someone like that for a mother.

When it came to parents relating to kids in all age groups, this particular individual was the first-- but far from the last-- of something else I had never encountered before: not only treating kids horribly in general, but the sickening way the so-called mothers virtually emasculated their sons. Not only was I appalled at the way this NRA spoke to and treated her adult-aged son, but I witnessed numerous examples of the same approach.

Not only did so-called mothers berate their boys, but it was also clear they held their approval-- 'love'-- as a "carrot on a stick" that regardless of what the sons did, they could never attain that carrot. Males of all ages were crawling and scraping for approval-- yet appearing to know they could never have it. Regardless of age, they were not *accepted* as the people they were, nor were they *respected* as adults.

168

This twisted approach was not only common in addicted mothers and their sons, but also males who were addicts themselves. One guy, for example, remarked: *"My mama and daddy are punishing me- so they took away my car."* Now this would have sounded odd if the speaker had been a young teenager-- but he was at least in his mid-fifties. And I heard similar types of remarks from a few other guys in his age group.

"Authority-trips" go way beyond destructive. Can anyone really wonder how or why individuals on the receiving-end of this type of treatment go on to abuse drugs, abuse alcohol-- and never become capable of relationships based on mutual respect?

The ignorant woman in question, upon noticing my twenty-year-old loved my computer, happily remarked: "You have an excellent way to *control* him!" It was one of those instances where I knew it was pointless to try to talk sense into someone who obviously had none.

There have been so many examples of NRA's inability to recognize human beings as human beings. When the subject is children-- of any age-- many NRA's appear to be unable to recognize them as individual people. Instead, they see them as nothing more than extensions of themselves.

In the real world, normal parents have an entirely different view of the parental role: the idea is one guides one's youngsters through their growing-up years, and when the kids become adults the parental role shifts to offering advice and opinions when advice or opinions are asked for. In the NRA world, however, it is much different-- and damaging to everyone concerned.

One day, when we were still living next door to the woman, she caught up with me in the driveway, directing a question to me: *"Why do you allow your children to ABUSE you?!"* she demanded. Clueless, I asked her what she was talking about, and she replied my kids addressing me as 'Mom' was *'abuse'*-- because, in her opinion, they should have been addressing me as *'Ma'am.'*

Although it was only one of numerous examples of how NRA's who claim they were 'abused' during their lifetimes have very odd ideas of what constitutes 'abuse,' my kids and I had a good chuckle over it. *"This is our family, not the military- if you want to go for that Ma'am and Sir bit, join the Army,"* I told them.

The point, though, was the woman did not like the fact that I didn't look at or treat my kids as my 'subordinates'-- that while we were not peers, we were all equals. She thought it was very strange indeed. And, similar to all topics that involve NRA's, the fact that it was not 'her' way meant that it was very, very wrong.

The mistake I made: as uprooting and relocating was a chaotic experience, I didn't discuss any of this with either of my kids. As is the case when dealing with any non-recovered addicts/alcoholics, there is always "something going on;" and a consequence of that is there is rarely if ever an opportunity to "sit down and discuss things." While there was also the issue of wondering how in the universe to explain a situation like that to kids who had spent their young years around mostly normal people, "sitting down and discussing things"-- either one-on-one or as a family unit-- was something that had ceased being a part of our lives since we fell into the chaos of living amongst NRA's.

NRA's and chaos-- NRA's and manipulation-- NRA's and "always something going on behind one's back"-- these gutter-crawling examples were very good examples of what a person may be up against upon meeting Oldtimers in 12-Step programs. If the lies, underhandedness, and so forth that I already described was not enough, there was more. The library in that city, similar to other public libraries I have visited, had a policy that only people who were actually residents of the city could use their computers. As I was not aware of the college library when I first moved there, this came to mean it was a relatively long time before I had the chance to check my email. I was told I had to have a utility bill with my name on it before they would issue me a library card, and a library card was required for computer use.

When I was finally able to check my email, I was stunned to find an email the woman had written when I was en route to

the city. One can assume she was aware of the library policy--
and that it would be a long time before I read it. In the email, she
admitted her plans for our living arrangements; and, equally
distressing, she admitted her plans for my adult-aged son: that if
everything went the way they planned, everything he owned
would be stolen, he'd be out in the street, and end up in a
homeless shelter some fifty miles away. With the warped sense
of status-consciousness common amongst these types of
individuals, they felt he was our 'defense' against them getting
what they wanted, and intended for him to be as far away as
possible. When their initial plans did not work because first one
and then a second couple helped us in finding living
arrangements, the couples also ended up on their 'shit-list.'

However-- sending an email they knew I would not
receive for a long period of time was another illustration of how
manipulative they were. Initially, I did not know what to make of
their phoniness; and, having never been in that area before, I
made the mistake of thinking it was that region's form of
"Southern hospitality." In other words, I initially believed the
odd "interest" they were expressing in my youngster may have
been a common approach to new people in that region. That was
why I initially allowed things to pass that I was uncomfortable
with-- such as bringing her oranges, asking if she wanted to play
with their dogs, etc. I thought perhaps that type of behavior was
acceptable behavior in that particular region. It moved from odd
and uncomfortable to way out of line when these two total
strangers told her they wanted to give her an 'allowance,' and
started telling her she should not trust her own family. What they
did not count on was my "Yankee-born" youngster was too smart
for them, did not fall for their manipulations, and came to me
about it. In other words, they found they could not con a
youngster with bribery and other nonsense; and, considering the
ways they successfully manipulated everyone in their midst, I'm
sure they were totally stunned to find it did not work with a
youngster who had not yet reached eleven years of age.

As for my friend who "believed in The Program," and
believed Oldtimers are naturally trustworthy and honest, I saw
quite a lot of this viewpoint in this particular location. While the

sick "couple" intimidated some people and ran roughshod over others, there were also some individuals who believed they were truly good people. Similar to 13th-Steppers in general, the "couple" generated this admiration by consistently being gutter-crawling phonies.

Of their many sponsees, one African-American woman in particular completely mindboggled me with her admiration of her "sponsor." This woman was a very pleasant, intelligent, kind human being-- and she was totally snowed by her sponsor's phoniness. One day, for example, she gave me a ride, and, in mentioning her sponsor, broke out in a wide, bright smile; with her head bobbing up and down, she exclaimed: "Isn't she *great?!*"

I'd also heard this woman speak at a meeting-- where she'd said her sponsor had 'loved her, until she was able to love herself.' Evidently, this woman-- as well as many of their other sponsees-- accepted at face-value the "couple's" hugs and fake pleasantries, with no idea how they were talking about their sponsees behind their backs. As one of the most nauseating examples, admonishing the female sponsor's youngster about how he should appreciate his mother taking the time to drive him to school in a different town so he 'would not have to go to school with all those n-ggers.'

I wondered if the African-American woman, and other sponsees of her race, would have held them in such high regard if they'd known their sponsors considered them nothing more than 'n-ggers' whose children were not fit schoolmates for their youngster.

The repercussions of this situation did not end after we relocated to other areas. Along with the ongoing concerns and anger, there were other problems attached to the situation.

First, my initial reaction to this particular location was that it was one of the most beautiful places I had ever seen; I had thoughts of setting down roots, building a solid life for myself and my family. Obviously, when the criminals were backed up by their purported 'connections,' it was impossible. It was not even relevant that some of the criminal actions these NRA's took against us could have resulted in very severe penalties to them--

172

because they were never held accountable. I shudder to think of what could have become of us if there had not been that one particular agency the criminals did not have 'in their pockets.'

Second, not only did it interfere with my own lawful liberty, but prevented me from helping others in need. The most heartbreaking example involved a young gay guy who was an online buddy for nine years. As my young friend was frequently on the receiving end of harassment, had no family members in the area, and suffered from a variety of serious medical conditions, on a number of occasions he asked me to go there to help him and be supportive. It was heartbreaking to try to explain why I could never go there-- although I had committed no crimes, harmed no one, to set foot in that state would have put me in danger. Approximately a year ago, my young friend entered the hospital for the last time, and passed away from cancer a few days later.

In that particular state, for individuals to interfere with the lawful liberty of law-abiding citizens is a crime punishable by life imprisonment, with the possibility of the death penalty. However, similar to unprovoked physical assault, knowingly making false reports to government agencies, and the various other crimes the NRA's perpetuated, it is only one thing more they got away with.

"UNDUE INFLUENCE"

The 'couple' in the previous section basically had a monopoly on the 12-Step program in that particular area. Not only did they themselves have a wide range of sponsees, the sponsees also sponsored a number of people. What it came down to was one way or another, nearly everyone was connected to the couple. And, as such, theirs was the only frame-of-reference most people ever heard.

There was one individual who clearly illustrates the *power* of NRA's. The first thing about this individual that creeped me out was the way she introduced herself at the meetings. While the custom is for a person to introduce himself or herself by saying "My name is ___, and I am an addict (or alcoholic)," this woman took an entirely different approach. Not using her real name here, she would state "I am an addict called Nora." It immediately occurred to me that her name-- and herself-- were only secondary considerations; that in her opinion, describing herself as an addict was the priority.

However, before I learned of her connection to the couple, there were other incidents that did not add up. First, when I was frantically searching for someone to talk to, I approached Nora at a meeting where I knew the couple would not be. I showed her the paperwork I had been given by CPS that stated the couple's lies had been investigated and found to be untrue, and her reaction almost knocked me over. "That only means they did not *find* anything," she said.

The second incident: Nora remarked that she was 'glad she was clean before she had her children.' Although I couldn't understand her tone at the time, she was insinuating that *I was not.* I mean she was insinuating that I had been an actively-using drug addict throughout my children's lives, and also was at that time.

How does this meet the description of *undue influence?* As Nora and her husband and their two children had recently moved to that location from a different state, it did not seem likely that she had known the couple for very long-- *yet* she was perfectly willing to simply take whatever they said at face-value. In this situation, it was not simply a matter of the couple's lies vs. my word, it was a matter of their lies vs. my word *and* the word of CPS and everyone else who had been involved in the investigation.

Similar to others who have been under undue influence by NRA's, *everybody except the NRA's* was 'wrong'-- and only the NRA's knew *'the truth.'*

Eventually, I learned another factor in how and why they had such power. When I happened to run into Nora one day, and she remarked that she was preparing to go to her clean date anniversary party, she commented about the woman: "She'd better be there- she's *my Sponsor!*"

What it came down to: this newcomer to the area, who, by the ages her children appeared, claimed to have been 'clean' for a decade or more, was unable to see anything beyond what 'Sponsor' said-- neither I nor individuals working for a government agency were to be believed when 'Sponsor" said otherwise.

THIRTEENTH STEP: NUMBER THREE:
"I MADE A DECISION"

At a specific point in time, I assessed life from three different angles: first, all of the chaos and turmoil that had led up to that present day; second, that present day itself; and third, what the future would hold. Seeing the "wreckage" that had occurred due to NRA's overrunning our lives, I realized that if we were to have any kind of worthwhile futures-- individually and as a family unit-- the decisions I made in that present day would be exactly that: *my own personal decisions,* rather than allowing the whims and manipulations of NRA's to determine the course of events.

My priorities were my family, obtaining a job and providing for my household, and looking ahead to the future. With these priorities in mind, I made a decision: for however long I was in this very negative environment, I would have no personal involvements-- specifically, that I would have no 'guy' in my life.

The mistake I made: rarely seeing my son, who lived on the other side of the city, and my daughter busy with school and activities, I didn't tell them about my decision. In fact, there should not have been any reason to. However, in looking back, I often wondered: how everything could have been different if I *had* said something-- if everyone had known the truth from the beginning, perhaps the nightmare that occurred afterward would never have occurred at all.

The specific point in time is relevant.

Why is the specific point in time so relevant? because something happened less than two months later:

When I made the mistake of accepting "a ride home" from someone I did not know, and this NRA refused to take me home, instead keeping me out against my will, I said "*I am not interested in 'dating' anybody, and I do not want a 'relationship'*." His reply: "*No, you're just not ready-- but we're in one now!*"

When I eventually did get home, I'd been forcibly kept awake for two and a half days and nights straight. Ignoring my request for him to leave, he approached the teens and presented himself as if he had a legitimate reason to be in my home. After being forcibly kept awake for that period of time, my mind blacked out.

And, both in terms of how the individual got into our lives in the first place, and everything that occurred afterward, the teens have never known the truth. He played them like pawns on a chessboard or puppets-- portraying me as the villain.

The situation:

I acquired a stalker. For nearly a year he had been (his words) "watching, following, observing, and researching" me without my knowledge. I'd never seen him, didn't even know he existed. I believed that I'd "accepted a ride home" from a total stranger, not knowing he'd essentially been in my life for almost a year.

It began with a phrase, expressed verbally and by actions: an individual *taking power in my life that he did not deserve.* More to the point: the sickest individuals often believe they "deserve" whatever they wish; in some instances, such as this, the "power" one believes they "deserve" means attempting to "veto" someone else's rights-- every right imaginable, including that of free will.

My "free will"? This 13th-Stepping NRA made me aware of his presence less than two months after I made the decision that I did not want anyone in my life; upon informing him of this, *he* informed *me* that nearly a year earlier *he* had decided he would "marry" me. In other words, he saw me when I first arrived in that particular part of the city, had been accessing my life ever since, while I was not even aware he existed. One of his statements was particularly alarming: "The only way I can get kids is to marry somebody who already has them." Upon realizing I was not going to go along with this, he simply circled around me and went after them.

Initially, I was clueless. As I had spent my life in the real world, amongst average people, the general idea is if you tell someone you do not want anything to do with him, to stay away from your home and family and out of your life, a normal person realizes that that is the way it is. I found this was not the case with an NRA: when he persisted in showing up at my home, he said: "See, I Keep Coming Back!" When I informed him this particular saying was a reference to program members and 12-Step meetings, he said he was 'working a program on a relationship.'

The ongoing tactic was sleep deprivation. It began with him forcing me to stand in one place for approximately five and a half hours; the second incident involved him keeping me forcibly awake for two and a half days and nights straight-- after which my mind blacked out and I don't know what happened. While the pattern of sleep deprivation included him showing up at my home and refusing to leave, and calling and texting me throughout the night, it didn't take long for my system to rebel-- I was no longer able to sleep more than a half-hour, when my system would "jolt" me awake, like the reaction a person has to a car backfiring. *When I informed him that being forcibly deprived of sleep was like being drugged against my will, he said he knew that.*

He attempted to instill fear and create dependency. He told me if I even walked up to the local convenience store alone in the middle of the daytime, it meant I 'want to get kidnapped, raped, and murdered.' He told me a tale about 'many women who looked very much like me' (same age group, build, hair color and hair style) having been found murdered and thrown in the river near my apartment. He said there was 'at least one serial killer' in the city, and that it was probably someone I knew. (Much later, when I approached two people with this topic, asking why, when none of this was true, someone would tell such tales, both people had the same response: *"To terrify and control you."*)

While telling me all of the men and women who attended that particular meeting were all bad, dangerous people, he zeroed in on one fellow who was likable, jolly, and friendly toward everyone-- telling me this particular individual was a 'serial killer.' Going by the man's habit of always offering people rides, and having many friends, he said what the man and his friends were really doing was trolling around the region in his van 'looking for victims.' He followed this by stating that one of the man's friends was "a hired killer-- in the business of Murder."

I could almost imagine how these guys would have reacted if they'd known how they were portrayed-- but, like in all situations, I did not have the opportunity to find out.

It went further-- he said he believed that some night, this 'serial killer' would try to break into my apartment. Stating that I had to be ready for such a situation, he showed up at my door carrying swords, and barged in. He strategically placed the swords throughout my apartment-- in corners, under the couch, etc. He then began swirling a sword around in my living room, saying I needed to be prepared to 'gut' the guy when he broke in-- to "leave his guts laying all over the floor."

Another common thread amongst NRA's is that on any given subject, regardless of how average, benevolent, or innocent it may be, they attach a 'sinister interpretation.' Various other former program members, whose vocabularies are a bit more raw than my own, describe it as a "mind-f*ck"-- the NRA's looking at any fact, and attempting to make it look like something much different.

One such incident also involved the same fellow who was pointed at as a 'serial killer.' What had happened one day was he and two of his friends-- one male, one female-- were driving along together on their way to a barbecue. The three of them asked if I would like to go along. When I replied I had to get home, they gave me a ride because they were going in the same direction.

The NRA heard about, and pounced on, this completely neutral incident. He said the 'serial killer' and his companions were not simply being kind and helpful by giving me a ride, but were doing so as an excuse to 'stake out' my apartment-- so the 'serial killer' would know where my door and windows were all located.

The bottom line, exactly as both a program member and a victims' advocate counselor later said, was the NRA was attempting to turn me into a dependent, paranoid, terrified wreck. And he did not like the fact that his tactics did not produce the results he wanted.

He said I wasn't safe in my own home either, because there were 'demons' in my living room, because someone had been 'murdered' in my apartment.

He also said meditating is dangerous-- "because you are emptying your mind and making it easy for the demons to get in."

Isolation took two forms. First, there were many instances when I was literally trapped; and second, he tried to scare me away from other people, and told other people outrageous lies about me. While he was telling me other people were all dangerous, sick, and bad, he was telling other people that I was abusive, mentally ill, and immoral.

Isolation was furthered by him telling me he had a variety of people spying on me and "reporting back" to him about my whereabouts, everything I said, everything I did. In legal terms, this is called stalking-by-proxy-- and, as such, everyone who participated in it was guilty of a crime.

He tried to cut my self-esteem down to nothing; this covered both my age and appearance, as well as my ability to do my job as a parent and do my regular job. He attempted to convince me that I was 'so messed up' that I could not perform either of these tasks.

He tried to cause me to doubt everything about myself: "The way you walk... the way you talk... the way you move... the way you breathe...;" and saying things such as "You have blind spots in your behavior" (that I was doing horrible things but was not aware of it).

Well, he said he'd 'learned all of the techniques of hypnotism, brainwashing, and mind-control.' One example was what he called his 'monotone voice.' It was difficult to describe. One thing he accomplished with this was getting me to do things I didn't want to do. An example that stands out in my mind: I was wearing a new necklace that I had recently purchased, and he told me to take it off so he could look at it. I didn't want to do this, and said I didn't. He kept repeating in that voice 'I want to see it, take it off,' and after he'd said this a number of times I felt myself doing what he told me to do. I felt like a robot-- like I was mechanically doing his bidding even though I didn't want to take off the necklace.

He had a goal, and one "means to the end" was to to try to cause me to flip out. He attempted to get me to believe that I had a variety of very serious 'traumas' in my past, but that I was so messed up that my brain was filled with 'repressed memories.' He said the fact that I 'couldn't remember' traumas meant I was 'insane.' The alleged traumas (which never happened) were all about sexual abuse.

Isolation was for two purposes: first, so I had no one to turn to; but also he also seemed to believe I'd 'crack' when the only so-called 'reality' I was faced with was his. He tried to get me to believe I 'couldn't face reality' because I did not acknowledge various incidents that didn't happen: he claimed my oldest brother had been killed in Vietnam, and that my niece had committed suicide. He furthered it by saying her suicide had been because of a 'hereditary mental illness,' and that I too probably had it.

Taking liberties with my body, he claimed that objections on my part also were 'signs of mental illness.' He said '*You're not objecting to what I'm doing- you're objecting to something somebody did to you in the past.*' He said because I objected to him putting his hands on me, I 'hadn't healed from the past.'

When I became angry over this crap, he said my anger, too, was a sign of mental illness-- and that it meant I had 'multiple personality disorder.' He said my anger was 'one of your other personalities coming out.'

There were also instances when he prevented me from eating; the reason he did so was he'd found out I had hypoglycemia-- when forced to go without food for a long period of time, my blood sugar levels go wacko and I end up with major hypoglycemic attacks. These attacks consisted of blazing migraines, extreme nausea, dizziness, and blurred vision. When these attacks kicked in, he told people these hypoglycemic reactions were actually 'signs of mental illness.'

With the exception of the way his lies destroyed my reputation, his tactics did not work. The only tactic that *did* work was consistently telling me if I were to take any action to get him out of the picture permanently, I would never see my teen again-- that she'd vanish into some other state and I'd never even know her whereabouts. While my mind was strong and stable enough to resist all of his other tactics, my love and concern for my family kept me in the position of a Victim.

One particular statement should make everything about the situation clear. Upon telling this freak to stay away from my teenager, he barked: *"NO! I'm not going to give her up because of you!"*

There was, though, another topic that bears noting; and, in fact, it is probably the most important question that any intelligent person should consider, because the sense of timing is very important. The NRA began alienating others against me, beginning character-assassinations and other lies behind my back, *immediately after* I met him and told him I was not interested in him. In other words, upon finding I would not cooperate, he did everything within his means to get what he was after *without* my cooperation-- even if it meant destroying me and my life in the process. An NRA whom I had just met, and who knew nothing about me, immediately began discrediting me behind my back-- and as the saying goes, it doesn't take a genius to figure it out.

Not long ago, something occurred to me: *words can, and do, make a difference.* As an example, an individual can use accurate, albeit evasive, words; someone else, such as a police officer, can use other accurate, but legal terminology; but there is much more personal impact when the accurate word or term is one of your own. The particular word that came to mind was *Accessed.*

To illustrate what I mean: an NRA *accessed* me for approximately ten months-- without my knowledge or consent. (The purpose: looking for any potential "weak spots" that would make me an easy target; and, as he said, the weak spot was being new to the area I didn't have a 'support system' or friends. The result: the vulnerable feeling similar to finding somebody has been living in your home without your knowledge). However-- the main point: *accessing* me for approximately ten months without my knowledge was the first step or stage of *violating my rights:* I was stripped of the right to make, on my own behalf, a free will, informed choice. Obviously, I could not make the "choice" of objecting to it, because I was not aware of it.

After he admitted he had been 'watching, following, observing, and researching' me for nearly a year, he also stated that I had been an ideal 'candidate' because I 'didn't have a support system.'

(I was later 'treated' to the statement: *"Secrecy is the venue of a perpetrator."* And an accurate statement it was.)

The second step or stage in *violating my rights* was his refusal to take no for an answer. Upon informing a total stranger that I was not interested, he felt fully capable of "vetoing" this with "We're in one (relationship) now!" and furthering it by claiming it was "an exclusive" relationship.

Although at that time I was sole parent to two kids and had been "the head of my household" for approximately twenty-six years, I was informed *"Women cannot be the heads of their households"*-- and that any guy can simply barge in and take over, regardless of the women's objections.

Third, he attempted to instigate "game-playing"-- claiming my refusal and lack of interest was only a matter of "You're just not ready." Clearly, his purpose was to try to get me to defend my position, "prove" something, with the either/or approach that I would certainly be willing to cooperate unless there was something wrong with me that prevented it. And, ensuring no one would learn the facts, that's the approach he presented to everyone.

One example can show how extreme this approach was. Not yet aware that he had been stalking me, the NRA 'invited' himself to spend the night in my apartment. When I informed him this was not going to happen, he claimed it was because I had "trust issues from the past." Now, if you had informed someone who to you was a total stranger that you wanted nothing to do with him, would you allow him to spend the night in your home? However, when I became angry and told him to get the hell out of my apartment, the response was "What is it from your past that has triggered your trust issues?" And that's the approach he presented to everyone-- that my refusal to cooperate meant I was 'messed up from my past.'

The next step or stage: I was *held* for nearly eleven months-- effectively *held* in a web of terror. While not only was my right to free will and virtually every other right violated, threats about a family member vanishing put me in the position of being unable to do anything about any of it. In addition, it left me unable to protect my family, and unable to defend myself.

The individual seemed to get a special delight over rendering me powerless and looking at the results-- I was consistently threatened, tormented, and then looked at as if I were a squashed bug, unable to free itself.

I was also "egged-on"-- consistently being *dared* to reach out for help and/or approach anyone with the truth.

While the other 13th-Steppers were sick, this particular NRA had the additional characteristic of being sadistic.

What it came down to: after *accessing* me for nearly a year without my knowledge or consent, when I had the misfortune of meeting this piece of trash in person he essentially presented me with two options-- if they could be called 'options'-- either I could cooperate, throw my life and everything and everyone in it out the window and hand it all over to him, or he would simply circumvent *me* altogether, attempt to destroy me in the process, and *take* what he wanted *without* my consent.

To clarify what my "decision" meant: I made the decision that I did not want some guy trying to hog all of my time, intrude into my personal space, disrupt my family, and create discord; however, when I had the misfortune of meeting this particular NRA, he informed me I did not have the right to make this decision.

And there was more to it. After I told him about my decision, I even went further to explain what it meant to me. As my youngest was still in High School, and did not have any specific plans for after High School, my plan was to abide by my agreement with her to stay in one location until she finished school, and when she was finished with her education I planned to move back to California. The NRA replied: "I hope you have a good life!" However, after a split-second for emphasis, he laughed, and informed me my plans were not going to happen. What would happen instead, he told me, was that he was going to buy some land out in the middle of nowhere, and I would be forced to live there-- never getting back into the city, and never seeing anyone else again. "I'm gonna fatten you up and turn you into a farm girl," he added. He said his goal was to get me so 'goofy' from sleep deprivation that I'd 'agree' to marry him-- and then would be 'stuck for the next thirty years.'

Now, going by either Program definitions or any other reasonable definitions, is there anyone who would think what I was on the receiving-end of could be considered "recovery" or "sanity"?

MONSTERS ARE MADE, NOT BORN

In between thirteenth-steppers, I acquired an opportunist. Unlike the thirteenth-steppers who had many years in programs and used what they had learned to manipulate people and manipulate situations, this particular NRA did not have that knowledge or expertise. Instead, he "played on my sympathies" for a free place to live, food, and similar necessities. The NRA had been hovering around, and zeroed in on me when my work hours increased-- meaning I had what he wanted: a means of financial support. The times I tried to get rid of him I did not succeed; the times I attempted to leave he followed me; I ended up being stuck with him for more than two years.

Initially, as his first bid for sympathy was claiming his life was in danger, with the approval of both of my family members I allowed him to stay at our place. However, it was my first experience with how difficult or impossible it is to get rid of an NRA. When I learned our landlady was pushing drugs, I approached a couple who were my friends. The guy told me his brother, who had a large house, was in the hospital, and offered my family a free place to stay in exchange for looking after the house. My friend made it clear the offer was *only* for my kids and myself-- that the NRA was not welcome. While this arrangement was fine with me, there was a complication that neither I nor my friends anticipated: the NRA visited the brother in the hospital, and manipulated the brother into extending the invitation to him, too.

An outside observer, who had evidently known the NRA for many years, remarked: "All he wants is some soft-hearted woman to support him." I was fully aware of this, and as much as told the NRA I had no personal interest in him. In an over-the-top instance of "rigorous honesty," I informed the NRA I had met someone at the meetings who meant the world to me, and the person's inability to see the 13th-Stepping couple for what they were was the only reason I allowed or tolerated his presence at all.

Similar to many situations with NRA's, though, it was not a matter of Me vs. Him. In separate instances, other individuals *In The Program* had a hand in the situations-- and, in both situations, the individuals insisted that continuing to 'help' him was 'the right thing' to do. In one instance, for example, an NRA told me I should do everything possible, including financial support, for this individual, 'so he could concentrate on working his program.'

Not only did this override my own judgment, but I made the mistake of listening to those *In The Program* instead of listening to people who agreed that getting him out of my life would be the sensible course of action. In other words, NRA's had a stronger influence than both myself and everyone else. Unfortunately, this eventually led to the mistake of actually defending this individual-- *'oh, this poor poor person who is so misunderstood.'*

Prior to meeting me, this ex-con had developed a habit: asking for "help" from churches. When my income was no longer sufficient to support him in addition to my own family, he returned to this habit. From rent money to cigarettes, he believed it was the place of every church he could find to provide for him. In some instances, he asked me to accompany him; and it was absolutely humiliating. He had the idea if he could claim a "family" needed help, he would have better luck than if he simply asked on his own behalf. In one instance, he remarked: "I'll even say the Sinner's Prayer-- if they give me money!"

By his own admission, he only went to 12-Step meetings for the free coffee-- and to see how many people he could hit up for money, rides, a place to stay, cigarettes, and similar assistance. He was especially noticeable whenever the meeting-places held holiday parties or parties to "honor" someone's "clean/sober date," because there was always large quantities of free food. If you recall "Jerry" from earlier in this book, this NRA admitted he attended Jerry's memorial service simply because there had been large amounts of food served to everyone who attended.

At one particular point in time he made a number of attempts to sign himself into a psychiatric hospital; each time, after being told he was not a danger to himself or anyone else, he was told he could not do so. He then approached an outpatient mental health clinic, and, after informing them he was a recovering addict, they ended up giving him a half-dozen different psychiatric medications. He stopped taking them, and soon after went back to drinking and using illegal drugs. I then bought bus tickets to "GTFO."

After his temporary employer fired him, he committed a crime. Still believing I should be his source of financial support, he composed a nine-page letter about how the crime had actually been a "set-up." I didn't know the facts about the crime until he was released from prison three years later and committed another offense in the city where I had relocated.

Like other NRA's I've known, this individual blamed everyone and everything but himself. Everything from substance abuse to the "lifestyle" that went along with it was always "somebody else's fault." However, if the psychiatric hospital had committed him upon his own request, he would not have been walking the streets to commit either of those crimes.

This, too, is a common occurrence: mental health practitioners who do not know that appropriate treatment for drug addicts and alcoholics is not giving them more drugs. Not only can they not function, they can pose a real danger to other people.

"YOUR DESTINY"

I recently read a statement that accurately describes my life-- or existence-- since I became involved with 12-Step programs: *"Your destiny will be determined by your relationships."* If you take the last word in its broadest sense, it is an accurate assessment: if there are NRA's in or around your life, that is essentially all there is. You are basically spinning in a fog, trying to survive; and, in addition to all of the other destruction, *your life is passing by while you are not actively participating in it.*

As one example, I knew very little about what was going on in the real world-- I heard next to nothing about the 9-11 incident and Hurricane Katrina, much less anything that was less tragic.

As a second example, I lost contact with nearly everyone who had been in my life, and had very little contact with others. This included longtime friends, and even many relatives.

Both the lack of stability in life due to the presence of NRA's, as well as manipulations by the worst of them, led to one huge transformation in myself and in my life-- and it was not a positive transformation. One of the most noteworthy parts of it involved the hope and optimism I'd initially had-- both goals and plans for my life that were all possible *at that time.*

It disappeared. While time can take away opportunities, horrible experiences and the consequences *took away even more.*

"THIS IS YOUR BRAIN ON DRUGS"

It must have been around two decades ago-- a commercial that occasionally showed up on television. The speaker tossed a couple of eggs into a frying pan, and, as the eggs began to sizzle, said: *"This is your brain on drugs. Any questions?"*

At the time, with no substance issues of my own, and not knowing anyone else it applied to, either, I simply brushed off the commercial, thinking nothing more about it until very recently. When thinking about it, another saying came back from the past: *"He fried his brain."*

A simpler way of wording it: if you abuse alcohol or other drugs, you will not come out of it unscathed. There is physiological damage from drug abuse-- brain damage being the main concern-- and even if you become "clean and sober," the damage cannot be reversed.

To compound the problem, many who engage in drug or alcohol abuse begin doing so before their bodies and brains are fully developed. Not only is their physiological development stunted-- so is their emotional development. The latter is why you will find many who are middle-aged and older with attitudes, beliefs, and behaviors that are on the scale of young teenagers.

Individuals who make an honest effort to recover often reflect this in their terminology. Instead of focusing on how many years a person has been clean and sober, he or she realizes his or her growth came to a halt when he or she began abusing alcohol and drugs.

However, experts also state that an addict's brain is different from the brain of a normal person in general.

While nothing can be done about the effects of drug and alcohol abuse on the body or brain, a true recovery process offers the chance to live as normal a life as possible. From how one sees oneself, to how one interacts with others, to how one lives in the world, a better life is possible.

"It works if you work it" is a popular saying. Unfortunately, even with all of the "tools" for recovery, many do not "work it." Instead, they keep their old attitudes, beliefs, and behaviors-- the same as they learned in active addiction.

'RECOVERY' IS A MONEY-MAKING INDUSTRY

Unlike many people who had much formal experience with the programs, and experts in the field, I initially did not know the entire subject is one huge money-making industry. One of the many examples is the wide range of books for individuals who are 'in recovery.' Early on, I learned about this from an

NRA who had many obsessions and addictions, one of which was his own large 'library' of this type of material.

Money-makers, greed, and taking advantage of individuals desperate for help aside, much of the material I looked into was stunning. One in particular comes to mind: a so-called "meditation" book. Paraphrased, a passage from the book tells people that even if something comes into their minds, this does not mean it necessarily should come out of their mouths; and even if they have a thought, this does not necessarily mean they should act on it.

From my point of view, it sums up one of the biggest problems NRA's have: they do not know what is and is not *appropriate*. Do adults really need "self-help" books to tell them it is not appropriate to act on their instincts? From my experiences, while such material rarely does any good, NRA's usually do not know these things. As "instant gratification" is the way of addiction, so is acting on instinct-- even when it is completely inappropriate.

And, instead of offering such people real help, the money-making industry cares only about filling its own pockets.

We can add this is done at the expense of individuals who need legitimate help. One example, which may or may not have started with good intentions but failed miserably, is the concept known as *"treatment"* or *"rehab."* As *rehabilitation* means *to restore*, it does not take much effort to see exactly *how* miserably it has failed.

Rather than achieving the goal of helping addicts and alcoholics move on to *productive* lives, it often has the opposite effect: with prescriptions for psychiatric medications in hand, individuals who go through treatment or rehab programs are then advised to apply for SSDI. With the claim that drug addiction and alcoholism qualifies a person as "disabled," not only is their recovery halted by more mind-altering, mood-altering substances, but they are urged to believe they cannot do anything productive with their lives. In other words, rather than being a *recovering* alcoholic or a *recovering* addict, they are simply deemed *disabled.* And, while human lives are destroyed because of this pattern, the so-called treatment industry and pharmaceutical companies are making "big bucks."

The problem: while many do "cheat the system" intentionally, from my experiences the majority who find themselves in these situations are only following the advice of misinformed health care practitioners and "treatment counselors."

Naturally, it gets worse: reliable sources have provided the information that a very large percentage of "counselors"-- both in treatment/rehab centers and on an outpatient basis--- are, themselves, "recovering addicts/alcoholics."

While there are surely many such people who have good intentions and back it up with education and applying what they learn, consider the implications when this is not the case: not only is it a matter of "the blind leading the blind," similar to "sponsorship" and general members, but there is the added factor of "authority." And such "authority" carries with it the potential of misuse, and harm to individuals who look in the wrong place for "help."

There can be other complications as well.

First, while I do not know how widespread this particular approach is, there are 'rehabs' which, after being made aware of a client's crimes-against-persons, do nothing whatsoever to make the client accountable for his crimes, nor protect innocent people. Rather than turning dangerous predators over to law enforcement, they simply close their eyes to it so the individual can "go his merry way" after he finishes his rehab program.

A second complication involves programs for youth. Numerous facilities take advantage of parents' desperation to find 'help' for their youngsters, and parents do not know exactly how dangerous the facilities are until it is too late. Youngsters are abused-- including being deprived of food and water, forced to participate in activity in dangerous environments, and many youngsters have died because of the abuse.

WHAT IS ADDICTION?

Addiction is generally defined as a combination of obsession and compulsion. In layman's terms, it can be translated to "*Gotta have it- gotta have it now- and gotta have more!*"

To further clarify, 12-Step programs define a drug addict as a person whose life is controlled by drugs; and an alcoholic as someone who cannot control his intake of alcohol of his own free will.

A program states that while no one can label another person as an alcoholic, there is a simple way a person can reach this conclusion for himself. Both the program and legitimate sponsors advise anyone who does not know whether or not he is an alcoholic to test himself-- to take one drink, and see if he can easily stop. The person is advised to do this an additional time, to be sure he has come to the correct conclusion. The person who is an alcoholic cannot easily put down a drink and walk away from it. This is the reason for the saying "One is too many- and a thousand is not enough." An alcoholic who takes one drink automatically wants and needs more.

For a period of time, I communicated with a 12-Step program member who could be described as a Winner. After asking me a wide range of questions, he advised me to try that little test that came directly from the Alcoholics Anonymous "Big Book." While I didn't have the opportunity to do so at that time, a few years later I did, just to satisfy his and my curiosity. I went to the liquor department of a local grocery store, and purchased a couple of small bottles. Each day for three days, I took one drink, and placed the bottles back in the closet. Naturally, as I'm not an alcoholic, it was not an issue; but on the third day I took an additional approach. I approached one of my kids and asked if there was anything different about me; the response was that there was not. When I informed my youngster that I had consumed some alcohol, the response was that drinking is stupid, but at least it didn't have any affect on me. Someone who is not an alcoholic can take one drink and stop; someone who is an alcoholic cannot easily do that.

Individuals who do not follow what their own programs teach do not pay attention to any of this. You may hear individuals say that someone who tried a drug once in the distant past, walked away from it and never looked back, is an addict; you may hear individuals say anyone who has ever consumed alcohol is an alcoholic. In short, they are paying no attention whatsoever to what they should have learned in their own programs. And from my experiences, the reason for this is they want a person to "come to believe" he or she has a serious problem-- and, worse, they want other people to believe it.

From my experiences, the reason for this is addicts and alcoholics who have made no real progress with their own recoveries feel the need for everyone to be as sick as they are themselves. In contrast, addicts and alcoholics who make real progress with their own recoveries are not threatened by people who do not have these problems.

WHAT IS A BEHAVIORAL ADDICTION?

Behavioral addiction is also known as psychic numbing.
While behavioral addictions are common in the NRA population, they are rarely able to acknowledge it as a problem. This is known as *denial.*

First, a behavioral addiction consists of the same obsession and compulsion as alcohol or drug addiction.

Second, behavioral addiction has an effect on the brain that is quite similar to the effect of drug or alcohol abuse. Engaging in a behavioral addiction actually alters the brain's chemistry. The most significant effect, though, is the behavior suppresses thinking and feeling.

An addict can become addicted to virtually any behavior. Similar to the denial experienced with drug and alcohol abuse, he will deem it "a hobby," "fun," "having a good time," or similar terms. Whether the behavior takes huge amounts of time or large amounts of money, interferes with everyday life, or involves any other sign of a full-blown addiction, he will not recognize it as such. In addition, similar to drug or alcohol addiction, an individual with a behavioral addiction is likely to become extremely defensive if anyone suggests he has a problem. *Defensiveness* is one of the main hallmarks of addiction, regardless of what one happens to be addicted to.

The first individual I met with a behavioral addiction claimed his t.v.-watching was his favorite pastime. Whenever he was not at work, he engaged in this "hobby" twenty-four hours a day, 'round the clock. When work did not interfere with his 'hobby,' he went for many days at a stretch watching videos and t.v. shows he had recorded.

Accumulating specific possessions, spending money, gambling, and virtually any other activity a person could possibly participate in, can become a full-blown addiction. However, without professional help, he is not likely to ever see it for what it is.

"MR.-BILLY-RUNNIN'-THINGS"

One of the first people I met in a Program came up with this saying, and it is accurate. Screwed-up individuals have the need to orchestrate other people's lives, and have their hand in other people's lives. It can be a need for power, the need for a "look-at-me" sense of self-importance, or both. In any case, the NRA makes it clear that he or she is "running the show."

While a large part of this covers meddling, interfering, and even taking over, it also covers undue influence: they want to persuade others to do everything 'their' way, regardless of the consequences to other people.

I encountered countless numbers of "Billys" in 12-Step programs. What it shows is few individuals in 12-Step programs take recovery seriously.

One example was being told I should get a hair cut. When I said I did not want one, the person made nasty remarks about my hairstyle, and said she would pay for a hair cut at her hairdresser's. When I said I was not interested, she persisted in calling me every single day to badger me about the hair cut. Eventually, she became angry, and said it was my decision to make. However-- the next day, she called again to tell me she had made the appointment with her hairdresser.

Over the years, I've been told what I should and should not wear, how I should wear my fingernails and hair, who I should and should not associate with, and so forth. If this is not bad enough, I noticed some of these "Billys" I encountered had the role of "sponsor" to numerous people-- taking full advantage of sponsees' misguided trust to essentially take over their lives.

"BUT THEY JUST WANT TO LOOK IMPORTANT"

From the "My Truth is the Only Truth" game to "Mr.-Billy-Runnin'-Things," what you have are little children in adult-sized bodies who 'just want to look important.' The catch, though, with having those adult-sized bodies-- and the years of experience to accompany them-- is these "but I just wanna be important!" games can result in anything from minor chaos and confusion to an amazing amount of destruction.

It can be summed up by a phrase you may hear from members of 12-Step programs: *Power in your life that they do not deserve.*

While that phrase is accurate, you will not find it in program literature. Similarly, you will not find "mind-games," "loaded language," or "psychobabble." The reason: none of these things are part of these programs-- nor are they condoned by the programs.

If you read the literature, two very important points should stand out: first, the entire scope of 12-Step programs is for individuals to share their strength, hope, and experience of what worked for them in their recoveries. It is noted that a newcomer in his first meeting is on the same level as an oldtimer who has been a member of the program for years or decades. Second, the entire scope of a sponsor is to guide the sponsee through the Steps. The literature also states that no member has any authority, and no member has any "special knowledge."

Individuals who are not working their own programs do not abide by these concepts. They attempt to run other people's personal and family lives, "diagnose" conditions and illnesses, and either prevent people from seeking necessary outside assistance or tell people to not listen to what their doctors and other professionals say.

One outrageous example involved a middle-aged guy who, shortly before being hauled away by the police for possession and use of heroin, looked at a social, boisterous little kid and commented: "Maybe she's *autistic*." In another instance, a woman who seemed to look at everyone she met as her own personal psychology project, said to a woman who was naturally quiet and reserved: "Maybe you have a *histrionic personality*."

All of these are issues anyone involved in a program should be alert to-- and watch out for. A special concern covers those who claim to be "armchair experts"-- that they know more and better than you yourself, or the professionals you have consulted. It comes to reading a book, taking a class, or seeing something on the internet, and the NRA's will do precisely what their programs tell them they cannot do: claim they have special knowledge and authority.

Personally, I think I've heard nearly the full range of this garbage and nonsense. "Underlying issues and causes," "new behavior and old behavior," "blind spots in behavior," a "crisis-awakening stage," and on and on. The point: none of it comes from the programs, and none of it is condoned by the programs. It is simply a matter of those who wish to look more important than they actually are-- and have power in other people's lives that they do not deserve.

Another of many asinine examples: the NRA who insisted anything that makes one uncomfortable is 'sexual abuse,' and that it is not enough to use that term, that one must call it 'rape. ' When I remarked that this is not what the dictionary calls it, she became huffy and stated that the dictionary is 'wrong.' And this approach, in fact, sums up NRA's: everyone is wrong *except themselves.*

It should not be difficult to see how this can be dangerous. This "My Truth is the Only Truth" approach attempts to cause people to doubt themselves, doubt everyone in their lives, and even doubt experts and professionals. NRA's who "only want to look important" pose a real danger to other people.

This subject is addressed by Dr. Robert Hare****:
Group therapy and therapeutic community programs are not the only source of new tactics psychopaths use to convince others that they have changed. They frequently make use of prison programs designed to upgrade their education; courses in psychology, sociology, and criminology are very popular. These programs, like those devoted to therapy, may supply psychopaths with little more than superficial insight and knowledge of terms and concepts- buzzwords- having to do with interpersonal and emotional processes, but they allow psychopaths to convince others that they have been rehabilitated or "born again."

AFFECT: THE FOUNDATION OF THE PROBLEM

Affect-- the ability to fully experience one's feelings and emotions-- plays a large role in normal human development. When babies and children are prevented from experiencing and expressing, and when his basic needs are not met, it further impedes the development of a conscience. In addition, as he is not treated as a full human being, he will go on to conclude that others are not human beings, but objects or sources from which to gain something. Whether these human beings are intimate partners, his own children, friends, or others, there is no connection on the levels of healthy emotion or compassion. A normal sense of empathy never develops.

Individuals who begin life in this manner are prone to running on primal instincts-- the same basic instincts animals need for survival: food, fight or flight, sex as nothing but a biological urge. If drugs or alcohol abuse enter the picture, any normal lingering emotions that may have attempted to surface are further shut down. Instead of being experienced, they are dulled. Expressed or unexpressed, he has fear and rage instead of normal emotions.

When a person does not develop this ability to fully experience one's feelings and emotions in his earliest weeks, months, years, it does not develop at all. In addition to not developing a conscience, there are other consequences: the inability to develop compassion; the inability to recognize and acknowledge other human beings as full-fledged human beings in their own right; and the inability to know what is appropriate and what is inappropriate.

The lack of affect also leads many to "make mountains out of molehills." They lack the ability to grasp whether something is extremely significant or very minor. Logically, this can result in a wide range of misunderstandings-- or worse.

The absence of affect results in the inability to differentiate between normal and abnormal. From not realizing there is a difference between foolhardiness and courage, to any other concepts and actions they easily mistake for something else, the bottom line is it is a jumbled-up mess. When individuals cannot recognize a difference between a minor annoyance and a disaster, all sorts of complications can occur. A disagreement becomes 'abuse;' an unpleasant task becomes something for which they need 'support;' and so on and so on. While it lends itself to a great deal of manipulation, it also prevents individuals from actually living their lives.

For the rest of us, it can be mindboggling to find NRA's cannot differentiate between fear and terror, anger and rage, love and lust, courage and foolhardiness, want and need-- and that they cannot grasp the rest of us having and expressing emotions that are normal.

And, from my experiences, individuals who come to believe 12-Step programs are the answer and solution to everything are much less likely to seek professional help for this problem.

DYSFUNCTIONAL VS. NORMAL

Most adults could state they have, or have had, two "families"-- the family-of-origin, and the family they formed and built during their adult lives. In recent years, I have been on the receiving-end of much negativity on both subjects-- including terms such as "dysfunctional."

"Psychobabble" can be very harmful and destructive-- especially in the hands of individuals who misuse it. The acceptable definition of this term: *"A Dysfunctional family is a family in which conflict, misbehavior, and often child neglect or abuse on the part of individual parents occur continually and regularly, leading other members to accommodate such actions."**

I've learned NRA's tend to use this and similar terms to mean "different from one's own"-- especially when resentments enter the picture.

Let me tell you about my so-called "dysfunctional" family-of-origin. As polar-opposites of what I've encountered in recent years, the themes were male and female are equal, children are people too, everyone has a voice, everyone has rights, and basic common sense is important.

One example comes to mind: when I was a child, one of my friends was a girl who lived across the street; I'll call her "Terry." In Terry's house there was playroom where she and her older sister had plenty of toys and a toy box. One toy in particular caught my eye: a small, plastic, gray-and-white panda bear. Every time I went to Terry's house I longed for that bear and wished it were mine. One day when Terry and her sister were out of the room I slipped the bear into my jacket pocket, and took it home with me. Almost immediately, my conscience started chewing on me; I feel it's important to note that I wasn't afraid of "getting into trouble" or "getting punished," it was a matter of "The bear belongs to Terry- therefore, I had no right to take it." I knew I'd done something wrong, and knew I had to set it right. Because I wasn't allowed to cross the street by myself (a main highway), I started nagging my mother to take me back to Terry's. When she asked if I couldn't wait until the next day, I said no, that I had to go back that day. After dinner, she escorted me across the street, and I went back into the playroom and put the bear back into the toy box. To the best of my knowledge no one ever knew I stole the bear, nor that I had returned it. I came to see this incident as a six-year-old having such a well-developed sense of conscience that I knew the difference between right and wrong, and when I did wrong I felt the need to immediately set it right.

When I hear or read about adults' stories of their childhoods, growing-up years, young adult lives, etc., it often includes a variety of mistakes, and sometimes has questions about how people tell their own kids about all of the awful things they did. Considering all of the people I grew up with were quite similar to myself, I don't think I'm in the minority when I say there's really nothing in all of those years that I'd be embarrassed or ashamed to tell my kids. My oldest, as a young adult, once remarked "You never gave me anything to rebel against"-- and that statement essentially covered my own growing-up years, also. For my kids and for myself, it was a matter of common sense-- there are things you do not do, simply because you don't. In other words, there's no need to 'rebel' or violate rules when there are minimal rules and the rules make sense.

In all of my growing-up years, there was only one incident that could remotely be described as "getting into trouble": when I was in elementary school, "chorus" was a required part of the curriculum; and, as a youngster, I hated my singing voice, so "chorus" was a class I particularly disliked. When the teacher told the class we were going to perform in a school concert, I told my parents I did not want to participate. The response was since I refused to participate in the concert, I would spend that evening in my room.

Between how minor the incident was, and how logical but minor their response was, it was an extreme contrast to what I've heard in recent years about individuals' growing-up experiences: for these NRA's, everything was based on blind obedience; and while they were regularly beaten, they had no real rules or standards.

Another extreme point of contrast was their needs were not met. The general idea was making kids fend for themselves would result in strong, independent people-- and I've seen countless examples of how this method backfired: they have no empathy whatsoever, and cannot make the smallest decision or action without "support."

This was not the way it was for me. One example was when I contracted the measles. For a period of time my fever was so high that my parents and doctor were not sure I would make it. During that period of time, my father took time off from work and sat beside me 24/7 until my fever broke and I was out of danger. He didn't raise a wuss or a weakling-- and neither did I.

Yet another extreme contrast is many NRA's were brought up with the belief "Children are to be seen, not heard." Forcing kids to shut down their thoughts and feelings can have many negative consequences. In contrast, even as a youngster I knew if I had something to say I could say it, if something was bothering me I could say so, and I was a human being regardless of age or gender.

One example occurred when I started the ninth grade; I so disliked one particular teacher that I told both of my parents and the principal that if I did not get transferred into a different class I'd quit school altogether. While I obviously did not have the ability to drop out at thirteen years old, they knew I was serious, and I received the transfer. The principal commented to my parents that I was a kid who never got into any trouble, never caused any problems, so whenever I did feel the need to take a stand about something, they knew it was something important.

However, you can take all of these subjects-- a solid conscience about right and wrong, sensible rules and sensible consequences, needs being met, and having a voice-- and this is what I'm told was a "dysfunctional family." I've noticed NRA's who assert this are those who did not have these benefits or advantages; not only do they resent the fact that I did, they also resent that I've passed the same benefits and advantages on to my own kids.

In contrast, NRA's who assert this kind of nonsense were from families that would truly meet the definition of "dysfunctional." While they were beaten over minor infractions, they were allowed to drink, use drugs, commit crimes, and all of those behaviors that can not only impact but permanently ruin kids' lives. As they continue throughout their entire adult lives to live with the consequences of such behaviors, they deeply resent those of us who did not do those things, and go further to attack the sense of structure we've had in our lives.

Now, I am not asserting that my growing-up years were a "peachy picnic of perfection"-- far from it. What I am saying is not only did the positive outweigh the negative and make the negative bearable, it also provided an excellent "point of reference" on which to build a solid life and weather the storms of life. Instead of being forced to build the foundation with child-sized hands, that foundation was *there*-- and so it has also been with my own family. And this definitely does not meet the definition of "dysfunctional."

Thinking about my experiences and experiences related by NRA's, it comes down to a person being the "product" of his or her background, upbringing, and early environment. In my case, those topics reflect the "old-skool" Dutch culture. Although I carry a variety of nationalities, races, etc., the culture I was most exposed to in my early years was what formed the person I became. It included such points as all people are equal, regardless of age, gender, race, or other factors; all people, including children, have a voice; deal with people in a fair, straightforward manner; excess and waste are negative; home and family are the priorities; and so forth.

In addition to NRA's having drug and alcohol problems, they all came from cultural backgrounds that were polar-opposites of my own. However, true to NRA form, none of those differences were seen as or accepted as differences, but something very bad indeed. Refusing to allow NRA's to walk all over me, for example, was considered very wrong by their definitions. What it came down to, though, was I was not raised to be a doormat-- and NRA's did not like that, at all.

In the words of a popular rabbi: *"Our homes mold and shape our beliefs, values, and character."* Only in the world of NRA's is this considered negative.

"BUT I HAVE NO REGRETS!"

A book on the nature-- and consequences-- of addiction would not be complete without a special section on this special issue. Directly and to the point, you can look at it as how actual recovery and the so-called "self-help industry" differs.

The topic: being responsible for, and accountable for, one's actions. A 12-Step program teaches this is something every addict/alcoholic must learn in order to recover; some of the "self-help" industry, however, teaches the opposite. While not all self-help material is negative, the nature of addiction places addicts/alcoholics in the position of choosing the approach that best suits self-will.

You will find large quantities of "self-help" material that does precisely this: material dedicated to advising individuals to never feel "guilt" or "shame." We can sarcastically add guilt and shame are considered "counterproductive" to so-called "healing." The Self need be the addict/alcoholic's only concern.

You may also hear "I have no regrets-- because everything has made me Who I Am!"

In recovery, an addict/alcoholic must take responsibility for his actions-- and to further it by making amends for his wrongs.

NRA's who wish to continue living in their disease find a convenient way to do so in self-help material-- for the "pop-psych" material consistently tells them they need never feel bad about anything they have done.

At one particular point in time, an acquaintance who regularly attended 12-Step meetings frequently raved about a book he had read. He said it was an excellent book, and had been very useful for him. With curiosity getting the better of me, I scouted every thrift shop and flea market in the area until I found and purchased a copy. My reaction was somewhere between "?" and "Damnnn!" As a longtime hobby of mine was scouting thrift shops for books, it did not take long for me to enmass a quantity of these "pop-psych," so-called "self-help" books. My reaction was generally the same as it had been to the book my acquaintance recommended.

Totally mindboggled, I approached an online friend who had had an entirely different background and lifestyle than myself, asking her if she was familiar with this nonsense, and whether she knew how long it had existed. She replied it had been around since we were children.

That explained it: I knew very little about the subject, because it was yet another factor in the "subculture" that I had never been a part of. When I was a youngster, an adolescent, and a young adult, my lifestyle and priorities were much different than those of my friend and others who started on the path to addiction and found "pop-psych" along the way.

One type of situation described in a pop-psych book clearly illustrates the NRA viewpoint, as well as the nonsense they listen to to back up their approach. In this particular book, written by a longtime popular "self-help" author, the reader was asked to consider a situation, and what he would do in such a situation: you go to a store needing one onion, and find the store does not sell onions individually. From the author's standpoint, the 'right' course of action is to break open a bag of onions, and take the one you want. The 'right' course of action involves no concern for the store's losses, or other customers' inconvenience. Heaven forbid the person inconvenience *himself* by going to a different store for an onion-- or, even worse, doing without something he *wants.*

And there you have it: when generations of NRA's buy into this nonsense, is it any wonder they fail to have any concern for the consequences of their actions, including the consequences to other people? The 'wreckage' they leave is much more serious than a mess in a grocery store-- they destroy other people's dreams, relationships, and *lives,* and 'have no regrets.'

"BOMBS AND MORE"

This is one of the creepiest things I experienced: there is always "something going on." If there is nothing going on around you, there is probably something taking place behind your back. If indeed there is not anything occurring at the moment, you can "bet your boots" there will be before long. In other words, you never know when the next "bomb" is going to fall-- causing some kind of disaster, or pulling everything out from under you. The consequences: you cannot make plans; you cannot be secure. I have experienced this time and time again with the NRA population-- including, but far from being limited to, the 13th-Steppers I met in three different locations.

What are the consequences to regular people ('normies') who get caught up in this? One consequence is you cannot plan anything-- not for next month, not for this evening-- because you never know when a 'bomb' is going to be dropped, nor do you know what's going on behind your back.

One example included a number of different situations that involved continuing my education; each time, it appeared nothing was going on that would interfere with these plans. However, '*appeared*' is an accurate word-- if I had actually followed through with my plans, the shortly-thereafter upheaval in my living arrangements would have resulted in financial disasters and other serious difficulties.

In the first instance, I had almost completed the required coursework for certification-- all I had left to do was participate in "clinicals" and take the final exams. An NRA who created constant chaos prevented me from doing so, and the individuals described in "Thirteenth-Step Number Two" made it impossible for me to do it at a later date, as I needed to leave the state entirely for my family's safety.

In the second instance, believing I was settled for a period of time, I was close to resuming my education, and planned to go the distance with it-- from taking credits I had already earned and eventually proceeding to law school. When all hell broke loose, it was necessary to relocate. What would the consequences have been if I'd enrolled in school, been dealing with financial aid, etc.?

Next, when I was stuck dealing with Social Services because I couldn't get a job, they presented the option of college. I was again close to making a decision-- when the building where we were living was sold out from under us and we had to move immediately.

My last attempt involved considering options in terms of time-frame-- as I didn't want to be dealing with my own education and financial aid when it was time for my youngest to start college, I opted for a much shorter line of coursework. As I planned to eventually move back to California where document-preparation by non-attorneys was legal, I thought it was a good option. The first problem was again losing a place to live; and the second was "Thirteenth-Step Number Three" intruding into our lives. Consequently, it took three years to complete a two-year course program.

From these and other instances I also learned even if you pay your rent, bills, etc., your living arrangements can still be yanked out from under you, often with no advance warning.

And, similar to everything else I'd been up against, none of these issues were issues prior to being mixed up with the NRA population.

Years ago, I happened to see a t.v. show called "One Tree Hill;" in one particular episode, the main characters were asked for one word that would describe what they needed most in their lives. For me, that word was 'stability'-- the specific definition being 'the absence of chaos.' Unfortunately, the chaos continued-- and, after April 2005, when I made a solid decision to make a stable life the highest priority, it only worsened.

"SOMETHING ABOUT COWS"

A saying from generations ago was "why buy the cow when you can get the milk for free?" In the distant past, it was generally a caution to girls and young women, advising them to not "put out" when they had not received the due respect of a full commitment in return. Amongst the NRA population and those they influence, there is no such advice.

Instead, girls and women are often treated as nothing more than prostitutes and chattel. They are expected to "submit"-- and treated like dirt when they do. Girls and women who expect better are labeled "gold-diggers," "game-players," and "drama queens."

Although I have heard the same remarks from numerous NRA's over the years, the very first incident had the most impact because I had never heard of such a thing: a middle-aged male, upon remarking that he had had sex with more than two hundred girls and women, shrugged it off with *"Oh, I just thought of them all as whores."*

In areas with high (no pun intended) NRA populations, concepts such as moral decency, self-control, and respect do not exist. You will find many-- both male and female-- who consider anyone who is unattached to be a "fair target." You will find many-- both male and female-- in "arrangements of convenience," simply living with someone until they move on to someone else. You will also find many-- both male and female-- engaged in the lower-class definition of 'dating": expecting others to meet their sexual "needs." In such areas, individuals may go through their adult lives without ever forming and maintaining a solid, healthy bond with another person-- because a solid, healthy bond with another person is something they have never experienced, and possibly have never even witnessed.

This nonsense about middle-agers and post-middle-agers having "boyfriends" and "girlfriends" often makes the news in terms of domestic violence. As a common factor in low-class environments is the notion that males 'have authority' over females, and males can 'own' females, there are countless instances in which girls and women attempt to leave their boyfriends or husbands-- and end up dead.

Oddly enough, so-called marriages can also be about "cows." What normal people look at as a mutual commitment where two individuals have a healthy bond and a life together, NRA's are not capable of this kind of relationship. In the rare instances when NRA's hold something up as a 'marriage,' it does not in any way resemble a normal person's definition of the word. Whether it is about a "power-trip," some other type of personal gain, or casual and pointless, it is an unhealthy-- and potentially dangerous-- arrangement.

The subject of 'cows'-- getting what one can, with no regard for the feelings, needs, and rights of others-- can, as any other subject connected to the NRA population, be so inappropriate that it totally stuns normal people. One NRA, for example, approached the subject from *both* angles: refusing to acknowledge importance where it *was* important, and making trivialities appear significant when they were not.

As this was one of the first NRA's I met in person, I was surprised when he mentioned all of the "fiancees" he'd had in the past. Not knowing what to make of it, I casually remarked it must have been awfully expensive, purchasing so many rings for so many women. Acting as if he had no idea what I was talking about, he elaborated on his experiences: the numerous women he referred to as his "fiancees" were simply women whom he had lived with in the past. In other words, "fiancee" did not mean any type of real commitment to this individual; he had not proposed marriage, presented them with engagement rings, or set wedding dates. Nor did he seem to understand that was what the word actually meant.

At the same time, however, he described numerous other women he had lived with as "old friends." He even went as far as to use that term to describe his ex-wife, with whom he had had a child!

While treating fellow adults as "cows" to "get free milk" from is bad enough, in environments where this lifestyle is common it often spills onto children, too. In the real world, a person is able to acknowledge that bringing a child into the world a) requires a considerable amount of adjustments in one's own life, and b) the ability to put one's child before oneself.

In these areas, however, those "plain facts" about parenting are unheard of. First, they make no adjustments for the sake of their children. A person may decide he or she "wants" a child, proceeds to have one, and proceeds to expect the child to accommodate the parent. This pattern does not only occur when a child is unplanned, but also when children are planned. A child-- even an infant-- must accommodate everything from his parent's social life to his parent's job.

Second, the NRA population-- referred to numerous times throughout the Program literature as "*self*-seeking, *self*-serving, *self*-willed"-- is less willing to sacrifice for their children than normal parents. If one does do something for a youngster, you can be assured he expects to gain something from it.

In this area particularly, I've heard the excuse that parents were "young." Age is not relevant. A young parent can be perfectly capable of being a good parent-- just as an older one can be capable of being a lousy parent. The actual issue is, as NRA's, so-called parents continue to believe they and their own wants must come first. It may be important to note when individuals are referred to as 'too young' to have kids, these individuals are not teenagers-- they are often people in their mid-twenties, who, by any sense of logic, should be adults. However, in these kinds of environments, becoming a genuine adult is something that rarely occurs. *And the cycle continues.*

Frankly, it is horrifying. When you see flocks of young people living on the streets-- many of whom were simply thrown away by their so-called parents, or left because of unbearable conditions; when young people take up their older generations' way of life and begin with drugs, alcohol, and crime when they are still children; and when the older generations do not want kids to be exposed to adults who never did these things, or a way of life that is better, safe, and healthy, what other word is there for it?

The realization finally came: *They do not love their own children...* not only do they lack the capacity to *love* another human being, they simply do not care. In many instances, children do not come into the world as welcome members of their families; instead, they are nothing more than consequences of a promiscuous lifestyle. One individual stated: *"Kids-- some live, some die- and there's really nothing anybody can do about it."* And by no stretch of the imagination is this acceptable.

"COWS" AND PREDATORS

Large numbers of "horror stories" covering experiences in 12-Step programs include rape and other forms of sexual assault. This is something that obviously must be addressed-- but there is a connected subject that also needs to be addressed.

While I am sure there are plenty of perverts, pigs, and other assorted creeps in the general population, I personally never knew or met any-- *without exception, all* of the deviants who believed they had some sort of entitlement to whatever they wished to extract from women came from one place: 12-Step programs.

The connected subject: in addition to committing sexual assault and rape, there are predators in the programs who use a special, insidious form of manipulation to get what they are after-- or to *try* to get what they are after. The goal: to get a woman to comply; the tactic: to break the woman down so she feels she has no other options.

The way I experienced this attempted trap in a variety of instances: an NRA chooses one particular "flaw" in the woman (or a perceived flaw, or a made-up flaw), and uses this flaw to pressure her into believing she cannot reasonably hope for or expect anything better than *him.* In other words, the NRA's beat women down in an attempt to make them believe they should 'appreciate' or even be grateful for the NRA's interest and attention.

The instances in which I was targeted for this tactic all focused on one particular topic these NRA's purported as being my 'flaw': my age. With no other flaws to go on, each and every one took the approach that since I was not a '20-year-old young chick,' I could not possibly hope for a decent man who treated women in a respectful manner. Various NRA's used this tactic-- and while it did not work in terms of them getting what they wanted, it certainly had a negative effect on my self-image and self-esteem.

The concept of a "package" has become popular-- and NRA's who wish to gain something from women take an entirely different approach. Rather than noting all of the assets a woman has, and everything that is positive about her, they hold out one thing that they claim to be negative. It was one of the countless NRA tactics and tricks that I did not fall for-- simply because I was over forty years of age, that did not mean I had no recourse but to "settle" for individuals in whom I had no interest, perverts, criminals, and other rejects. However, if I, as someone who was stable and without any addictions, encountered this situation time and time again, it should not take much to know how women who are struggling with addictions and other serious issues are completely vulnerable to these tactics.

"CONNECTIONS BETWEEN ADDICTIONS AND ABUSE"

You may have heard being under-the-influence lowers a person's inhibitions and impairs his judgments; however-- what about NRA's who are *not* currently using substances, and claim long periods of "sobriety," yet continue to abuse other human beings?

The nature of addiction includes an exaggerated and misguided sense of "self"-- self-importance, self-will; the inability to ascertain right from wrong; and a variety of other characteristics. These characteristics are not going to simply go away solely because someone is 'in a Program.'

Unfortunately, the word and its variations are tossed around with such regularity that it's become common practice to misuse it. As described by the American Psychiatric Association, "abuse" is defined as *"behavior which is designed to control and subjugate another human being through the use of fear, humiliation, and verbal or physical assaults."*

Another definition that should be equally simple to understand is my own personal definition: ABUSE starts when someone throws your rights and free will out the window, and either verbally or by behavior attaches an *'or else'* to it.

It happens too often-- and it should not happen at all.

However, as you have seen throughout this book, NRA's appear to be clueless about this subject. Similar to other topics, I never knew whether they were simply engaging in game-playing to manipulate others, or whether they were so screwed-up that they didn't even know what the word meant. If I had to guess, I'd guess it was mostly the former, combined with some of the latter. But the most important part of it, in my opinion, is that NRA's who routinely misuse the word were likely lying about their own histories. After all, when individuals make asinine statements such as a child calling a parent 'Mom' instead of 'Ma'am,' giving a youngster one easy chore to do, or setting reasonable rules for kids' safety amounts to 'abuse,' perhaps those individuals are not telling the whole truth when they claim they were Abused earlier in their lives.

DONNING MASKS

Not all NRA's are sociopaths. During my years of involvement with 12-Step programs, I knew many individuals who did not have any wrongful intentions, and had no desire to harm other people. However, as sociopaths are most definitely represented within the 12-Step programs, the subject must be addressed.

From my experiences, sociopathic NRA's don masks. It is no different from the way average people have wardrobes of clothing, putting on whichever outfit is appropriate for any given situation. Whether a sociopath wishes to intimidate someone, ingratiate himself to someone, or appear "good" when there is nothing good about him, he has a ready mask to present the image he wishes to present. This characteristic can also be looked at in terms of abusive situations in general-- a nearly universal factor in abusive situations is for an abuser to present himself as a wonderful human being to the majority, while only showing his abusive nature to his victims.

One "mask" I have seen numerous times is that of 'Christian.' As is the case with any mask a sociopath presents to the world in general, there is nothing genuine about it. We can look back at the popular saying *"What Would Jesus Do?"* and easily see there is nothing Christian or Christlike about sociopaths' attitudes, beliefs, and behaviors.

Instead, as with all other masks, these NRA's don this phony mask *because they feel it gives them an advantage*-- most specifically, an advantage over other people. One example was the NRA who claimed that being a 'saved Christian' meant he could commit another murder, and not be held accountable for it. Another example as an NRA who put a great deal of effort into trying to take away my rights and my role, claiming 'the Bible says' women cannot be the heads of their households, 'the Bible says" women must be submissive and silent, and 'the Bible says' any male can claim authority over any woman.

Although masks allow them to claim an advantage over others, it can allow them to feel superior to others, too. As an example, one NRA dismissed people who were not 'Christians' as "riff-raff" and "scum."

And both of these characteristics fit in perfectly with the definitions and descriptions of *sociopathy*.

Taking great liberties with paraphrasing, I came across accurate descriptions of "the way sociopaths see themselves and others:

They believe they are Superior to others, and that others are potential targets;

They believe others deserve to be victimized, because others are dumb;

They believe others deserve to be victimized, because targets have consciences and emotions that the sociopath deems stupid;

A target's conscience and emotions are considered useful, because they make the target easy to exploit;

They believe it is entirely reasonable to exploit others whenever it means the sociopath gets what he wants.

These characteristics show why it is not possible for these individuals to be rehabilitated-- because they cannot see there is anything wrong with them, and simply believe they are above and superior to other people.

In other words, in the minds of sociopaths, human lives are nothing more than a game, and human beings are but objects to exploit for their own purposes.

When sociopaths do not get their own way, the result is rage-- and it can be extremely dangerous. When they do get their own way, they sneeringly dismiss their victims as fools.

There was something I could not understand for a long time. As I'd spent my life in the real world, which consisted primarily of straightforward people, I could not understand the emphasis on manipulation, sneakiness, underhandedness. Because I had no experience with either these types of individuals or these types of behaviors, I initially dismissed them as losers-- along the line of "What kinds of losers cannot get what they want in life by being honest and straightforward?"

Eventually I learned that was not the issue. What the issue was, was whether or not NRA's had the ability to gain by honest means, to do so would have lacked something that they evidently considered all-important and essential: the warped thrill of "winning," combined with the equally-warped thrill of "defeating" someone else in order to "win."

These types of NRA's *play games with human beings' lives.* The power they feel from being able to orchestrate other people's lives is even more important to them than their eventual 'goals.' It is like they actually gain a sense of exhilaration by creating wreckage in other people's lives-- and to human beings themselves.

"LIE, CHEAT, AND STEAL"

This phrase is sprinkled liberally throughout 12-Step Programs, as is the saying "manipulate people and manipulate situations." The reason these phrases are used so frequently is they are amongst the most prominent hallmarks of "the disease of addiction." While the Programs explain that they are tactics used by the addict population to gain drugs, they add that many who become addicts had these and other "features" long before they ever began using drugs or abusing alcohol.

Many learn young how to "get what they want," and to "get away with" things. Rather than embracing true recovery and change, they continue to manipulate-- to be sneaky, devious, and underhanded.

What it comes down to is the NRA population does not attempt a real recovery process-- *because it benefits them to not do so.* Whether someone is seeking to gain something he or she has no right to, harm or exploit other human beings, or persist in criminal behavior, they can find a ready, easy "cover" in 12-Step programs.

Lie, cheat, and steal; limits and boundaries; an additional factor is NRA's often seem completely unable to differentiate between what is and is not theirs, what they do and do not have rights to. While it was an ongoing issue, the very first experience I had with this topic involved the very first NRA I met in person. The situation: the NRA had taken a ring that was very important to me. While it may not be relevant that the ring had not been extremely expensive, and was one of my most prized possessions that I'd planned to pass along to my own kids, I had purchased it years earlier and it was mine.

With all of those facts in hand, the NRA exclaimed: "But I like it- why can't I keep it?!" and had a great deal of difficulty grasping my response: *"Because it isn't yours!"*

The fact that something is not 'theirs' is a fact NRA's completely disregard. Similar to this one particular individual, they believe 'wanting' something means they can claim it.

"CREATING AN ENVIRONMENT"

Many years ago, I read an article written by the daughter of a popular celebrity. At the time, I was clueless about what she meant. She said her father *'created an environment of chaos, so he could always have control.'* I eventually learned what the woman meant: NRA's often "create an environment" of chaos, or an environment of hostility, or numerous other environments-- *because* they enjoy "having the upper hand," and enjoy watching other people "spin in a fog" or "scurry around like chickens with their heads cut off."

Creating an environment of false security can be even worse: something is bound to happen, but you never know what or when. An additional "environment" includes pitting people against each other-- often by telling each person a different "story."

There was yet another example that occurred on a number of occasions, but I've hesitated in including it here because I have no idea what the word or term is for it: when NRA's do not want you to know about, find out about, or notice something way out of line that is going on 'behind your back in front of your face, the tactic is to cook up a phony emergency or crisis to distract your attention. Your attention is on their scam, rather than being able to pick up on what is really going on.

NRA's who do not want to live in the real world-- or do not want others to-- have no trouble "creating their own environments." And it can make existing a living hell for the rest of us.

TOMBSTONES-- OR NOT

One example of "manipulating people and manipulating situations" was the frequency of which I heard "suicide threats."

As it was another oddity I was not familiar with before I became involved with 12-Step programs, I made the mistake of taking such "threats" as they were presented. The "threats" did not come from troubled persons who were actually considering ending their lives, but was nothing more than another manipulation tactic. Along the line of 'go along with what I want, cooperate, or I'll kill myself,' this tactic when presented by adults was nothing more than a grotesque take on a tantrum-throwing toddler threatening to hold his breath 'til he turned blue.

In fact, a phony suicide threat was how I ended up boarding that bus from a familiar environment to the unknown in August, 1998-- against my better judgment.

A second individual made two such threats. In the first instance, he claimed if I were to remove him from my life permanently, he would go to the nearby Transportation Center and 'lay down in front of a train.' In the second instance, he held a box-cutter to his wrist, threatening to slash his wrists.

The third individual also threatened me with 'throwing himself in front of a train.' After inappropriate behavior toward me, he demanded I tell him if he had "dishonored" me, stating that if I were to say yes, he would end his life in that violent manner. I made the mistake of brushing it off, because, like with the others, I believed he meant what he said.

Phony suicide threats are yet another means of "manipulating people and manipulating situations." In none of these instances would the NRA's have carried out their threats to do away with themselves-- and they were all counting on the fact that I did not know this.

"STAYIN' ALIVE"

Call it a healthy sense of self-preservation: *"Do not poke a poisonous snake with a stick."*

What I mean is there are a variety of ways in which to deal with NRA's, while staying alive and intact. You can avoid them altogether-- and if you have any choice in the matter, this is definitely in your best interest. You can fight back, showing your strength, even if only verbally. However, there is an additional response which I refer to as placating-- merely brushing it off as much as possible. When what you have to say is not something that an NRA wants to hear, you have nothing to gain and plenty to lose by "asserting yourself."

If you find yourself dealing with someone who clearly has no marbles left in his pouch, do the sensible thing and refrain from "poking a poisonous snake with a stick."

In some instances, a situation can be serious enough that the only recourse is "placating"-- to try to prevent the situation from becoming worse, or more dangerous. While it can leave a naturally-straightforward person feeling like a hypocrite, it is the only option when there are no other options.

NINES

Years later, struggling underneath the "wreckage" the last 13th-Stepper caused, the same thought comes to mind that has been pestering and tormenting me ever since the incident first occurred: *What would someone else have done, or done differently, if they had been in my situation?*

That question is not only directed toward "know-it-alls" who would insist they would have automatically known what to do, but also those who continue to buy into and repeat lies because they have never been willing to listen to the truth. And that question has pestered and haunted me for years: *What should I have done differently- what could I have done differently?* Not once have I had an answer to that question.

What did I do? with more than four decades of life behind me, and those decades having consisted primarily of reasonable, stable, sane people, I used the only approach I knew: *logic.* While it was the most asinine and useless approach possible, it was the only one I was familiar with.

Logic fails when it is used toward an NRA who is so twisted that he fully believes you have no rights (in addition to making a point of frequently saying so); logic also fails when said individual thoroughly believes that no consequences to you are relevant or wrong, so long as he gets what he wants.

When someone has his head on straight, he understands and respects the meaning of the word 'No.' When someone has his head on straight, he realizes and acknowledges that human beings have rights-- including that right to say 'No.'

In contrast, an individual who is sick and twisted does not acknowledge any of this-- instead, he will 'veto' your rights, both in word and action, proceeding to both sneak behind your back and threaten you to your face.

For a long time, I was bothered with the thought *"How could anyone be gullible enough to believe all of this crap?!"* It was a matter of people only hearing what he wanted them to hear-- and what he wanted them to hear was his lies, and to dismiss any idea of listening to me instead.

In addition to the basic mindboggling gullibility, there was another factor that figuratively kept me shaking my head in disbelief: it would seem the people who were caught up in those lies should have wondered what lies were being told about *them, too.* However, I knew there was no point in saying anything, because they'd been manipulated into not believing me, anyway. Still, I was fairly certain they would have had an entirely different view of the entire mess if they'd known how the NRA was trying to turn *me* against *them.*

Perhaps individuals in the local 'program' did not know me well enough to know truth from lies-- but those who were the main focus of the scam *should have* known.

It was about an NRA's systematic attempts to reduce me to an animal level, where nothing existed but survival instincts.

From the onset, it was "about" ripping away what Maslow covers in the "safety" level, with the result being the levels on top of it also crumbling.

From the onset, I had no 'safety'-- security of body, employment, resources, morality, family, health, property-- I was told I 'had no rights,' and it was consistently backed up by actions.

When the programs say addiction affects every area of one's life, it turns out they are not only referring to individuals who are addicts/alcoholics-- but also those of us who are sucked into "the disease of addiction." You find many who seem to devote their lives to "manipulating people and manipulating situations," with no concern whatsoever for the consequences to anybody. And the point: even if you walk blindly into the quicksand, you will eventually find it is much harder to get out-- the nightmare that occurred after I made my decision is clearly proof of this.

Recovery, and better lives, are possible for people who want it-- and are willing to do what it takes to recover. I met people like that-- but there were very few. Others simply plod on through life *creating* wreckage, and *leaving* wreckage. They do not know the difference between right and wrong-- or do not believe such concepts apply to them. They are the truest definition of the word 'sociopaths.' Between August 1998 and March 2005, these were the types of individuals I associated with-- and exposed my precious family to. *In April 2005, when I made the decision "No more!"-- all you need to do is look at the results of that decision.*

I sometimes think of things I should have paid more attention to in the beginning. One that comes to mind was a statement made by a middle-aged woman shortly after I began associating with individuals in the programs. *"God forgives us- and gives us a second chance,"* she said. My mistake, as often happened in those days, was not paying much attention to what she said. The reason: in those days, if I had thought clearly about her statement, and thought clearly about how it applied to *me*, I would have noticed there had not been much in my life that I needed forgiveness *for*-- nor a *second chance.* There were no examples of that nature *until I became involved with 12-Step programs and their members.*

I am certainly not saying I made no mistakes whatsoever in my life prior to becoming involved with the programs-- but the fact is the mistakes, errors-in-judgment, and devastating consequences of mistakes and errors-in-judgment *all* came as a direct result of my involvement with the programs.

I am also reminded of a remark someone made in the distant past: *"Hate is the b*stard child of Fear and Misunderstanding."* And frankly, from my experiences, that statement accurately sums it up: while there are individuals in the programs who Hate because they have Fear, it is not nearly as destructive as people who Hate because they Misunderstand. And, from my experiences, Hate based on Misunderstanding is the worst part of the nightmare that shows no signs of ending.

At that New Year's Eve party, December 31 1999, a girl addressed me by saying: *"Everybody deserves a chance!"*

Should that include me, too-- the chance to try to set things right, and the chance to be heard?

THE MODEL: PART TWO

I think the most logical question would be: why did I continue my involvement in these programs? While making the mistake of looking at individuals as individuals, and not realizing they represented the majority, was the common thread, there were some other points that were also relevant to the question.

First, when I began meeting 12-Step members, I took the approach that similarities were more important than differences. This, unfortunately, allowed me to overlook a considerable amount of negativity that I should not have overlooked.

Second, after being badgered to attend my first meeting, I concluded most of those members were good people-- and, in fact, they were. While they were misguided, and totally cowed by their 'sponsors,' most of the members in that particular location were sincerely trying to overcome their addictions and build better lives for themselves.

Third, after I attended a meeting at the second location "by invitation," I was later approached by a women who did not attend the meeting. It took very little for her to assess my situation, and caution me by saying this city "will eat you alive." She then proceeded to assign a close friend of hers the role of my 'bodyguard,' saying that I would be safe in his company. During that period of time, where he went I went-- and mainly where he went was the 12-Step meetingplace.

When the woman's friend moved to a different city for a new job, I acquired a replacement. Although the first 'guard' was helpful, the second was even more so, because most people were afraid of him. He referred to me as his 'sister.' While many people got the wrong idea, I let them think whatever they thought, because my safety depended on it. However, an NRA used 'every trick in the book' to get rid of this person. As he was afraid to confront the person himself, he began by barking at me "I object to him being in your life- get rid of him!" My friend was not so easy to get rid of, but the NRA eventually succeeded, and then I had no one.

The other factor occurred when I made some personal decisions, and decided to walk away from the meetings. That was when an acquaintance asked me to take care of his meetings in his absence. However, there was one point about this particular situation that eventually came to bother me very much: as much later I was informed this acquaintance had been a longtime friend of "Thirteenth-Stepper Number Three," it led me to wonder if it had been a set-up from the beginning. In other words, I wondered if the acquaintance who had presented himself as my friend helped the creep access me by asking me to look after those late-night meetings where I would be alone and with transportation. It is something I suppose I will never know the truth about.

So, to clarify the time-span of "the model," it can be described this way: in 1994, without any drug or alcohol issues, and having not had a drink at all in more than six years, I met a woman who belonged to the Program, who stated I could have a life of Choice if I 'worked the twelve steps.' Going by the definition of 'sobriety dates,' as explained by another woman, my not drinking at all ended up being more than eleven years.

After approximately eleven years without a drink, and no drug history, and never having seen a 12-Step meeting, a woman in another Program claimed an allergic reaction to a normal dose of cold medication meant I was a Drug Addict-- that I'd 'relapsed,' and was 'in denial.'

Earlier in this book I made a couple of references to a third 12-Step program. Not only was the NRA who made these asinine claims responsible for my introduction to Narcotics Anonymous, she was also responsible for my introduction to the 12-Step program for sexual abuse survivors. Her claims of what constituted 'sexual abuse,' 'incest,' and 'rape' were absolutely mindboggling. It was one of the many examples where, while I was always armed with the facts, an NRA attempted to 'screw with my perceptions,' and, failing at that, simply badgered and badgered me to apply terms she chose to those experiences. Not only did she insist I was a 'survivor' of those words and terms, but also insisted I had post-traumatic stress disorder.

While none of what she said was true or accurate, it may bear noting that she insisted she was qualified to make these assessments *through the mail.* In other words, the NRA attempted to cause me to alter my vocabulary to suit her, and make diagnoses, when she had never met me in person nor spoken with me.

Going back to what the second uninformed woman called my 'sobriety date,' I consumed alcohol three times in a twenty-five year period. That twenty-five year period included approximately four months of attending N.A. meetings in one location because I'd met good people in a new city, and approximately a year of attending A.A. meetings in another city-- first because I thought it was a safe place, and later because an acquaintance asked me to take care of his meetings. The last time I had a couple of beers was more than eight and a half years ago, although my life has been torn to shreds for the last eight years, and I have had no involvement with the Programs or anyone in the Programs for the last seven years.

What it comes down to is I had nothing to 'recover' *from*-- and everything about my life is *much* worse because of 12-Step programs than before I ever heard of them.

"POWER IN YOUR LIFE THAT THEY DO NOT DESERVE"

There was nothing whatsoever about "the world of addiction" that I had any experience or even knowledge about prior to becoming involved with programs. There was one particular topic that was amongst the most distressing: prior to programs, I had never heard the term *'control'* used or applied in the context that NRA's use and apply it. As a common tactic of NRA's, it is one of the many terms they apply to anything they personally do not like, while insisting it is something they themselves do not do.

In my own life-- in the real world-- the general viewpoint is sensible rules, policies, and laws exist for a sensible purpose. They do not violate the unalienable rights of anyone, regardless of age, gender, or personal situation. This viewpoint, for me, goes as far back as my growing-up years, and continued in my early adult life with other normal people. In fact, prior to programs, I was only familiar with the term in two different contexts: first, when it is preceded by the word *'self-;'* and second, when referring to something such as putting a leash on a dog before taking it out for a walk. Within the programs, though, the second example is closer to the facts-- although we are talking about *human beings,* not animals. The way I described my program experiences was like being a butterfly pinned to a corkboard.

Dictionary definitions of the word include: *the power to make decisions about something and decide what should happen; to exercise restraint or direction over; to dominate; to command; to hold in check; the act or power of controlling, regulation, domination, or command; the situation of being under the regulation, domination, or command of another."* Now, by what stretch of the imagination could any of this be considered "o.k."?

The most important point to bear in mind about the situations in which I experienced 'control' was that the individuals involved were strangers-- individuals whom I had never even met before. Yet they claimed this kind of 'power.' *As soon as I set foot in their world,* I began encountering it: individuals whom I did not even know began "issuing orders." It took a long time to see it for what it was: NRA's wanted to keep me away from People, and to keep People away from me, so I would have no one to go to for help, and so no one would see the situation for what it was and possibly help me.

In one particular situation, initially I did not have a phone in my apartment, and did not have home internet. I was unable to stop him from showing up-- at my apartment or elsewhere; nor was I able to get rid of him. I stated that I wanted him out of my life, away from my home and family; and his reply was: "I do not *wish* to get out of your life!"

Again, does anyone-- or at least anyone *normal*-- really believe any of this was o.k.? My turning point came when I had the opportunity to speak with a police officer. The officer did not give a damn about 'programs,' programese, psychobabble, fundamentalist christians' so-called authority, or any other such nonsense; instead, he asked me to describe incidents, and when I described some of them, he informed me what the law calls such incidents. *Some* of the terms the officer used included *stalking, harassment, criminal trespass, kidnapping, and unlawful restraint.* And the creepiest thing about the entire mess was that while 'the law' was on my side, people who should have been were not.

In fact, the latter part of that last statement was the one and only deciding factor-- why there was nothing I could do. Instead, I had no viable alternatives but to continue tolerating the intrusions into my life, a variety of forms of abuse, and endless verbal taunts and threats.

226

Naturally, as is generally the case with any situation that involves NRA's, it got worse. One particular incident illustrates how extreme these situations can become; and, even more relevant, assuming very few people knew about it. I assume none of the individuals who were directly involved, nor "bystanders," nor even the few individuals who felt truth and doing the right thing were important enough for them to offer their assistance, none were aware of how a related mess occurred. To the best of my knowledge, only two individuals knew about it-- myself, and a judge who offered his opinion and advice.

Upon granting me a temporary Restraining Order, and stating I had solid grounds for a permanent order, he advised me to not follow through with it, and to seek other options. Although there were no other options that I was aware of, he stated his reason for this advice was upon assessing the situation, he believed the people who should have backed me up were so manipulated by the NRA that they would probably lie under oath in court to defend him. Considering the way everything had been going, and the fact that this opinion and advice came from a county court judge, I believed his assessment was accurate, and I dropped the order. So instead of a tiny bit of security and justice, I dropped it so the individuals in question would not be in the position of committing perjury.

However, as in any NRA-related situation, I can guess that anyone and everyone who had knowledge about the order and the fact that I dropped it came to different conclusions-- either intentionally, or simply because they did not know the facts. I assume the people who offered to back me up thought I was a spineless coward for not following through with it, while those who were directly involved thought I was a fool. However, similar to the sh*t I tolerated and went through, dropping the order was for the same reason: believing it was the only thing I could do to protect some of my loved ones. What it came to was the judge's assertion that you cannot even trust loved ones to be truthful, when they have been so manipulated.

On the subject of "power in your life," there is a connected topic on which many former members related their experiences. Although my experiences with the topic were different from theirs-- probably because they had a considerable amount of experience with 12-Step meetings-- the consequences were essentially the same: human beings being made *helpless,* unable to stand up for themselves. Whether one describes it as manipulation, brainwashing, or torture, all of those definitions would be accurate.

What all of the individuals experienced: in any situation, regardless of how extreme a situation may be, the normal response-- anger-- is not an option. People are told they cannot *become* angry, and cannot *express* anger. Their universal experience involved being told "Anger is *not Spiritual."*

In other words, regardless of the harm someone else is inflicting upon you, you are merely supposed to silently "take it."

It really should not take much to understand exactly how destructive this approach is-- it violates one's rights, it violates one's place as a human being, *and* it places *power* in the hands of those who not only do not 'deserve' it, but use such power to continue harming others.

'POWER' ON A LARGER SCALE

An average person might assume if he never walks into a 12-Step meeting, he is unlikely to ever encounter NRA's. Nothing could be further from the truth. The NRA population exists in government, law enforcement, the justice system, social work, and the health care community. What the issue comes down to is like my friend said: "Everybody deserves a chance"-- and the fact that the NRA population is not exactly in this category. Instead of making good use of their opportunities to recover and build better lives for themselves, there are many who simply misuse their authority.

"ON A SIDE NOTE..."

"The titles of the last two sections are based on a popular Program saying." *No, they aren't.* When I began meeting large numbers of 12-Step program members in one particular area, individual after individual used that line-- to me, and to others. It seems the concept is if someone harms or wrongs you, you 'gave' the individual the 'power' to do it.

While it's obviously an asinine and potentially dangerous approach, there's a catch: upon relating the saying to large numbers of former program members all over the United States, I found that no one had ever heard of it. Evidently, it's something program members in one particular location dreamed up-- yet repeating it and repeating it as if it is legitimately connected to the 12-Step programs as a whole.

The psychobabble you may hear frequently in the programs has sources as diverse as so-called self-help material and Charles Manson. And, in addition, other quotes and sayings that NRA's often parrot are not from the programs, either. They 'borrow' lines from everybody from Albert Einstein to Joan Baez, regularly using the quotes as if they are program-related.

"WHEN ANYONE ANYWHERE REACHES OUT FOR HELP..."

This book would by no means be complete without a very important warning: every 12-Step group is autonomous. What this means is there is no higher authority-- and no one to turn to if wrongs are committed within the groups. If you happen to be a newcomer, either to a program or an area, you are one-hundred-percent on your own.

In the second 13th-Stepping incident, I didn't actually turn to anyone for help because I didn't know what was going on. In addition to the odd ways I was being treated, various other people commented that their "Sponsors" had told them to not say anything, to not speak up in my behalf. Those "Sponsors" were the two individuals who had committed the 13th-Stepping.

In the third instance, however, I did reach out for help. While still unaware that the NRA had been stalking me long before I had the misfortune of meeting him, finding I could not get rid of him led me to try to contact nearly everyone whose phone numbers I had. *Not a single one even bothered to return my messages or find out what was wrong.*

It was almost a year later when I happened to meet up with two program members. One said many other people had known the individual had been watching and following me way back when it started. Not a one of them bothered to bring it to my attention or to warn me I was in danger. "*We knew he was up to no good,*" the person said.

The bottom line is many in 12-Step programs may be willing to talk about drugs or alcohol, but if you are in a position of danger most will do nothing to help you-- they will either look the other way or dismiss your cry for help.

In contrast, at different points in time I reached out for help elsewhere. The results: two police officers, a detective, a police sergeant, and two counselors with victims' advocacy services, all advised me to obtain a restraining order. They all believed the situation was serious enough that I, my family, and my household needed legal protection. One of the victims' advocacy counselors said: "All of that talk about murder and serial killers- he's obviously crazy and dangerous!" and her coworker nodded her head in agreement. I asked why anyone would say such things-- certain of the answer, but wanting to hear it from an 'authority'-- and received the response: "*To terrify and control you.*"

The incident with the detective may also bear noting, primarily how a detective ended up showing up at my door one night. What had happened was some young adults had come to visit, and while they were playing some games in the living room an NRA popped up at the door. Almost in unison, they said I should call the police. As I had the backup of numerous young adults, I did so; and, as I was talking to the officer the NRA reappeared, strolled nonchalantly up the sidewalk, and made a threat to me. The officer then took him aside, and whatever the NRA said to him alarmed the officer enough to send a detective to my apartment a few hours later. The detective said she "strongly advise" me to immediately get a restraining order against the NRA.

Eventually, the NRA's remark to me was "Go ahead and get your ass down to the sheriff's office and get a restraining order- and watch it all blow up in your face!"

The title of this section is a reference to a popular saying, and it is even printed on 12-Step program brochures: *"When anyone anywhere reaches out for help, I want the hand of A.A. to always be there- and for that, I am responsible."* Unfortunately, I had been so "sucked into" the ways of 12-Step programs that initially, I believed it-- and believed that was the way longtime members of the programs saw it. Months earlier, an Oldtimer had advised me that if I intended to attend their meetings, I should ask someone to be my 'sponsor.' While I had no actual reason to have one, I followed his advice. The woman whose name I chose told me she was usually very busy with work and family, so if I ever needed to get in touch with her I should leave her a message and she would get back to me. However, near the onset of this nightmare, when I found I could not get rid of this individual no matter how hard I tried, when I was still able to get out of my apartment periodically I "hid out" in a downtown park, frantically sending messages to the woman. She never got back to me.

When it became clear the person who said she wanted to be my 'temporary sponsor' was not going to respond to my requests for help, I sent messages to a half-dozen or so other program members whose numbers I had. No response from any of them, either.

One of the women advised me to speak with the intergroup secretary. The person responded by sending a "mass email" to all of the local chairpersons, telling them they needed to get together with me and deal with the situation. None of them ever contacted me. As he'd sent me a copy of the email, I recognized one name in the "Cc" list and contacted that particular person directly. Her response: "Don't you ever contact me again!" And, although she had been badgering me to call her in the past, she irately told me to tear up her phone number and email address.

Much later, I contacted the main offices of the 12-Step programs. I asked if there was something I should have, or could have, done differently. I was told there was not-- that under the circumstances, I had done the right thing. I was told that one's local "grievance committee" was responsible to deal with situations like this; but, even more distressing, was told if a person has any kind of 'sponsorship relationship,' that the sponsor should take whatever legitimate means possible to "prevent" situations like this- and to step up to the plate and help if it does occur.

So what it came down to was those who asserted 'program' authority on local levels did not do what they were supposed to do-- but simply sat back and did nothing.

Eventually, a few individuals did reach out to try to help. I guess they were no match for the NRA's.

Specifically, though, was being told from the General Services Office: "*It is indeed regrettable that members of A.A. are amongst those who act inappropriately toward others... good sponsorship is the key in helping the newcomer avoid such pitfalls...*
Clearly, there are times within A.A. that the newcomer or any other member may face the kinds of difficulties and abuses that are encountered in life in general, and good sponsorship helps in resolving these and other problems appropriately."

LIES ARE THE ROOT OF ALL EVIL

A phrase I heard occasionally was "lying by omission." The phrase was misused for the purpose of attempting to gain information that was no one's business. I have known other former members who were manipulated with the same tactic. However, it can also be used by intentionally twisting the facts to achieve an outcome that is not based on the facts. One of the most extreme examples was an NRA who employed this method so individuals with whom he communicated would believe "his Truth" instead of "the Truth."

There is nothing quite like destroying someone's credibility when one wishes to gain power-- and nothing quite like perpetuating lies when one wishes to destroy someone's credibility. In many instances where abuse is the issue, including this particular instance, the quickest route to gaining power by destroying someone's credibility is by attacking the person's mental stability.

In fact, it is often the foundation of battering and other forms of domestic violence, not only situations within 12-step programs-- a victim is consistently told he or she cannot reach out for help because no one would believe him or her; and, in many situations such as this one, "people" are actually manipulated to believe the lies.

If you do some research or ask victims or experts, you will see abusers lying about their victims' mental stability accounts for one of the main reasons victims cannot get away, and cannot see any constructive means to deal with the situations.

In this particular instance, there were two topics: a 'large number of abusive men in my past,' and 'early childhood sexual abuse,' allegedly resulted in being "insane"-- which in turn resulted in being "in denial" and being "unready for a committed relationship." You can go back to the description of this particular 13th-stepping incident to see exactly how the "non-relationship" occurred-- but I feel for the sake of clarity the lying should be specially noted.

First, my experiences with 'abusive' individuals essentially began when I became involved with 12-step programs. I take exception to the terminology, though-- there is no such thing as 'abusive *men*,' because an individual who intentionally harms or injures someone is not a 'man.' However, whether we are talking about individuals who commit physical assaults, sexual assaults, or dominate women, this is a range of experiences I knew little to nothing about before I became involved with the programs. The NRA concocted this lie as a means of leading people to believe that my refusal to become involved with him was based on a wide range of horrible experiences from which I had never 'healed and recovered.'

The second topic was equally outrageous: asserting that I had never 'healed and recovered' from childhood sexual abuse. Specifically, an incident occurred when I was four years old: a neighbor, who was mentally ill and mentally retarded, of an indeterminate adult age, lured me out of my back yard and exposed himself. While this incident was minor but confusing, the lingering effects were from the "story" he told me so I would not "tell on" him-- his threats caused me to have nightmares.

However-- when the individual learned I'd eventually sought help for the nightmares, and that they had eventually ended, he took the tack of asserting that my mind was permanently gone because of this incident. First, although I'd struggled with the sole symptom of nightmares, I had never been diagnosed as having Post-Traumatic Stress Disorder or any other mental condition-- his response was that he could effectively "diagnose" mental conditions even when professionals did not. He went as far as to say I should go to a counselor so I could 'prove' there was nothing wrong with me; but, after I made the asinine move of doing so, and said the counselor concluded there indeed was nothing wrong with me, I was told the counselor was wrong-- and 'counselors are all crazy, anyway.' I was also informed this particular incident was misrepresented-- that people were being told I had agreed to go to counseling 'to get help for all of my problems.'

Second, continuing with the "special knowledge" that 12-step programs warn against, he said it was actually a matter of "delayed stress"-- that even though the nightmares had ended decades in the past, and I'd never had any other repercussions from that one minor incident, at some point it would all cave in on me and I would blow sky-high.

In addition, he said I needed to be "in therapy" for the rest of my life-- and that if I believed the professional input I received decades ago had resolved the issue, I was only fooling myself because I "only had a cap on it."

In other words, he asserted that a minor incident that had occurred more than four decades in the past meant my mind was gone permanently, and that at some point I would completely fall apart or explode-- and refusing to acknowledge this nonsense as fact meant I was "insane."

As nearly any abuse victim can probably tell you, this tactic is very effective-- claiming your mind is not working properly is the surest way to destroy your credibility. If people believe you are unstable, no one will believe you-- and no one will even listen to you. It is the surest way for an abuser to get whatever it is that he wants. To further compound the problem, an abuser's lying often includes a "Jekyll-and-Hyde" appearance-- *no one but his victims know the facts or know what he is really like.*

MORE ABOUT PREDATORS: FINANCIAL TOPICS

This book has already discussed financial predators in terms of NRA's who exploit the vulnerability of people who are flat-broke and in need of jobs; there are also those who make people vulnerable by lending money or other assistance so they can use 'owing them something' against the people; but there is another financial topic that must be addressed.

If you have income-- either from a job, government assistance, or other regular source-- you are likely to have experiences that I had on a number of occasions. You may be approached by NRA's who claim they need your 'help,' have a personal interest in you, or are looking for 'roommates.' What this translates to is the NRA wants to live off your money. If the NRA has income of his own, he will expect you to cover his expenses for him, while he uses his own money on his addictions-- if not drugs or alcohol, whatever obsession he is addicted to.

The very first NRA I met in person was also this type of financial predator. His first approach was to inform me he had moved into a new, expensive apartment, and wanted me to move to that area, get a job, and, as he worded it, 'get him out of the hole.' His second approach was to sign up for government assistance, using my and my family's names and information so he could obtain what he wanted for himself.

Upon relocating to another city, I found a plethora of financial predators claiming they were looking for 'roommates.' Fortunately, I'd had more than enough experience to see the scam for what it was, and resisted each attempt.

However, it is somewhere between difficult and impossible to resist a scam when you do not see it for what it is; and, with that in mind, I was 'taken' a number of times. One situation in particular bears noting, because the scam I was on the receiving-end of later played out with other innocent victims.

The NRA in question remarked that he was 'clean,' trying to get sober, and had no other concerns beyond putting his life back together so he could be a good parent to his small child. (Much later, I found none of these things were true). Upon pestering me repeatedly to invite him to my home for dinner, and finding I had a fairly decent apartment that was well-stocked with food, and dinner on the table at a specific time, he began showing up at that time-- regularly. He stated he needed my help so he could put his life back together for his child's sake. His next tack was to state his 'bad eyesight' made it dangerous for him to walk home after dark, and asked if he could stay at my apartment. I made the foolish mistake of allowing him to do so-- fully believing I was 'helping' him-- until he drained all of my resources and moved on to his next victim. His next victim was a teenage boy who had "aged out" of the foster care system, and was working hard to build a solid life for himself. The young kid didn't see the scam coming either-- and weeks later approached me with tears in his eyes, saying "Everything is *gone!*" After the NRA drained the kid's resources, he moved on to a mentally-disabled boy who was on SSDI-- showing up at the boy's home each time his disability checks arrived, urging the boy to give him the money for beer and drugs. Before he took the boy for everything he had, the boy gushed: "I can't believe somebody like him wants to be *my friend!*"

Another individual also took me completely off-guard. I guess if you have spent your entire life without knowing many scammers, it's difficult to recognize a scam when one begins. In this particular instance, an NRA whom I did not know very well 'offered to help' when I needed a small amount of cash to put toward a security deposit for an apartment. Although I was very uneasy about accepting help from anyone, I believed he was on the level when he wrote and signed an agreement for the terms of repayment: he would lend me the small amount of cash, and, in a few weeks, I would pay him back.

However-- as soon as I left the manager's office after giving her the money, the NRA looked at me, expressionless, and said: *"It isn't true."* Not knowing what he meant, I asked him to explain, and he replied that he would not accept the repayment, instead *"I will ask you to put me up for a week."* As I had already given the money to the manager, I had no options.

These two incidents are how I ended up with two NRA's camping out in my apartment for short periods of time. In each instance, they only left when their employers paid them, so they no longer needed my resources. In each instance, though, the NRA's managed to completely drain my resources to the extent that I had nothing left to eat. The last time it occurred was the only time I ever had to go to a city food pantry-- so my teen continued to have meals, even though I went without. For two solid weeks I had nothing to eat, and nothing to drink but coffee, until the coffee too ran out.

I knew another woman who was victimized. While she was around my age, she was more worldly and sophisticated than I. At the onset, 'Mary' (not her real name) was expressing how happy she was: "He wants to *marry* me!" she exclaimed. A few months later, the consequences of Mary allowing the guy to move in with her had included the guy beating her, taking everything she owned, and causing her to lose her apartment and end up on the street.

Financial predators-- opportunists-- do not care whether the individuals they take advantage of are male or female, what their ages may be, *or* the fact that the individuals need their own resources to support themselves and/or their families. The only concern an opportunist has is that he gets what he wants.

The entire situation put me in mind of a book I read many years ago, written by a young man who had grown up in the inner-city slums. He wrote about the way older guys had taught him to view women-- that 'all women are *bitches.*' One friend advised him: "If all a b*tch has is a penny to buy milk for her child, take it- she can always get more."

And that, in fact, is the way NRA's view human beings-- not only women, but males and youngsters, too-- as nothing more than b*tches to use and discard. To NRA's, human beings are but objects from which to gain something.

NRA opportunists come from every direction. As an example, there was a period of time when I was looking for a full-time job, but needed money in the interim. An individual, whom I later learned had the habit of 'trolling' for people at 12-Step meetings who desperately needed a few dollars, hired two other people and myself to do some work for him. For a few days in the sweltering summer heat, the three of us scrambled up and down ladders, crawled around a roof, stripping old roofing and cleaning up debris. After we had completed the job, the guy claimed he 'couldn't cash a check on the weekend,' and disappeared entirely without paying us. I cannot speak for my acquaintances, but I needed that money to buy school supplies for my teenager.

However, the guy was only one of the two opportunists in this particular scenario. One day, one of the older NRA's approached me, saying he had known the guy for a long time and would get my money for me. Did he follow through with it? No-- because, like all NRA's, his 'offer' to help "had strings attached."

"THINKING OF BARBARA GRAHAM"

Something came to mind: when I was around thirteen years old, I watched a very old movie on television. The title was "I Want to Live!" and it was the story of a woman who had been executed in California long before I was even born. An actress named Susan Hayward played the leading role; the woman's name was Barbara Graham.

As I'd never heard of Barbara Graham before, I mentioned the movie to some of the older generation who had been around back in those days. They expressed that the general consensus of most Americans was Barbara Graham did not commit the crime she was accused of, convicted of, and executed for. While Barbara Graham had had a hard life-- a difficult childhood, many mistakes, even committing some serious crimes-- the general belief was she was innocent of the murder.

The reason this scenario came to mind was a comment that had followed-- referring to the woman being executed for a crime she did not commit, the comment was that all kinds of horrible things can happen when a person associates with the wrong people.

"Guilt-by-association-- you are judged by the company you keep" was considered to be the sole reason Barbara Graham was accused of, convicted of, and executed for something she had not done.

Looking back at the last eighteen years, I can relate.

While I've never been accused of murder (not that I know of, anyway), I've been accused of virtually everything else under the sun-- from criminal behaviors to immorality to addictions-- for no other reason than 'the company I kept.' The fact that I never did any of the things I was accused of, well, that fact didn't seem to be relevant to many individuals.

Before getting mixed up with 12-Step programs, the childhood caution to "keep good company" was rarely an issue-- most of the people I knew when I was growing up and when I was a young adult were "good company." During my growing-up years there was only one incident when this subject was addressed, and it was not about any individual people but about staying away from the wrong kinds of places.

In high school, I had an acquaintance whom I will call 'Susie.' She was a pleasant girl, and her parents owned a diner not far from our school. The catch was the diner had a bar connected to it. One day Susie said if I'd stop at her place after school, she would teach me how to play pool, adding that there were rarely any customers in the bar at that hour of the afternoon. My parents did not like the idea, but did not forbid it, either. However, a good friend whose husband was a minister urged me to not go there. She said even if I did not do anything wrong, being in a bar at all would give me a bad reputation-- a reputation that was not in tune with my values and lifestyle. While I did not fully understand her viewpoint, I decided to not go to the bar with Susie anyway. Looking back, she was right-- even if you do not do anything wrong, you get a bad reputation from being in the wrong places. In my adult life, this fact did not cover bars-- it covered 12-Step programs.

A quote from a book I read a long time ago sums it up. Before I was even born, a book was written about "lifestyle differences." A person the author interviewed accurately described the attitudes, beliefs, behaviors, and way of life of most NRA's I've known: "They are not simply immoral; they are not even unmoral; they are completely amoral." And, as one is judged by the company one keeps, it's a very bad place to be.

Whether it is people or places, many years ago a woman tried to put it into perspective. As is the case with many who become involved with the wrong kinds of people and/or the wrong places, the woman was age-indeterminate. What I mean by that is there were no clear cues about her age, but everything about her gave the impression that she was much older than she actually was.

She said: *"I used to be just like you."* She had been casually assessing my nice clothes and neat appearance, and that my priorities were my family first, with my job coming in as a close second. She remarked that if I were to continue associating with the wrong people or being in the wrong environments, I would eventually become 'just like her.'

The woman, who was probably somewhere around forty years of age, appeared to be ten or fifteen years older. She wore a huge, shapeless, oversized housedress, not only inappropriate for someone her age, but appeared to be something she had acquired from a rummage sale. Her hair was chopped off short, uncombed, and completely gray. Her inappropriate appearance included old tennis shoes, and tattered old ankle socks that were once white. In addition, she lived with a guy who frequently beat her, and what food she did not obtain from various charity sources she obtained from garbage cans.

All I knew about her past was she had been a professional, well educated, and, like me, was in no way prepared for the new environment she entered or the individuals in that environment. I saw a woman who had had a fairly good life, and opportunities in life, but lost everything by becoming involved with the wrong people in the wrong places. While losing her career, income, and opportunities was bad enough, what immediately occurred to me was that she had lost *herself.* And I did not understand whether her comments were meant to be a warning, or simply a casual observance that I, too, would lose everything.

While the woman's "significant other" was actively using drugs and a practicing alcoholic, I found those facts were not nearly as relevant as the programs make them out to be. The reason: the attitudes, beliefs, behaviors, and lifestyles of NRA's in 12-Step programs can be as destructive as the attitudes, beliefs, behaviors, and lifestyles of those who make drug or alcohol abuse the focus of their everyday lives. For many in the programs, those factors simply do not change-- and to say it is a nightmare for those of us who become involved with such individuals is an understatement. Not only can you lose yourself, your life, and everything in it by associating with actively-using addicts and alcoholics, you can *also* lose yourself, your life, and everything in it by associating with those who claim to be "clean and sober."

SITUATIONAL DEPRESSION

An individual studied me from a couple of feet away. In a voice that was halfway between feigned concern and sarcasm, he remarked that I was 'dying.' Assuming I knew what he meant, but wanting to clarify, I asked if he meant it literally. He nodded his head and said yes.

Situational depression is very common amongst abused women. Unlike clinical depression, which is a mental health issue that can respond to a combination of medication and therapy, situational depression is a direct result of a specific situation-- something the person can do nothing about. Amongst abused women, it generally consists of an overwhelming sense of hopelessness, helplessness, powerlessness-- caused by being trapped, with no real options.

Claiming I was literally dying, the individual remarked that I did not have to die-- that all I had to do was going along with what he wanted, and 'things would get better.'

Not only did the situation cover the violation of my rights and free will, it was a callous disregard for my life itself.

"SELF-WILL RUN RIOT"

I've concluded there are three types of addicts/alcoholics: those who, with or without a 'program,' realize they have problems, and "do the footwork" to overcome them; those who try, but do not succeed; and the majority, who are no different 'in recovery' than when they were in active addiction. The books talk about this: the lying, cheating, stealing; the manipulating of people and manipulating of situations. In active addiction these traits were for the purpose of getting whatever they wanted with no concern for the consequences-- including the harm caused to other people. NRA's do not give up these characteristics-- so whether they are actually "clean & sober" or not, it does not matter.

One incident comes to mind. Upon moving to a new location, I was glad to make friends; however, as it was before individuals 'in programs' began dumping the nonsense on me that we "cannot judge" others, and "must accept" others, when I learned someone had an earned bad reputation, I simply did not choose them as friends.

One individual in this category was a young woman around my age; and, although I had never expressed anything negative, either verbally or by action, she picked up on this and decided it was "not o.k." One night "Melanie" showed up at my door, and when I politely informed her she could not come inside, she barged in anyway, lifted her leg, and kicked me. As she was wearing very heavy boots, I later found she had broken a bone in my hand.

While this could be seen as lousy behavior from an individual who was bent on getting her own way, the next part of the situation make "the ways of NRA's" even clearer. Although the normal course of action would have been to a) have Melanie arrested for barging into my home against my objections, and the unprovoked physical assault, and b) have her held responsible for paying my hospital bill, I found I could do neither. The reason: I was informed Melanie's unwelcome visit was not simply Melanie-- she had a number of her "friends" hiding in the bushes outside, and they stated they would counter anything I charged her with by claiming I had instigated the attack.

As you can see by many other examples in this book, a person who is harmed by an NRA is often *victimized twice:* first by whatever they do to you; and second by having a "ready game-plan" so you cannot stand up for your rights and demand justice.

And, as you can see by other examples in this book, I have been on the receiving-end of these tactics numerous times-- NRA's who want something, or wish to get their own way, *plan in advance how to get away with it.*

Other situations come to mind, also. In one instance, an NRA was persistently harassing me, so I was attempting to call the police from a pay phone. In getting the telephone receiver away from me so I could not complete the call, the individual twisted my arm, causing a minor injury. He then rushed out of the room for a few brief moments, and returned with a scratch on his face-- saying if I were to call the police, he'd claim I had attacked him.

In another instance, an NRA called the police, saying I had 'tried to strangle him with his necklace;' he then informed me he had done this because I had simply refused to cooperate with something he wanted me to do.

Manipulate people and manipulate situations-- I was totally unfamiliar with these concepts, or the types of behaviors it included, until my life was overrun by "the NRA population." What little I saw of it before also involved addicts or alcoholics, but I was clueless because it did not directly involve me. One example was a woman who, despite never loving or caring about her young child, used the little child as a pawn to get revenge on her husband for leaving her. It was a matter of 'you did something I didn't want you to do- so now you will pay'-- resulting in kidnapping the youngster and committing "Parental Alienation."

Similarly, the individuals described in the 13th-Stepping incidents used the tactics of manipulating people and manipulating situations-- to get what they want, and to not get caught.

"WINNERS" STEP IN A DIFFERENT DIRECTION

One of the first people I met who belonged to a 12-Step program made a comment that surprised me at the time. She said: *"A.A. is a Selfish program."* While all she meant by that was if a person has serious problems due to alcohol (or drug) use, it is essential for the person to consider recovery his priority.

Although I suppose that is a logical approach, NRA's use a different angle-- and are backed up by both their Programs and the pop-psych nonsense that many NRA's "live to the letter." Rather than emphasizing *recovery*, they take the concept of being *selfish* to a different extreme. And, in fact, it was the same angle that started NRA's on the road to addiction in the first place.

The angle: nothing outside one's own skin matters; and there is no worth in anything outside one's own skin, unless one can personally benefit from it. Regardless of age, or period of "sobriety," NRA's are like unsocialized little children who place themselves at the center of the universe. One NRA summed it up accurately: *"If it doesn't involve me, why should I care?"*

The subject came to mind when I was reading a book that brought back some incidents in my childhood. One incident in particular involved a girl who was annoyed that her favorite television show was not aired that day, because it was replaced by Robert F. Kennedy's funeral. I was slightly exasperated, thinking the girl 'hopelessly childish and immature.' The catch, though, was she *was* a child; and, although she was only a year younger than I, it was perfectly natural and normal for a youngster to not comprehend the importance of world events, and not understand that something which did not affect her was a higher priority than her own personal interests.

For most people, the theme "putting away the things of childhood" is accurate. At some point in time, healthy, normal people realize they and their personal interests are not the center of the universe. For people who are properly socialized, this knowledge generally comes long before they are adults.

While NRA's do not grasp this concept during their childhoods or youth, many *never* grasp it. While individuals who step in the direction of *recovery* are able to recognize other "people, places, and things" as important, NRA's do not. Whether the topic is one's own family, community concerns, or significant events occurring in the world, *"If it doesn't affect me, why should I care?" is* their approach.

Not only is a generation of apathy negative in general, I have a great deal of difficulty with it from a personal standpoint. The sense of isolation is horrible, and it comes from the fact that there is no one with whom I have anything in common. Their lives are their *programs,* their other addictions, and the attitude that the rest of the world be damned.

"NORMIES" ARE AT THE BOTTOM OF THE DUSTPILE

It did not take me long to realize the less I said about this subject, the better-- the better for me, anyway.

One experience I had occurred when I knew almost nothing about 12-Step programs. At the time, various people in my new location were talking about "sexual abuse." While I did not have any credentials at the time, and nothing more than the desire to help others, the fact that I was not a "survivor" myself did not come up. However, when I expressed interest in starting a group, it was not my lack of personal experience nor my lack of credentials that disqualified me from doing so. Instead, I was told I could not start and lead a group for sexual abuse survivors because there was one requirement that I did not meet: a group leader was required to "have a year's sobriety in Alcoholics Anonymous." It did not matter that I was not an alcoholic-- the fact that I did not participate in *A.A.* meant I was not qualified to hold this position.

Upon pressing the issue a little further, it was even more outrageous: the NRA told me that if a member were to become suicidal, I would not know how to help the person. The notion that a recovering alcoholic would be more capable than I was completely mindboggling.

There was another incident in which I learned NRA's see themselves as *above* 'normies.' In this particular instance, I was preparing to give up my involvements with the programs entirely, when an acquaintance asked for some assistance. The acquaintance, who had been leading a late-night meeting, stated that health problems were interfering with his ability to continue doing it. Although another member was rather upset by my volunteering, stating that I absolutely should not put myself through the inconvenience and danger, I made the mistake of volunteering anyway.

When any of the Oldtimers showed up, I turned the meetings over to them. However, when they did not, I was in the position of leading the meetings myself. The catch: even when I performed all of the general duties of a chairperson, I was not to call myself one. I was only to be a "co-chair," while the initial chairperson was absent.

I approached an Oldtimer, asking what this was all about. He stated that anyone who did not have a year's sobriety in A.A. 'was more likely to steal money from the collection basket.' I honestly could not recall when, if ever, I had been so insulted. Similar to the first experience, the view that recovering alcoholics are more responsible and honest than non-alcoholics was, in fact, insulting.

However, while we normies are at the bottom of the dustpile, addicts and alcoholics who leave the programs and succeed-- either on their own or through other recovery methods-- are basically in the same category. Regardless of their success-- both overcoming their addictions and building better lives for themselves-- you will hear NRA's sneering that they are only fooling themselves, and will eventually fail. In fact, NRA's love the thought of others failing.

"RED FLAGS"

A logical question would be why did I not simply walk away when I first started seeing all of the "red flags"? In addition to looking at each individual as an individual, there was the factor of feeling that other people's lives were their business, not my business. Unfortunately, this approach backfired in a number of different ways. First, when I did not speak up about something being wrong, NRA's made the mistake of assuming I condoned their behavior, or even participated in similar behaviors myself. In many instances it was an honest mistake because they did not know different; in others, though, "the company you keep" and "guilt by association" were intentional misrepresentations by those who knew better. Second, while I was eased into the indoctrination-- like being hit in the head with bricks, repeatedly-- it did occur. As with numerous other subjects, I continued knowing the facts, but NRA's 'monkeyed with my perceptions.' Even from the very beginning, it reeked of cult tactics-- although the NRA's in the beginning seemed to only be passing on what they, themselves, believed.

One of the most important points: the individuals I knew in those early years were not newcomers; the majority claimed "double-digit clean/sober time." This itself should have been a red flag. What I mean by that is surely individuals who put years or decades into drug and/or alcohol abuse could not 'recover' overnight, but it would have seemed logical that those who had put a decade or more into The Programs should have "come to their senses"-- to know the difference between right and wrong, and to know what one is and is not responsible for. Instead, though, they continued to do whatever they chose to do-- and use The Program as an excuse.

The very first example was not only filled with red flags, but virtually the entire scope of Program excuses. There was a woman who was almost middle-aged, and she was the mother of a young child. First she related that her husband had beaten her child severely. *"But that's His Inventory,"* she said; *"and I cannot take his inventory!"* When the child disappeared a period of time later, she remarked that it was God's will-- *"God must have big plans for her!"* she exclaimed.

Obviously, bad things can happen in life-- although they are, without a doubt, more common within The Programs-- but the more relevant point is the approach these individuals take to "bad things" that happen. They simply do not seem to grasp the difference between right and wrong, and do not feel responsible for anything. Brushing off horrible child abuse as the abuser's "inventory," and the disappearance of a small child being "God's will," were the first examples I ever encountered of these warped approaches. They were, however, far from the last.

As you have probably gleaned from this book, red flags were everywhere, and they were on a wide variety of different subjects. Another of many examples came when I arrived in a new city. While I was very tired from a long trip, had a youngster who was not accustomed to traveling, and had no clean clothes because my luggage did not arrive at the same time, an NRA who said I certainly wanted to meet people in the city should accompany her to 'her meeting.' Now, if you relocated to a city where you had never been and did not know anyone, getting to know local people may be one of your priorities-- however, if you'd never had drug or alcohol issues, would you figure a Narcotics Anonymous meeting would be an appropriate place? A community center, PTA, or ballgame, perhaps, but not an N.A. meeting.

Red flags, again, were everywhere, in a variety of forms. However, even when they put a figurative knot in my stomach, I never saw any options but "go along to get along." Depending on the particular situation, I felt that speaking up would either be a matter of interfering, or of 'offending' someone. And, when I did reach the point of speaking up, I was verbally attacked-- accused of being narrow-minded and worse. *The Programs:* it's a place I never should have been.

"PROGRAM" IS NOT MEANT TO BE A VERB

There are people who have no "voices," those who have small or timid voices, and those who are as visible as they can possibly be-- many, many people who, for well over a decade, have been speaking out against 12-Step programs, and some telling their own stories. Evidently, their "voices" are not being heard. Shortly before I finished writing this book, I happened to notice various other books had been written-- from one person who collected an assortment of stories from a large number of former program members, to experts ranging from anti-cult activists to psychologists-- as well as numerous websites, online groups and forums, *all attempting to inform people about the dangers of 12-Step programs.*

In addition to everything I wrote about, something occurred to me last night: in the eighteen years since I first heard of "programs," one "message" was particularly damaging, particularly harmful: the message that "my life did not count."

This "message" came in two different forms. One approach was what could be called "one-upsmanship"-- various NRA's who engaged in heated arguments about who had had the worst backgrounds, and who had suffered the most. I had nothing to contribute to these "discussions."

The other approach was initially explained to me by an NRA who treated every person she encountered as if they were her own personal psychology project. She stated that regardless of the facts, a person is never supposed to say his or her experiences were not as bad as someone else's experiences. Misusing a psychology term, she said to do so is called "minimizing."

In other words, the NRA pressured everyone she could to lie, to misrepresent, to exaggerate, to "make mountains out of molehills." The truth-- the facts-- were simply not relevant.

What it came down to was: *tell the truth, and you will be disbelieved, ridiculed, shunned, resented.* They simply did not want to hear that anyone was never abused, sexually abused, neglected, tormented-- the same as they did not want to hear that anyone had never had drug or alcohol problems, did not have mental problems, did not engage in promiscuity or crime. They simply "needed" everyone to be worse off than themselves.

NRA'S AND PARENTAL ALIENATION

** *From "A Brief Introduction to PAS" by Dr. Richard Gardner: "The 8 Points of PAS":*

* *"A campaign of denigration"*-- the child is taught to hate the parent, often to the extent of wanting to eliminate the parent from his or her life;

* *"Weak, absurd, or frivolous rationalizations for the deprecation"*-- any difficulties or problems that actually exist between the parent and child are blown way out of proportion-inappropriate reactions to what would be considered minor difficulties in the absence of PAS;

* *"Lack of ambivalence"*-- full-scale, all-or-nothing;

* *"The 'Independent Thinker' Phenomenon"*-- the child has been programmed and/or brainwashed into fully believing both the hatred he or she feels toward the parent and the rationalizations for it are all his or her own ideas;

* *"Reflexive support"*-- the child automatically "sides" with the individual who is manipulating him/her against the parent, and believes the individual is in the right and can do no wrong;

* *"Absence of guilt over cruelty to and/or exploitation of the parent"*-- neither the child nor the manipulator can see that abusing the parent is in any way wrong;

* *"The presence of 'borrowed scenarios'"*-- using memories, thoughts, etc., which are not the child's own, to produce hateful thoughts in the child toward his/her parent;

*: "Spread of the animosity to the friends or extended family of the parent"-- the child will begin to dislike and have negative opinions of the parent's friends, associates, and/or relatives.

At a specific point in time, I received a letter. The young woman wrote to me, asking if I would conduct her wedding ceremony. As the city where she lived was not far from where I was planning to relocate, I agreed to do this favor for her. I would officiate at her ceremony, and proceed on to where I planned to move.

As is often the case with NRA's, what was presented was not the way it was, and not what I encountered when I arrived. She informed me that she and her boyfriend had broken up sometime earlier, and that she had other reasons for wanting me to go to her home. When we were driving to her apartment from the bus station, she motioned toward a number of different places, saying they would be good places for me to obtain temporary work. Shortly after we arrived at her home, she asked if I would like to accompany her to one of her 'meetings.' Before then, I was aware she had a drinking problem, but did not know she was a full-blown alcoholic, used drugs, and belonged to 12-Step programs-- nor did I know she was neither 'clean' nor 'sober.'

To say the situation was a nightmare would be a gross understatement. The most important point, though, was that most NRA's have what they call an agenda, and the young woman was no exception. She informed me that if I wished, I could live in her apartment and go on welfare-- *but* if I were to proceed with my plans to move a few miles north, I would not be taking my teenager with me. The sick, twisted young woman said: *"I want to take her- and raise her as my own daughter."* It was one of the many instances in which my ability to hold my temper in a situation where it was certainly justifiable prevented a very messy scene.

To backtrack: although I barely knew the young woman, the last I'd seen her was well over a decade earlier; she'd dropped in for a short visit when my family lived back East, and my youngest child was a baby. More than a decade after that brief

252

visit, she got us to her home under false pretenses, with the intention of 'taking' my teenager.

The onset of Parental Alienation started when I myself was a teenager, and the young woman was only four years of age. I witnessed the abusive way she was treated by her so-called mother, shortly before the mother kidnapped her. Using the term loosely, the 'mother' engaged in a consistent, all-out campaign to turn the girl against her father-- and the rest of his family. By the time I arrived at her home, she was thoroughly messed up by Parental Alienation Syndrome-- and since I was a member of her father's family, she was set to destroy me and my teenager, too. The only way we were able to get away from her was by my slipping out to a nearby restaurant and calling the police.

Parental Alienation is not a child's fault. Regardless of a youngster's age, gender, or relationship to an alienator, a youngster is no match for the underhandedness of an individual who wishes to turn the youngster against his or her parent and destroy the relationship between the youngster and the parent. However, how useful could her 'recovery' program have been if someone did not see the situation for what it was and advise her to seek help to deal with it? I could only assume that by the time she became involved in Programs, she had been so indoctrinated with unwarranted hatred toward her parent that the horrible lies she told us were simply believed by those who did not know the truth.

Wondering why the Program did not help her was only a split-second thought. It did not take long for my viewpoint to change-- upon considering my own experiences with 12-Step programs. The bottom line is the Programs *are not concerned about the truth.*

Not only was her life destroyed, so was her father's-- a decent human being who loved his child. In the distant past, I witnessed interactions between the two of them-- the grand, happy time she had when she was with her father. I also witnessed the abusive way she was treated by her mother-- physically, emotionally, and verbally.

Initially, the girl resisted Parental Alienation. One of the earliest examples occurred when she was being pressured to address her maternal grandfather as "Grandpa-Daddy." *"I don't WANT to say that- he is NOT my Daddy!"* she exclaimed. In another instance, she was pressured to stop using her given name and go by her mother's maiden name instead. She was very upset when relating that she did not want to do that.

However, whether Parental Alienation wears a person down quickly or takes time, it eventually leads to full-blown Parental Alienation Syndrome. By the time of my unfortunate visit, she was not only making numerous remarks about how she hated her father, but his entire family. She went as far as to say she was waiting for her paternal grandmother to die, so she could 'get some money.

One day she asked me to pick up a prescription for her at a local store. The lady at the store said "Oh yes, *Miss* * called and said you would be picking it up." I asked the young woman about it, and she informed me she had indeed reverted to her mother's maiden name. When I remarked that she had used her given name on the letter she'd sent me, she informed me that she only used her given name when she had to communicate with members of her father's family-- to stay on their good side, and ensure that she would continue receiving gifts and money. The same kind of manipulation and underhandedness displayed by NRA's everywhere.

ANOTHER LOOK AT "SANITY"

If you look around the programs you will hear that word, and see it clearly stated in "Step Two." However, the word can be misused; and, in the programs, it often is. It is likely the common definitions of the term is what is meant in the programs: the ability to think and behave in a normal and rational manner; sound mental health; reasonable and rational behavior. It is also

254

possible that doing what it takes to recover from any addiction can lead to it.

The catch: far too many do not "follow that path"-- and that common definition of "sanity" does not occur.

What we have instead can be looked at from the perspective of the M'Naghten Rule: by the original legal definition, *"at the time of the committing of the act, the party accused was labouring under such a defect of reason, from a disease of the mind, as not to know the nature and quality of the act he was doing; or, if he did know it, that he did not know he was doing what was wrong." (Queen v. M'Naghten, 8 Eng. Rep. 718 [1843]))*

If you look at the many examples I have described in this book, you can see two factors that make the legal definition of insanity inapplicable. *First, individuals who meet the M'Naghten definitions of 'insane' cannot go to the extremes these particular individuals went to to plan their actions in advance; and second, cannot go to the extremes these particular individuals went to to cover their actions so they would not be caught.*

In other words, none of the individuals who perpetuated crimes against others could be dismissed with "They know not what they do."

"Sociopaths" would be a more accurate term. *Clearly knowing what they were doing was wrong-- by both legal and moral standards; and having no conscience for the consequences to other human beings.* Using "Bear" as the first example, the NRA's showed they are incapable of remorse, incapable of feeling any sense of personal responsibility or accountability, and incapable of any sense of compassion or concern for their victims.

ANOTHER LOOK AT 'SANITY'-- PART TWO

The first time I encountered *animals*, I was forty-two years of age. As I had never encountered such individuals or situations before, I was left with a large amount of guilt over not being able to effectively deal with the situations. While the feelings of guilt remained, further encounters made it clear that an average human being *has no* means of effectively dealing with it. The reason: when an average human being is confronted by that degree of threat and danger, we *are not equipped* to deal with it. Instead, our human capabilities shut down-- and there is nothing left but the base instinct for *survival.*

In this first instance, an *animal* committed an unprovoked physical attack on a member of my family. Under normal circumstances, I would have instinctively assisted my family member. However, as the attack was on a completely animal level, I was unable to do so. Instead, I "froze in place"-- I could not move, I could not speak, I could not do anything.

To compound this particular situation, the attack was witnessed by another animal. She simply stood there silently, watching the attack, and when the instigator had sufficiently terrorized both my family member and myself, she said to the instigator: "O.K., that's enough." Turning to leave, she remarked to me: "Everybody has their quirks."

Similar to future attacks by animals, the entire situation was *staged.* Not only did it contain *intent,* it also consisted of *manipulation.* First, a period of time after the attack, the instigator approached me, apologizing profusely for his behavior. He was *so, so sorry*-- he said. Even at that time I duly noted the person he had *not* apologized to was the person he had attacked.

Shortly after, I witnessed the instigator speaking in one of his 12-Step meetings. When it was his turn to 'share,' his phony sincerity was mindboggling: with his head in his hands and tears in his eyes, he moaned: "I acted *just like an animal!"*

The catch: while his 'apology' to me was not real, neither was his 'confession' and phony contriteness that he made to his group. While he had been telling me and his group that he was so sorry for his horrible behavior, he was telling another member of my family that the person he had attacked had actually been at fault.

Why did this *animal* so viciously hate my family member? Similar to other NRA's, he resented the fact that this person had not screwed up his life with drugs, alcohol, or criminal activity. In this instance, though, it went further: upon offering to "buy" my family member a prostitute, and "coach" him about illegal means of dodging his student loans, the young adult stated that he was not interested-- he did not wish to participate in anything immoral or illegal. And these issues were enough to cause Oldtimers in 12-Step programs to viciously hate him-- even to the extreme of committing an unprovoked physical assault.

Unfortunately, this horrible incident was not my only experience with *animals* in 12-Step programs. The common thread was every incident was staged-- so anyone who did not actually witness the incidents were easily convinced the wrongdoers were innocent and the victims were to blame.

The other common thread: when one is confronted by something that is no more than a predatory animal, one's survival instincts kick in-- and they are completely involuntary.

In each situation, I experienced an involuntary, instinctual reaction that one might find amongst wildlife. Most people are familiar with the concepts "fight or flight;" but there are some situations where neither of these reactions are possible. In these kinds of situations, the instinctive, involuntary reaction is to *'freeze.'* Amongst wildlife, this reaction is a sort of "playing dead"-- in hope that the predator will lose interest and go away.

To me, this reaction was as terrifying as the situations that caused it. In each instance, it was as if I were completely paralyzed-- no part of my body would move except my eyes-- and as if my vocal chords, too, were paralyzed.

The first incident occurred when the animal attacked a member of my family; the other incidents occurred when I myself was *trapped*-- unable to get away from an individual, and unable to get away from the situation. There was an additional incident when, being unable to get away, my entire body convulsed as if I were having a grand mal seizure.

It should not take a lot of thought to realize exactly how threatening situations must be to cause a person to be unable to respond in a rational, human manner, and be completely taken over by the involuntary reaction for *survival*. Equally important, the animals involved in these situations all claimed "double-digit" clean/sober time in their 12-Step programs.

There is an additional point that comes to mind. The people in my present-day life-- important people, regardless of location-- could, if they think clearly and their memories serve correctly, recall the stark contrast between my survival-instinct reactions and the manner in which I'd always dealt with others who were out-of-line. During the period of time that I was involved with NRA's, there were three other individuals whose behaviors were out-of-line. In each instance, direct confrontation was the logical course-of-action, and direct confrontation was the approach I applied. While it did not produce any results, in each instance I stood my ground. I had gone "eyeball-to-eyeball" to individuals who deserved to be "told off," and did not back down. I simply did not allow anyone to push me around.

More recently, though, I was sneered at and told I was 'afraid of confrontations.' My history-- both in and out of 'the programs,' proves this to be untrue. The logical conclusion should be that there were other factors-- factors which other people were not aware of, and did not witness-- that caused a person who had always been strong, direct, and able to defend herself to *appear* like a coward.

BATTLING THE SICKNESS

The first part of the last section accounts for a large part of the problem I had with the NRA population: average people with average backgrounds are simply not equipped to effectively deal with, or even reasonably cope with, the kinds of sickness one can encounter in the 12-Step programs. There is simply no approach we are familiar with that is in any way effective-- it is a losing battle.

The attitudes, beliefs, behaviors, and lifestyle of NRA's-- individuals in Programs who do not care about true Recovery-- can put a person in a position where he or she has very few options. One option is to buy into the craziness, and "become one of Them." The other option is to try to crawl or climb out of the darkness. While it irked NRA's to no end that I refused to accommodate their craziness by becoming one of them, the second option was rarely an option at all, because "wherever I went, there they were."

However, attitudes, beliefs, behaviors, and lifestyles that come out in words is something an average person has no means to cope with, either. You may remember some examples from earlier in this book: "I hope you die alone in your own private hell!" and "I guess the only way we'll end up together is if one of your kids ends up dead." When your coping skills were developed over a lifetime in the real world, how do you react to remarks like that? Being so stunned that you cannot reply is taken as cowardice-- but it is nothing more nor less than the inability to process how anyone can have minds that are so twisted that they can utter the most outrageous, atrocious remarks without a second thought.

And, as is the case with any subject that involves the NRA population, there was no end to it. Whenever an NRA made himself or herself visible, there were streams of sick remarks from individuals with twisted minds. It was yet another aspect of the Quicksand that I had no natural ability to deal with.

One example: one NRA, upon noticing I had some tattoos, remarked that I "love pain-- you're addicted to pain;"

Another example: an NRA, upon hearing I had scars from minor skin biopsies in the distant past, remarked "I know you have scars- but it's from being whipped, and I know you enjoyed it;"

Another example: after commenting that he didn't like women to use cosmetics and hair dye because women should look 'natural,' the NRA remarked "I don't want you to look too good-- because I don't want guys looking at you."

And another example-- this coming from from a female program member who began writing to me out of the blue, an individual I'd never met and knew nothing about: "I will never abandon you."

These are only a few of the many examples I heard from NRA's. Is it any wonder how someone who spent their life in the real world, amongst normal people, was unable to cope with this craziness? And, similar to all of the other warped b.s. I encountered in 12-Step programs, these particular NRA's and others who made equally-outrageous remarks were Oldtimers-- individuals who had belonged to 12-Step programs for decades. One can easily see while "recovery" is like a book they never read, the same can be said for "sanity."

It often includes the gross indifference to human life-- and humans' lives-- that are essentially 'trademarks' of sociopaths. Not only do they not care about human suffering, death, etc., they attach a bone-chilling sense of contempt and scorn to such situations. In the twisted minds of sociopaths, human suffering and even death amount to nothing more than 'they deserved it.'

In one instance, an NRA talked about a local businessman who had committed suicide. "He was weak," the NRA said. In another instance, an NRA talked about someone who had allegedly been a friend at some point in the past, commenting about how she had shot herself to death. With no expression of regret or sadness over the end of a young human life-- even one who had been a friend-- the NRA snorted with contempt: "She was a drama queen to the end- I pity the poor bastard who found her." In yet another instance, I witnessed a conversation between an NRA and another person, in which the NRA was offering to 'do away with' someone the person did not like.

There are many NRA's who are not sociopaths-- but an important point to keep in mind is there are also many who are. And, an additional point: as there are many non-recovered alcoholics/addicts who, despite all of their other problems, do not take a cold-blooded approach to human suffering, it shows there must be much more to sociopathy amongst the NRA population than alcohol or drug addiction.

Attempting to battle their sickness-- even by trying to get away from it-- is a losing battle. As one NRA accurately described it, I was "like a wild animal in a trap- chewing off it's own leg to try to escape."

"YOU WILL KNOW THEM BY THEIR FRUITS"

A friend who is also a minister often quoted this line from the Bible, and it is accurate when referring to individuals in 12-Step programs:

"Beware of false prophets, who come to you in sheep's clothing, but inwardly they are ravenous wolves. You will know them by their fruits. Do men gather grapes from thornbushes or figs from thistles?"

In other words:

Consider the way an individual assesses and presents himself; his attitudes, beliefs, and behaviors; and his dealings with others.

Consider whether those particulars reflect Step 2 'sanity' or not; and, if not, then "recovery is like a book that has never been opened."

Recently, I commented to some friends who were fortunate to 'escape' 12-Step programs that it was good to be away from the insanity. They all agreed. My comment, though, was preceded by an incident that summed up the types of situations I was talking about: when one is involved with the programs, or with individuals who belong to programs, one is never supposed to say anything is 'wrong.' To claim anything is wrong-- or immoral, illegal, harmful, etc.-- results in being admonished that one is "taking someone else's inventory," or "judging others." Consequently, no matter how bad, horrible, or warped something may be, one is expected to remain silent-- as if condoning it.

The point: from my view, it's a "two-parter": not only no longer needing to cope with the b.s., but, even more important, no longer being in the position of "acting as if" b.s. is o.k.

Although there have been countless examples over the years, the incident that resulted in my comment consisted of finding something I was not aware of before recently: cemetery information with details about an NRA's death and burial, which allegedly took place more than nine years before I met the individual. My first reaction was perhaps he had not been the person he'd said he was, and that he had stolen a deceased person's identity; afterward, though, the conclusion was that it had been a scam. In other words, the NRA had designed, purchased, and set up in a public cemetery his own tombstone-- having his 'clean date' inscribed as his 'date of death.'

A "good, funny joke"? "Symbolic"? One thing I recall about this particular NRA-- and it is common amongst NRA's-- is he'd asserted the individual he was during his drinking and using days 'was not him'-- it was just *his disease.* I have heard similar remarks from numerous other NRA's-- strongly asserting they were in no way responsible for anything they did in their actively-using days, because it was their 'disease' and their 'old behaviors,' not themselves. While this particular NRA obviously went way overboard with his symbolism, it is exactly the way NRA's see it. And it bears noting that while they go to great lengths to differentiate then vs. now, I did not meet a one who made any significant changes in their lives. Their attitudes, beliefs, and behaviors, and the way they deal with others, are no more 'sane' than they ever were.

If you have read this book, you have seen there is not much that reflects 'sanity' when it comes to Oldtimers in 12-Step programs; and there is not much that reflects 'making amends to people they have harmed.' Instead, it continues to be about "lie, cheat, and steal; manipulate people, and manipulate situations"-- exactly as a 12-Step program describes the addict/alcoholic population that has never touched 'recovery.' Yet you will hear them say they are 'sane' because they are 'in a program.' I guess it can be summed up with the saying that makes its way around: *"Denial isn't a river in Egypt."*

Upon seeing the listing for that tombstone, and realizing what it was all about, my comment to my friends included the feeling that I had finally come full-circle. Since 1994, I'd been wound-up in the insanity of 12-Step programs-- beginning with a wide variety of individuals, long before I was virtually dragged to an N.A. meeting in October 1999, and was 'invited for coffee' to an A.A. meeting in 2004; and, while I was fortunate to meet many good people, it did not in any way take the focus off the sheer insanity of *programs,* nor the population I describe as NRA's.

Full-circle, unfortunately, does not come to mean closure. In April 2005, I attempted to achieve that closure; and that was when my rights were violated to an extreme that I had never experienced before. There cannot be closure until the truth is known, accepted, and acknowledged; and, considering the nightmare of the last eight years, I do not know if it will ever happen.

"Beware of false prophets, who come to you in sheep's clothing, but inwardly they are ravenous wolves. You will know them by their fruits. Do men gather grapes from thornbushes or figs from thistles?"

HOW DO THESE ATROCITIES OCCUR?

Many average people, former program members, and professionals in various fields have long expressed the viewpoint that 12-Step programs are dangerous cults. Many have also been urging the general public to take this seriously. While I am personally "on the fence" about the viewpoint of it being a cult, there are other factors I believe are equally, if not more, important.

From my experiences, I believe the main reason these types of atrocities occur within 12-Step programs is there is no accountability. Whether a victim is a newcomer to a program, someone who has been involved in a program for a period of time, or a chosen target who does not even belong to a program, what the individual is up against is:

1. There are no requirements for any individual to begin a 12-Step group. So-called requirements are treated casually, in terms of "all you need is a coffeepot and a resentment." Thus, anyone who wishes to do so can simply decide to start a group-- and will be approved by the program's main office to do it.

2. Similarly, there are no requirements for "chairpersons." While an individual group may have a policy such as "one year of sobriety," there is nothing that is actually required to hold these positions.

3. The policy that every group is autonomous means even the main offices that issue approval have no authority. Furthering this, it is stated every group can operate however it chooses "as long as it does not interfere with other groups, or the program as a whole." Further yet, it is stated nothing is officially out of bounds so long as it does not violate the program's "principles." If you look at what these "principles" are, they are nothing more than "the desire to stop using drugs or drinking," and similar statements.

What all of this comes down to is if someone is being harmed, he or she is completely on his or her own-- "offenders" are not removed from groups or meetings, not held accountable for their actions, and, in most instances, other members simply look the other way-- or blame the victim.

4. Between the "anonymity" factor in general and the trends of "drug courts" and similar means of getting anyone and everyone involved with 12-Step programs, there is virtually unlimited leeway for what individuals can "get away with." Groups, however, pass this off as anyone who has-- or pretends to have-- the desire to get clean/sober is a welcome participant.

"ON THE GOOD SHIP LOLLIPOP"

I sometimes think back to the guy who said I needed to "get the hang of how to be ornery." Unfortunately, I paid little attention at the time to what he said-- not only was I used to dealing with people in a direct, straightforward manner, and that manner having positive results, but I also could not understand how being 'ornery' could possibly be an asset.

The first reason I didn't understand the relevance was my life had, in general, been spent with normal people-- and normal people do respond in a positive manner to being treated fairly. Second, though, was until I read 12-Step literature, I was totally clueless-- I'd spent years with the mistaken viewpoint that each individual *was* an individual, not knowing they had "the nature of addiction" in common with each other. My lifelong habit of giving people the benefit-of-the-doubt resulted in not being suspicious when I should have been-- or, what would have made more sense, avoiding them altogether.

So I was essentially defenseless. Whether in terms of their actions and behaviors or their manipulations, I didn't know what the hell to make of it-- or how to deal with it-- because normal approaches and responses only work when one is dealing with normal people.

Consequently, any and every approach or response was wrong. From "Think whatever you think- I won't correct you, because there's nothing I can say that would force you to see the facts" to throwing cons of my own to try to determine what was really going on, everything backfired. Evidently, my old acquaintance who said "Keep an addict/alcoholic talking long enough, and eventually the truth will fall out" was mistaken.

I thought back to something someone said to me when I was young: that whenever she felt she was in a position of danger, or wanted to get rid of an undesirable, she would simply start skipping, and, in a little Shirley Temple voice, start singing *"On the good ship lollipop."* Perhaps I should have gone to that extreme-- but instead, unscrupulous individuals saw an average, normal, middle-aged mother who had no experience with "the nature of addiction"- and zeroed in on me like vultures.

Looking back, I wish I'd taken the remark about being ornery seriously. If I'd been armed with such comebacks as *"What the hell makes you think you know anything?!"* and *"It's none of your damned business,"* perhaps the NRA population would have got the message. *Maybe.*

WATCHING THE FALL

There's a word I recall from days-gone-by: *Wasted.*
It accurately sums up the consequences of drug and alcohol abuse.
I have known consequences such as suicides, overdoses, murders, vehicular fatalities, life sentences-- all because of "mind-altering, mood-altering substances." Lives have been ended; lives have been lost.
And those who ended up in "programs," their fate has been no better-- although many delude themselves into believing it is. They began by forfeiting their lives for the sake of mind-altering, mood-altering substances; and, due to the

266

consequences, forfeited the *rest* of their lives for the sake of *"Programs."*

Deluding themselves into believing they have recovered from their addictions, they resent the fact that most of the population never had addictions.

Some go further-- expressing a nauseating sense of smugness. One individual, commenting on the death of an acquaintance: "That's what he gets for using drugs." Another individual, noticing a number of people walking into a bar, smirked: "They're doing my experimenting for me." In other words, there are those who are somehow capable of dismissing one of the most popular slogans in 12-Step addiction programs: *"It was your best thinking that got you here."* They are capable of smugly dismissing death, suffering, and normalcy-- as if anyone who is not *"in a program"* deserves whatever they get-- somehow forgetting how they came to be in a program in the first place.

Wasted. Dead or existing, there is not much difference-- because many who are not literally deceased simply never learned how to live.

LOOK AT THE ENVIRONMENT

Some areas have much higher rates of alcohol and drug addiction than others. This fact alone should be cause to investigate the reasons-- and to start making changes.

One factor is the age at which individuals begin using these substances. The younger a person is when he begins using drugs or alcohol, the more likely he is to become addicted-- and suffer irreparable damage.

One research study concluded individuals who began drinking before reaching legal age have a forty-percent chance of becoming alcoholics, whereas the risk of becoming alcoholic drops significantly for individuals who do not consume alcohol until they reach adulthood.

A second factor is the way drug and alcohol use is seen in the community. In areas where it is considered acceptable, fewer individuals will avoid it.

A third factor is the stark contrast between moderation and excess in lifestyles. Areas where excess is the norm in every part of life breed more alcoholics and drug addicts.

And, from my experiences, such environments also do nothing to encourage individuals who have alcohol or drug problems to do anything to change or recover.

The Minnesota Department of Transportation also states: *Underage drinking is linked to mental health problems. Not only do teens who use alcohol often progress to addictive behavior later in life, according to an article entitled "Alcoholism: Clinical and Experimental Research, published in August 2005 from Albert Einstein College of Medicine, "They are at a higher risk for developing mental illnesses such as depression, suicide, and psychoticism as adults."*

Teens aren't prepared to deal with the risks of alcohol. Teen alcohol use is not an inevitable rite-of-passage. Parents can make a powerful difference in their child's decision to remain alcohol-free by learning and applying the research-proven skills of bonding, boundaries, and monitoring."

From my experiences, though, the biggest threat to young people is not what is commonly known as 'peer pressure.' A *peer* is someone who is approximately the same age as an individual. Instead of pressure from peers, young people are often on the receiving end of pressure and influence from individuals who are older than themselves-- older acquaintances, and sometimes even their own parents.

The earliest example I encountered: a woman with a large family occasionally boasted about her kids' drinking habits; while none of her kids were adults, she did not like the fact that one of her kids had no interest in alcohol and refused to consume it. Attempting to shame him, she retorted: "Even your little brother *drinks!*" I duly noted at that time the 'little brother' she was referring to was *eight years old.*

As a parent, I encountered similar adult-to-adolescent pressure, both in terms of my own family and other families. From older individuals sneering at a teen: "You don't drink- oh, right, you're just a *little kid!*" to parents who, quote, 'party' with their youngsters, adolescents and young adults today have more to battle than peer pressure.

And these instances only involve alcohol; you can find the same pressure and influence when it involves illegal drugs. Whether NRA's are actively using drugs, or 'clean,' they have no qualms against pressuring young people to try the drugs, claiming there's 'nothing really wrong with' illegal drug use.

The longterm effects of drug use were discussed in my Junior High health classes. I did not know what to make of it, because no one I knew used 'mind-altering substances.' While I took what we were taught at face-value, it was not until I began meeting NRA's in person that I began to see the reality of mind-altering substances' after-effects.

I met a variety of individuals who, despite years of being 'clean,' were paranoid, psychotic, unable to determine what was 'true,' unable to determine what was 'real.' There were individuals who could not determine that what they saw, witnessed, or experienced, was, as a Program book says, not based in reality.

The bottom line: influencing young people to use alcohol and drugs is an ongoing pattern that must be stopped. In addition, individuals who have drug or alcohol problems deserve help-- that is, individuals who actually *want* help. And, in addition, as the Minnesota Department of Transportation has said, parents and other adults who both try to set good examples and steer young people away from mind-altering substances should be seen as "doing the right thing."

"ADDICTION IS A FAMILY DISEASE"

Most people use this phrase to accurately describe the effects drug and alcohol abuse have on the families of alcoholics and addicts.

However, as addiction affects families, so do 12-Step programs-- *and not in a good way.* Nearly everyone who has been involved with a 12-Step program and walked away from it is likely to relate how it affected his or her *family.*

Many people have related how their families were torn apart by wrongdoers in 12-Step programs-- I am by no means unique.

It would be equally appropriate to say "the 12-Step Program *is a family disease."* Not only have I heard from many individual people regarding their experiences with this subject, some of the professional experts in this book's Appendix section have also addressed it: a 12-Step program does not only put a person in danger, but also the person's family.

From my own experiences, NRA's have a very odd "take" on the subject of families-- what is and is not right, what is and is not healthy, what is and is not appropriate. One NRA, for example, upon hearing my parents did not raise their kids to be criminals, exclaimed: "Oh, they must have been *so Controlling!"*

I have also heard parents cannot give their youngsters any rules, cannot expect a youngster to do a chore, and must give their kids every single thing they want-- and if a parent does not take this approach to the kids, the parent is *"Controlling and Abusive."*

There was something about this warped angle that did not occur to me until quite recently: the claim that kids should always have and do whatever they wish came from NRA's who had stated they had been *abused* when they were youngsters. However, if this is the NRA outlook, perhaps what they meant by *abuse* was that they did not always *get their own way.*

When thinking about it, a situation from many years ago came to mind: a friend of mine had "grounded" her young son because of some misbehavior on his part; afterward, the boy hollered out the door to her: *"You're not my mother anymore!"*

The catch: while kids often do not like rules, and eventually desire more and more freedom and self-direction, there are NRA's who exploit these normal aspects of growing up for their own purposes. Kids are led to believe if they do not like rules, they can simply "ditch" their own parents and take the approach my friend's son took. In an area with a huge NRA population, a young woman who worked with the area's youth remarked: *"This kind of thing happens all the time around here."* She described the nightmare of families being torn apart by individuals with wrongful motives-- as well as the hopeless outcome of most of these situations.

Going back to my friend's situation-- as there was no one in their lives to take advantage of her son's brief annoyance, their lives resumed normally. Unfortunately, minor disagreements can be blown way out of proportion-- and lead to families being torn apart-- when NRA's take advantage of such situations.

IS ADDICTION A "DISEASE"?

When I began writing this book, I had heard no other viewpoint than *"Addiction is a Disease."* Although this viewpoint came from the 12-Step programs and individuals who participated in the programs, it was the only one I was familiar with at the time. In what I have gleaned from research, the concept of addiction being a disease began with the physician who wrote the introduction to the Alcoholics Anonymous Big Book many decades ago. It seems the general idea was alcoholism (and, later, drug addiction) was a) something a person has no control over in general, and b) that when a person has the 'disease,' he has it for the rest of his life. And while Narcotics Anonymous states "We *do recover,"* the disease concept has remained.

In recent decades, many-- from experts in the field of addiction to groups to individuals-- have been asserting that addiction is not a disease at all. Many believe people *can* control their addictions, and *can* completely recover.

Rather than debating in favor of either viewpoint, there is another angle I feel is much more relevant: there are those-- most notably NRA's in 12-Step programs-- who, while continuing to label themselves as "having the *disease*" of alcoholism or drug addiction, use this as a ready, easy excuse to claim they are in no way responsible for their behavior. At its worst, others are expected to tolerate the most atrocious behaviors from NRA's, as NRA's claim "their *disease*" is responsible, rather than themselves.

With that angle in mind, there are a couple other points to consider-- both of which should eliminate the "disease model" for alcoholism and drug addiction. First, think about common *diseases*-- cancer, for example. While there are risk factors for developing cancer, having a risk factor does not necessarily mean a person will develop the cancer, and not having the risk factor does not guarantee he will not develop it. I could mention an uncle, who chain-smoked nonfilter cigarettes for fifty years, suffered no health effects whatsoever, and passed away shortly before his 90th birthday; other smokers developed cancer at a young age; and people who did not smoke and had no other risk factors developed it.

This is not the case with addiction. You cannot become an addict if you do not use drugs; and if you do use them, you will become addicted.

The second point: if a person has developed a *disease*, there is virtually nothing he can do about it himself. One must rely on medical professionals-- and even that is not a guarantee of 'recovery.'

This is not the case with addiction, either. While addiction is difficult to overcome, many many people have successfully done so. The primary reason NRA's do not overcome it is they 'choose' not to-- either preferring to continue active addiction, or replacing it with something else.

There are those who claim drug addiction and alcoholism are diseases that are in the same category as "diabetes, cancer, and tuberculosis." Now, is there anyone who has, has had, or knows someone who has any of these conditions who believes gathering together with others who have the conditions and "working steps" makes any difference in whether or not they "recover"?

"TRUST": ANOTHER DANGEROUS MANIPULATION

There is another dangerous manipulation you may not be prepared to deal with if you are not aware of it in advance. A long-ago friend once remarked that a person should never *trust* anyone *until* that particular individual has *earned* the trust. At the time, I felt my friend was being rather cynical in his approach to fellow human beings-- but that was *before* I met NRA's in 12-Step programs.

Not only will NRA's *demand* your 'trust' without doing anything to earn it, you may even find those who claim there is something wrong with *you* if you do not extend your full trust automatically.

When it comes down to it, it is no different from any other manipulation that comes from the NRA population: they want what they want, and if you do not willingly give it they assert that it is some kind of 'defect' on your part. Perhaps some details about what some NRA's wanted will underscore the extent and potential dangers of this manipulation: NRA's who wanted my bank account information, access to my family, and details of my personal life which were none of their business.

Logically, these are types of information and access you should not provide "upon demand." Refusal, though, results in the usual NRA tack of claiming there is something wrong with you if you do not comply-- if you did not have trust 'issues,' or 'unresolved issues from your past,' you would allegedly comply without hesitation.

One of the first program members I met cautioned: "Be careful who you trust in these programs." She was definitely on-target. I have learned there are very few people in 12-Step programs who *deserve* anyone's trust-- and those who *demand* it are certainly not in this category.

It is simply another way NRA's attempt to get rid of everything a person has learned, knows, and holds as basic common sense. When it comes to so-called 'issues,' the fact is that it is less likely to be about your trust being violated 'in the past' as it is about your life history containing cautions and common sense. If you are like most people, your cautions and common sense consisted of "Don't trust strangers," "Do not give your personal information or details to someone you do not know well," and "If someone has not proven himself to be trustworthy, you should not trust him with anything."

Unfortunately, as you have seen throughout this book, NRA's are "master manipulators." When they do not get their own way, or do not get what they are after, they automatically try to put you on the defensive. If you are up against such a situation, ask yourself if the individual's behavior warrants your trust-- and what he has done to earn it. Also note the types of manipulations the individual hauls out if you refuse to comply.

Saying "No," and even saying "It is none of your damned business," are not 'trust issues'-- they are common sense.

There is another point to keep in mind about this subject-- the misuse of the term. It is one more oddity of NRA's that I saw time and time again: individuals who want something to which they are not entitled, want their own way, or want to infringe on your rights, may claim it is a matter of 'trust.' Although trust is not the issue at all in these situations, it is another way NRA's attempt to portray everyone other than themselves as defective.

YOUR PLANS VS. THEIR GAMES

You can pick a situation-- any situation. When any given situation involves your *unalienable rights,* you can bet that NRA's will use any means available to them to undermine those rights, and attempt to take them away entirely.

One particular issue involves your *right* to be let alone, and to not have your life interfered with or intruded upon. When your *rights* are consistently or severely violated, you may find yourself in a situation that I first encountered with the first NRA I ever met, and a number of times thereafter: NRA's who do not respect *your* rights do not respect anything else, either.

NRA's believe your rights do not exist. If you assert your rights, you will be sneered at, attacked, or a variety of other negative responses. If it is extreme enough that the law and the courts become involved, NRA's will sneer at them, too. This is the case with Restraining Orders, sometimes referred to as Protective Orders. Similar to the way NRA's sneer at, and proceed to trample over, your rights, they do the same with court orders. Similar to the way NRA's do not care about other people's rights, they will not allow the law or the courts to stand in the way of what they want, either.

In each and every instance, the NRA's in question violated the court orders. In each and every instance, getting and doing what they wanted was their only priority, and their only concern. These types of situations show 'recovery in 12-Step programs' for the sham that it is: while countless numbers of individuals can and do recover, for NRA's it is a matter of "Once a criminal- always a criminal." Regardless of their "clean and sober time," they do not care about the law, and they do not care about other people's rights. In fact, they see court orders as a violation of their own, self-perceived rights-- which by no stretch of the imagination do they have at all.

At its worst, obtaining a Restraining Order can result in an abuser becoming outraged to the point of violence. At its least, an abuse will simply "walk through" it, and proceed to do whatever he wishes anyway.

WHO IS THIS "GOD OF YOUR UNDERSTANDING"?

While 12-Step programs claim a person can "choose" and rely upon "the God of his understanding," this is one topic on which many who became disillusioned with the programs found what was initially stated was not the way it really was. One common example: as many 12-Step meetings have the policy of either beginning or ending meetings with The Lord's Prayer, it should be clear the programs are designed to accommodate *one, and only one,* "understanding" of God.

Logically, this places many people at a disadvantage from the very beginning: when only one concept of God is respected, where does that leave Christians of other denominations, Jews, atheists, and those of other "paths"? One is expected to *conform*-- regardless of his or her own personal beliefs.

As another example, I knew a number of 12-Step program members for whom attending church was a regular and important part of their lives. These members were told by Oldtimers in the programs that they could not engage in a church sacrament known as Communion. Specifically, they were told that the tiny amount of wine that was part of Communion amounted to 'blowing their sobriety,' 'relapsing,' and 'not working their Program.' In other words, there were indeed not free to practice their own religions.

If this is not outrageous enough, it gets worse: what many NRA's *do* with their "understanding."

One example is the program concept *"there is no such thing as a Coincidence."* One incident I encountered involved a woman who encouraged everyone to make a "God Box." Good-hearted, albeit misguided, she told everyone that whenever they had a problem they could not resolve, or an important question they could not answer, they were to write it on a small slip of paper and place it in their Box. She furthered this by saying they should take the next event that occurred in their lives as God's "answer." Not only can such a viewpoint be confusing-- depending on the circumstances, it can be dangerous.

276

A second situation involved a couple who was being pestered by one of their friends; they were busy, and did not want the guy bothering them. When one of the guy's acquaintances happened to walk around the corner and they went off together, the woman exclaimed: *"That was Divine Intervention!"*

Personally, as a Jewish woman, I do believe in God-- and I believe He is capable of many things. However, it is certainly not in the best interests of anyone to believe that anything and everything that occurs is "God's" doing, or "God's" will.

Also, as a Jewish woman, I encountered negativity about my religion-- my beliefs and practices. The worst example was a predator who *demanded* I adhere to the so-called teachings of "Paul." I was manipulated, berated, and ridiculed over the fact that *my* beliefs have nothing whatsoever to do with this particular individual from the New Testament. Although it was a question I never asked anyone, I wonder how many other women in 12-Step programs found themselves up against NRA's who *demanded* they be 'submissive, silent, and obedient.' It is definitely a recipe for disaster.

Personally, my range of ancestry included individuals who left their homelands for the purpose of finding "religious freedom" in the United States. Religious freedom covers the right to believe and practice as one chooses-- without undue influence, and without forced conversion. In addition, for more than eleven years I have belonged to an organization dedicated to religious freedom. However, despite the programs presenting themselves as open for every individual's "God of your understanding," it is not what I found, nor what many other former members found.

Instead, the 12-Step programs are only compatible with the beliefs and practices of Fundamentalist christians. In fact, as you will see in the References section, the entire idea for the programs originated with a fundamentalist cult.

Those of us who refused to comply with these beliefs and practices encountered a variety of abuses-- from basic disrespect to being told there was something wrong with us. "You're not willing to change and grow!" was one remark. Darned straight I wasn't. If my ancestors uprooted themselves to gain religious freedom, I was certainly not willing to allow NRA's to take mine away.

When it comes to NRA's, an additional angle is the way many shirk their own responsibilities-- rather than taking constructive action when it is appropriate to do so, they simply shrug it off with *"I turned it over to God!"*

Many who became disillusioned with, and walked away from, 12-Step programs consider the programs to be a "religion" in itself. At least in terms of examples I described, that viewpoint could be considered accurate. The programs *claim* a person is free to adhere to his own interpretation of God-- but almost immediately it becomes clear this is not true. The programs *claim* they want recovering alcoholics and addicts to develop personal responsibility-- but it eventually becomes clear this is not true, either.

Instead, they are "strongly encouraged" to forfeit their own beliefs (or lack thereof) about God, and, essentially, "turn their will and their lives" over to *the program.* And those who refuse to do so are open to a wide range of negativity.

Without a doubt, the subject of "the God of your understanding" can become very messy in 12-Step programs. I encountered many examples, but the one that stands out as the creepiest was the NRA who told his sponsees to remove the names 'God' and 'Higher Power,' and insert *his* name instead. Some examples I was given-- not using his real name here-- included *"Joe,* grant me the serenity..." and "Made a decision to turn my will and my life over to the care of *Joe...*" and "Praying only for the knowledge of *Joe's* will, and the power to carry it out..." Think about that degree of power... and the implications.

I have had quite a few personal experiences with this topic. The most important point I have learned: the approach NRA's have toward virtually everything in existence equally applies to 'the God of one's understanding.' Some experts refer to this approach as *"WIIFM"*-- *"What's In It For Me?"* In other words, they do not look at 'the God of one's understanding' as a personal belief, but in terms of what they can *gain from* it.

I learned: when individuals in the programs express interest in a religion or beliefs that are not their own, such "interest" is one-hundred-percent phony. As an example, I experienced two NRA's who claimed they wished to convert to my religion. With no legitimate interest whatsoever, the sole reason for this approach was assuming they could "get on my good side" by claiming to be interested in something that was very important to me.

I learned: NRA's often have the "cafeteria" approach to 'the God of one's understanding.' In other words, they pick-and-choose what suits themselves. The first experience I had with this involved a woman who asked what "faith" I was. Upon mentioning I felt regret over doing something my religion did not agree with, she commented that I should simply change my religion.

I learned: amongst NRA's, there *is no* respect for beliefs or practices that are different from their own. Some will go as far as to try to convert you-- and label your refusal to do so a 'character-defect' or worse. In one instance, an NRA had the gall to state that he *would* convert me; however, when all of the underhanded attempts failed, he resorted to the popular NRA mind-game-- simply telling people I was a member of that particular religion, as if his lie was a fact.

I learned: within the programs, there *is no* 'God of your understanding'-- if you are not willing to comply with the status quo, becoming involved with the programs can result in a considerable amount of trouble. I have met plenty of former members who went into a 12-Step program with different beliefs, only to find outrageous disrespect; and those whose belief in God was shattered because of their 12-Step program experiences.

Naturally, it can go even further. Although the programs state they are open to people of all beliefs and people with no beliefs, and that The Program respects whatever one's personal beliefs may be, there is another way one should look at the approach The Program takes: if you read some of the literature,

you may see various references to 'a power greater than oneself'--
one is told he can look at his sponsor or his group as that 'power.'

In general, but regarding the steps specifically, replace the
terms 'God' and 'Higher Power' with these alternatives: "Turn our
will and our lives over to the care of *my Sponsor (or Group)*,"
etc. And look at the implications of such statements.

While the NRA I referred to as "Joe" was one who
actually did prod his 'sponsees' in this direction, The Program
itself not only condones but encourages it.

The bottom line: while there are plenty of "pat" slogans
used to pressure people into not relying on their own logic and
not following their own free wills, you may be equally
discouraged against relying on "the God of your understanding."
Instead, you will be expected to surrender your will, your mind,
and your life to the sponsor, the group, *The Program.*

'GOD' MEANS *WHAT?!*

When I first read a statement on a blog, I initially thought
it was one individual's odd way of looking at the subject. When I
read further, it said the statement was a common slogan in the
Program. Upon doing some research, I found quite a few
references to it: the utterly offensive statement that *'G.O.D.'*
stands for *a Group Of Drunks*.

I had already been acquainted with the viewpoint that a
Program member could call his 12-Step group his *Higher Power*,
but this one went way over the edge. Unfortunately, for the
NRA's who are thoroughly indoctrinated, it is essentially the way
they see it. And I am sure I am not unique with the belief that
equating God to 'a group of drunks' is offensive, warped, and
destructive.

You might think it could not get weirder or worse. Of course it can. Within the groups, individuals who 'are just not ready to accept' fundamentalist teachings are, as I mentioned, often advised to consider their 'sponsors' or the 'group' or 'the program' as their 'Higher Powers,' there is another common approach that is equally ludicrous: telling such individuals they can even consider inanimate objects to be their Higher Powers. From what I have learned from many former members, the two most common objects presented for this purpose are lightbulbs and chairs.

Unfortunately, I am not joking. Individuals who are either clueless about 'higher powers' in general, or merely do not have any beliefs, are offered this so-called option. Think about how outrageous this option is: are you going to 'turn your will and your life over to the care of' a chair, or 'pray for the knowledge of' a lightbulb's 'will'?!

What is the purpose of this outrageous approach? Think about it clearly: it is to give individuals the false security of *believing they have control over their own choices*. If you continue reading through the literature, though, you will see references to the idea that 'you will eventually see and do things *our way.'* It is only one more example of how 12-Step programs have *'Cult!'* figuratively written all over them.

TAKE IT FROM THE SOURCE

"Take it from the source" is a saying that was popular in my grandparents' era. What it meant was before believing something or agreeing to something, consider the source-- how credible and honest the source is, and how the source has demonstrated his or her credibility and honesty. In other words, look at the person's history-- history, specifically, of relating to and dealing with other people.

The NRA's are those who lie, cheat, and steal; manipulate people and manipulate situations. Even their own 12-Step program books say this.

And then there are the rest of us-- individuals who have always tried to do the right thing, albeit sometimes failing; who relate to others in a straightforward manner; and who place the people we care about as our priorities.

A person made a comment that was very accurate. Regarding NRA's, she said: *"They define themselves by their problems."* They do not even have names, without connecting *'alcoholic'* or *'addict'* to it. They believe they have a *disease-- and* that it makes them exempt from basic standards of decency, honesty, and concern for others.

In contrast, I am a parent and a writer. The former has been my role and my priority for nearly thirty-four years. I do not expect any special treatment, entitlement, or consideration-- only respect for who and what I am, and what I have put more than three decades of my life into.

However, when it comes to "taking it from the source," I can look back at some of my earliest experiences in the 12-Step programs to see exactly how clear the contrast really is. As one example, the very first time I heard the statement that one 'cannot judge others,' it came from an NRA who had covered up the murder of his own child. The first time I heard the statement that one 'cannot take someone else's inventory,' it came from an individual who dismissed extreme child abuse. And these are only a couple of the examples. When it comes down to it, it is a very good idea to assess the integrity of anyone who tosses "pat" phrases and slogans-- and ask yourself what kind of people they really are.

"LITTLE PINK HOUSES"

Something occurred to me; oddly enough, it did not occur to me until quite recently. After I became involved with NRA's, one of the many forms of chaos that affected my entire family as well as myself could be summed up in a casual question I heard from a teenaged program member many years ago: "Where does your family *stay?*" Initially assuming it was nothing more than regional terminology, I replied "We *live* a few blocks from here."

It was not entirely about regional terminology; instead, it covered the NRA lack of stability in all matters-- including one's living arrangements.

What occurred to me: after becoming involved with the NRA population, the concept and practice of people having a consistent, stable place to *live* was no longer a part of my family's lives *for more than six years.*

One consequence of this upheaval was the loss of 'people, places, and things.' As only one example, it did not occur to me until recently that of everything I owned before I left New York, all I still have are two shirts and a few pictures. Some of the losses were due to relocating on the spur of the moment, and others were due to flat-out theft. And this was not only my experience, but my kids' experiences as well.

In addition to losing friends we'd met along the way, there was also the loss of locations where we could have "set down roots."

Upon becoming involved with the NRA population, there was disaster after disaster. While you have read about most of these situations in this book, what each and every situation came down to was: when I was not on my own to make solid decisions that were in our best interests, and consistently under-the-influence of NRA's, even if solid decisions were made they could not effectively be carried out. From jobs that did not exist to moving because of a variety of bad circumstances, for more than six years the chaos of NRA's stood in the way of *stability* in our lives-- even when it came to having a place to live. In addition, I found that allowing *any* NRA's into one's life results in them bringing *more* in.

Whether you look at it in terms of NRA's inability to make solid decisions, or the WIIFM attitude, it is all about *chaos. And* the only way to end the chaos and rebuild stability was to keep NRA's out of our lives, and attempt to eliminate their influence.

Naturally, it did not work out that way. Upon making my decision, I learned NRA's are like cockroaches-- even if you make it clear you do not want them in your lives, they will, one way or another, crawl in and take over.

The subject brought something else to mind. When a person sees a situation which, to them, is very unusual, the person's comments can be quite a revelation. I had an experience like this nine years ago. The person and I went into a grocery store and proceeded to shop for some items. I noticed she was looking at me quizzically as we did our errands; and, as we were on our way out of the store she stopped me and commented: *"You look so happy!"*

For a person who has lived with you for every day of her fifteen years to consider that an usual, rare occurrence, is indeed a revelation-- up to that point, this person had never seen me 'happy' before. That day was like a split-second in time-- preceded by years of NRA's and their chaos, years of NRA's as albatrosses around my neck-- and, like all good things, did not last long. One summer day, nine years ago, I was happy-- and not since.

"JACKIE KENNEDY GOES TO HARLEM"

It is an exaggeration-- I in no way claim the celebrity or status of one of the most famous and best-loved women in American history-- but that statement is the way I've come to look at the entire situation: *culture shock;* and, with it, the inability to cope or function in the middle of a very negative culture that was nothing like anything I had ever seen or experienced before.

Within the programs, I personally knew two categories of people: there were individuals who had made mistakes-- including, but often not limited to, drug and alcohol abuse-- and were, as one person called it, "doing the footwork" to overcome their addictions and their problems, and build better lives for themselves.

The second category involved individuals who refused to acknowledge their mistakes *as* mistakes. Taking into consideration all of the stories told by these individuals, the common factor, both past and present, was what they could "get away with." This was how they initially approached drug and alcohol abuse-- and the way they continued to approach everything else in their lives.

These NRA's made it a "lifestyle choice." And attempting to interact with such individuals was like bashing my head against a brick wall, trying to survive in a "subculture" that was very strange indeed.

I did not grow up in the subculture-- nor did it ever hold any appeal to me. Consequently, I was totally at a loss as to how to deal with such individuals, or the environment in which they existed. For the most part, it was a matter of coming from a "Leave it to Beaver-ish" background, and falling into an environment of "Drugs, Sex, Rock'n'Roll."

However, unlike most normal cultures, differences were never seen as, nor accepted as, differences. Instead, they were looked at as something to sneer at, resent, and take advantage of. On one side, I learned "live and let live" did not cut it, and asserting oneself did not cut it, either. On the other side, I spent many, many years figuratively going around with my jaw on the ground and a question mark over my head. One person accurately assessed my position by saying it was as if I went around with a neon sign on me, consistently flashing *"There's one!"* to every NRA who was seeking a vulnerable target.

From drug and alcohol abuse to the lifestyle that often accompanies it, it was a 'world' I had never participated in, and did not really know existed. There is a huge difference between human beings who make mistakes and/or have problems and do what they can to rise above it, and NRA's for whom "getting away with it" is a way of life.

Me, all I am and all I have been is a strong, stable human being-- and a strong, stable mother. Never in my worst nightmares did I ever dream of the possibility that more than eighteen years of my life and counting would be torn to shreds by gutter-crawling criminals; and, even more important, that my family would be exposed to such a way of life. Perhaps if I had had the foresight to investigate what 12-Step programs are all about, and the types of individuals I would encounter there, perhaps we all would have had a way of life that was in tune with our standards and values-- a way of life that was compatible with who we really are.

"SUPERMARKETS"?

Individuals who continue to uphold the Programs sometimes compare them to "supermarkets." I have heard such individuals claim a person is no more likely to find any kind of negativity in a 12-Step meeting than he or she would find in a supermarket. They claim you can encounter "dysfunctional people" and "dysfunctional situations" in any grocery store.

Yes, one can have the misfortune of encountering thoroughly messed-up people and thoroughly messed-up situations anywhere. However-- you are not likely to encounter them with such regularity as you will find in the 12-Step programs. In addition, though, other factors are involved.

First, if you walk into your local supermarket, you are probably not in an extremely vulnerable condition. In contrast, a person who approaches a 12-Step program is usually extremely vulnerable, for one reason or another. As the most common example, the majority of people who walk into a Program are at "rock bottom" from years or decades of substance abuse, often with their entire lives in disarray, desperate for help, and hoping they can find someone they can trust; many have health or mental health issues that contribute to their vulnerability. While my situation did not involve any of these factors, simply being an "anonymous" person in a new place led me to be vulnerable. Any of these factors leave a new person in the position of being a "sitting duck" for predators.

Second, when you walk into a grocery store, you are not likely to be confronted by total strangers insisting you "trust" them. Nor will you be up against NRA's who attempt to manipulate you into believing not 'trusting' total strangers means you have 'character defects,' are 'sick,' or that you are 'not willing to work the program.' In a supermarket, you will not find strangers claiming there is something wrong with you if you do not comply with their demands to open your mind and memories, wallet, home, family, and life, to them.

Third, if you do encounter a messed-up individual in a supermarket, right-- and *your* rights-- are on your side. You will not be told you must tolerate-- or 'accept'-- inappropriate behaviors against you, nor to 'look for your part' in it, nor to keep it hush-hush in the name of Anonymity. Instead, depending on the particular situation, you may receive help or back up from others in the store, or receive help from the police. Only within the programs are individuals told they must shut up and take it, blamed, and left to cope with the consequences without any assistance or support.

"SHOW SOME RESPECT"!

I'm aware that communicating styles can vary, due to such factors as culture, upbringing, the area where a person grows up, etc. However, non-recovered alcoholics/addicts bring an additional factor. While their communication styles vary, too, the goal differs from that of the normal population. While normal people generally wish to settle differences, the entire purpose of the NRA is to "win"-- to win at someone else's expense; to win by making someone else lose.

With this in mind, I encountered a variety of styles. There were NRA's who were "screamers and yellers;" those who "threw low-blows;" and those who worked by intimidating others. And I was completely unfamiliar with any of these approaches.

While intimidation can include actions, words, or behaviors that threaten the listener, there was yet another form of intimidation I was not familiar with before: getting one's own way by lying. Specifically, making untrue remarks such as "Yes, you did," or "I never said that." I found the only way I could cope with this type of power-trip was to simply say nothing at all. I mean there is no point in speaking up for yourself when NRA's will simply state that either you or they said or did something you or they did not say, or did something you or they did not do. It is but another example of NRA's power-trips-- manipulation.

IS A 12-STEP PROGRAM A CULT?

In recent years, everyone from former members of 12-Step programs to professionals have been using the word *Cult* to describe Alcoholics Anonymous and other 12-Step programs. As I have stated throughout this book, as my own formal experiences with "programs" was minimal, I do not feel I am qualified to make a judgment-call on this particular issue. While many experiences related to me by other former members point in that direction, my personal experiences conclude:

1. There are two specific factors in 12-Step programs that coincide with cults. First, there is the aspect of "offer people

288

what they *think* they want or need... and then it's *'Gotcha!'.*"
There is also a great deal of manipulation in terms of getting
people to *believe* it is what they want or need.

Second, what is *presented* is not what one often finds
after one becomes involved. One example is the slogan "*To thine
own self be true.*" This may sound very appealing-- but after
becoming involved, one finds something entirely different.
Within the programs, one is *not supposed to* "be true" to oneself;
one is not supposed to tell the truth about himself, nor to *be*
himself. Instead, members are encouraged to do the exact
opposite. You may find you are badgered and badgered to
present yourself in a negative light when it is not accurate,
"admit" things that are not true about yourself, "remember"
things that did not happen; and if you fail to cooperate, you will
be accused of "not being honest" or "not working the program."

2. Whether the programs are cults, cult-ish, or cult-like,
experiences I have had involved *individual* members who
displayed those behaviors and definitions. In the appendix of this
book, some of the reference material I included is based on the
work of experts in the fields of cults and related topics. In fact, I
was in situations where virtually *every* point the experts covered
was present. In addition, many other former members have
reported similar experiences.

So, while so many experiences in common can make
referring to 12-Step programs as cults a logical conclusion,
whether it is the "fault" of the programs themselves or individuals
therein is not, in my opinion, relevant. Instead, *our* experiences
should serve as a warning: *if you become involved with a 12-
Step program, this is what you can expect to encounter.*

WHAT EVERYONE NEEDS TO KNOW ABOUT STALKING

Not only from my own experiences, but experiences related to me by other former members also show how common stalking and similar behaviors are within the 12-Step programs. In fact, as you will see at the end of this book's reference section, it is such a serious and common issue that a program's general service trustee brought it to their attention.

The Julian Center, based in Indianapolis, provides a clear definition:

What Is Stalking?:
It is mental assault.
It is intentional.
It is a crime of power and control.

Contrary to other crimes that usually consist of a single act, stalking consists of numerous incidents spread over time. By definition, stalking involves actions used to make a person feel threatened, intimidated, annoyed, or afraid. It is meant to terrorize, frighten, and make a person feel defenseless.

When writing an article on this subject in the past, I was granted permission from the state attorney general's office to use quotes from their material. It provides a great deal of insight in general; but the most important factor is it makes it clear that when certain acts are done either without your knowledge or despite your objections, it is not justifiable, it is not 'bad behavior,' it is a *crime:*

Some Things Stalkers Do:

Follow you and show up wherever you are;
Repeatedly call you;
Send unwanted gifts, letters, cards, or emails;
Monitor your phone calls or computer use;
Threaten you or someone close to you;
Drive by or hang out at your home, school, or work;
Find out about you by using public records or online search services,
or contacting your friends, family, neighbors, or others;
Repeatedly show up for no legitimate purpose at places where you are; and
Other actions that control, track, or frighten you.

You, as a human being, have the right to live in peace, safety, and privacy in your own home; you have the right to move about freely and peaceably in your own neighborhood, conducting your daily life; you have the right to be free of any and all unwanted intrusions. If someone is displaying the behaviors listed above, contact your local police immediately. Do not make the mistake of wishing or assuming it will stop; and above all, do not try to deal with it yourself.

WHOSE LIFE IS THIS, ANYWAY?!

There are many ways in which the goings-on of 12-Step programs mimic domestic violence and abusive relationships. You do not need to be in an intimate or other type of personal relationship with an NRA to encounter situations and experiences similar to domestic violence. An abuser can be the same gender as yourself or the opposite, older or younger than yourself, a sponsor or another member, and any number of other variations. The most important similarity, though, is that extricating oneself from an abusive situation is best accomplished with help or 'support' from others-- and, also similar to domestic violence situations, the lack of help or support can make getting away from an abuser and moving on with one's life difficult or impossible.

Most people of reasonable age are entirely capable of directing their own lives; in fact, it is one of those rights spelled out in that famous document. Priorities and preferences may vary, but most people would agree it boils down to those *certain unalienable rights*-- life, liberty, and the pursuit of happiness. Similar to domestic violence and other abusive relationships, you may find your rights cease to exist when you encounter undue influence and intrusion from NRA's in 12-Step programs.

Personally, I had been directing my own life since I was a young adult-- and, if you will excuse the expression, I'll be damned if I'd allow a bunch of crazies in 12-Step programs to claim I could not do that anymore. However, as an individual who works with victims describes it: a person notices her *lack of life* and says "What happened to ME-- where is MY life?!" Perhaps it bears noting again that in each and every situation that involved NRA's running roughshod over my rights and my life, they were individuals whom I had just met. They were not friends, they were not people who had been in my life for a period of time, they were total strangers-- strangers who knew little to nothing about me.

A couple of the many examples illustrate some of the extremes to which NRA's go when they wish to *violate someone else's rights.* In these examples, I was tracked and monitored by "control-crazy" NRA's. The first NRA used a beeper to monitor my whereabouts at any given time. The second NRA used a cellphone-- not only for the same purpose, but also to monitor who I communicated with on the phone.

Naturally, though, as is the case with anything involving the NRA population, the way the devices were presented was much different from their actual purpose. First, I was initially told that my carrying a beeper could help the NRA, because it would allow his employer to get in touch with him through me whenever necessary. After I agreed to this foolish arrangement, though, I found it had nothing to do with the employer-- the NRA wanted it to hold me accountable for my whereabouts.

Second, I was initially told a cellphone was necessary in case my family members needed to get in touch with me. However, I was then told my calls and texts would be monitored, and I also found the NRA was using it to always know my whereabouts-- the same as the first NRA.

These types of abusive situations did not stop with interfering in my everyday life. I was also told by two NRA's that they had the power to "veto" my end-of-life directives. One NRA said he could stop me from being an organ donor; another said he could stop me from being cremated. In other words, NRA's running roughshod over your life and your rights may not even stop when you are dead.

In these types of situations, where exactly are "You," and where exactly is "Your life"? Similar to any other type of abusive situation, "You" and "Your life" cease to exist-- your "certain unalienable rights" cease to exist.

We can go back to the previous section and see how many experiences I had are clearly covered in both the Julian Center's and the attorney general's definitions-- *"It is mental assault... It is intentional... It is a crime of power and control;" "Actions to control, track, or frighten you..."*

One example involved an individual I had just met, and covered two incidents that illustrate how NRA's do not take no for an answer. First, upon informing me he had a job that often required him to be out of the area for periods of time, he dropped a handful of quarters I front of me, telling me I must go to a pay phone at least once per day and 'check in' with him. When I replied to his comment that this was what his girlfriend did by saying I was not only not one of his girlfriends but had no role in his life at all, he shrugged it off as if I hadn't said it. Next, he said as he frequently drove by my apartment at night, I must keep the lights on in my apartment so he would know I was there. Initially, I developed the habit of keeping the lights off, doing housework and writing by the light of my computer monitor, but that did not work. He would approach my door, and demand to know what was going on, if anyone was in my apartment, and why I had not followed his orders.

A second example: he seemed to always know when I left my apartment and where I was. In these instances, he showed up wherever I was, demanding I accompany him. When I'd refuse to do this, he simply followed me all the way to my destinations, catcalling at me the entire way. In one instance, this occurred when I was walking home from a local Walmart. I ducked into various businesses, trying to throw him off the track, but he was always waiting for me when I came out. When I spent time in a fast-food place, noticing he was not around when I came out, I thought I'd finally gotten rid of him. However, while I ended up walking approximately six miles to get home, he was sitting on my street when I arrived.

A third example: I made the mistake of accepting a ride to the store, but after the car drove away he said he was going somewhere else first. I told him I did not want to accompany him to his friend's house, opened the door when the car was stopped at a light, and put my foot and leg out to exit the car. He responded to this by hitting the gas, shooting the car forward into the traffic. The only way I could have gotten out of the car would have been to jump out of a speeding car in a stream of traffic. After forcing me to accompany him to the friend's house, and satisfied with being able to do so, he turned the car around and drove me home.

After I assumed he was finally out of the way, away from my home and family for good, I found this was not the case. There were incidents where he was sitting across the street when I came home from errands, sitting across the street long enough to alarm my neighbors, and even an incident where he put a card in my screen door. The clear message he was giving was 'I am still here- and I still have power.'

However, when it comes to NRA's, false security is nothing more than false security; the most recent example occurred when I had not personally seen the individual in years. One day, only a few months ago, I was walking up to the local convenience store, and the NRA appeared to be driving past me. The catch: after he passed me, he quickly cut into the next side street, turned around, and passed me going in the opposite direction; and then quickly cut into another side street, turned around, passing me again; he continued this behavior of passing me back and forth, back and forth, five or six times, before I reached my destination.

And these are only a few of the many examples covered by the Julian Center and the attorney general's descriptions. And again, where exactly were *my rights?* Well, as expressed from the viewpoint of a so-called Fundamentalist, I have not *had* any rights-- because I am female.

"HAPPY, JOYOUS, AND FREE"?

When I first heard that expression, I approached a longtime 12-Step program member and asked him what it meant. He said it was a reference to sobriety-- a person would be "happy, joyous, and free" because he was no longer controlled by the need to drink or the effects of alcoholic drinking. Not long after, though, I was approached by a member of a different 12-Step program who sneered derisively at 'all of those fools' who believed that "happy, joyous, and free" was a possibility. (While I do not elect to go into it in detail, these instances sum up yet another asinine factor: not only do many NRA's believe 'normies' are thoroughly messed-up individuals with their heads in the sand, there are also NRA's who take the same view toward individuals who belong to programs other than their own.)

Back to the point of this section: it is like the old saying "Misery loves company," and there are none so miserable as those who refuse to take any steps to put their own lives in order. They cannot stand to see anyone happy-- or even reasonably contented-- with his or her life. So they will do everything they can to drag you in, and drag you down.

As an administrator of an online forum for 12-Step program survivors says: "The program of *A is indeed a damaging, harmful, dangerous, and deceiving organization. The damage and harm occur in many ways, depending on the person, their upbringing, their beliefs system, etc."

If you have a specific problem that needs to be addressed, a bunch of strangers with no expertise cannot provide answers or solutions. Instead, you will find even the most minute problem blown so out of proportion that a basic question looks like a disaster. The concept of resolving problems does not exist, because you are expected to live with and in the problem for the rest of your life. Equally outrageous, if your life is essentially the way you want it to be, and you are living it as you choose, NRA's will haul out the psychobabble to inform you why there is nothing about you or your life that is acceptable at all. In other words, "happy, joyous, and free" are included in the bait-and-switch trap-- if they get you with these air-filled 'promises,' what you find afterward is altogether different.

In the meanwhile, what do 12-Step NRA's approach as their own "happy, joyous, and free" states? There are NRA's who forfeit lives, or refuse to build lives, in favor of their 12-Step programs. *The Program* becomes a substitute for life, family, making a contribution to the world they exist in. Many use their Programs as an excuse to not work. In one particular area, 12-Step meetings were a "hang-out" spot for homeless people, and others who had nowhere to go. Others yet use 12-Step programs as a place to seek victims.

If you want to be happy, joyous, and free, it may be possible. Depending on your situation, talk to a member of your family, a longtime friend, or a doctor. But if you want to resolve problems, improve your life, or even retain the good life you currently have, stay away from 12-Step programs.

QUICKSAND

"I didn't have time to think..." Most people use this common phrase at one time or another. For me, though, it was more accurate than one can imagine. For many years I didn't have the time, freedom, or breathing space to collect my thoughts.

Unfortunately, this also meant I didn't have the time, freedom, or breathing space to communicate any of it to the important people in my life. There was always "something going on"-- as I referred to it, it was like spinning in a fog. It is the chaos which is the life of NRA's-- the chaos which they create, and take full advantage of. .

It was as if I'd stepped into quicksand-- stepping off into the darkness of the unknown. None of it was a part of my familiar world-- but although I knew none of it was o.k., I didn't know what it was or what it was all about.

I also did not know how to extricate myself-- for once I stepped into the quicksand every attempt to move away from it only sucked me further in.

I made mistakes. In fact, I made *many* mistakes. One mistake I made was looking at each person as an individual. I told myself that just because Person A did wrong, that did not mean Person B would be the same. I dismissed each one's individual wrongs and oddities as their own personal quirks-- failing to see how similar they really were. In other words, I granted the benefit-of-the-doubt where it was not deserved.

Another mistake I made was to "try to understand." The fact of the matter is not only at the time, but even looking back, I find numerous instances where I had no ability to discern whether they were intentionally lying, playing a game of manipulation, or whether they were operating under delusions.

My other mistake was attempting to bargain for my life-- the feeble futility of pleading with someone to go away, to stop his wrongful behavior, to 'give' you your life back. In seeing the increased sense of Power a crazy person gets when someone is virtually begging for her life, I learned the only way to deal with those who play a game with your life is to refuse to play.

Refusing to play their game brought the attack that I was 'insane.' In the world of NRA's, there is something very wrong with you if you do not silently go along with what somebody else wants. *It is all about compliance.*

The non-recovered addict/alcoholic needs weak people-- codependents whose entire lives and identities revolve around him. A weak person is easy to dominate. The non-recovered addict/alcoholic cannot tolerate a strong person-- someone whose stability and personal identity gives her the strength to say 'no.'

That last sentence sums up my turning-point. For years I had walked blindly into bad situations, been manipulated, been conned, had my sympathies played upon, and numerous other tricks and games of NRA's, suffering consequences each and every time.

In the last instance, however, there was an entirely new and different factor: I said 'no' from the onset, and my 'no' was dismissed as if I were as inconsequential as a bug which could be shrugged-off. It was made clear at the onset that I had no rights-- that I would either comply, or everything would be taken from me against my will, under the guise that my refusal to cooperate meant I was crazy.

And, I made yet another mistake. Having no other framework than that which I was familiar with, that was the manner in which I attempted to communicate with these individuals. I learned that such characteristics as honesty, fairness, directness, tactfulness, and all of the other characteristics which had been positive throughout my life did not work when the recipients were NRA's. In fact, what those characteristics resulted in was to set me up as a target.

There was another characteristic, though, that made matters much worse. As I recall one program acquaintance remarking: "There is only one thing I don't like about you- and that's you hardly ever talk about yourself!" While my immediate reaction was that 'myself' wasn't exactly a fascinating topic, there was something about her viewpoint that bears noting: *people did not know me well enough to know I was on-the-level.*

When some anonymous stranger shows up from some anonymous place, there can be a couple of normal reactions. A person may think: "This is someone I'd like to know;" or a person may think: "I don't really want to know this individual." However, wrongdoers in the NRA population do not take either of those approaches; instead, they see the fact that you are essentially an unopened book, and proceed to fill it in with any and all outrageous claims that will damage your reputation, destroy your credibility, and utterly ruin your life. And, as you have read from some of my experiences, they will conduct their character-assassinations behind your back, without your knowledge, so you cannot defend yourself.

There is another point, though, that should be the clearest point of all. Like the t.v. celebrity said, the best predictor of future behavior is past behavior. The only intelligent way of looking at the subject is to look at the person I was prior to *Programs*-- not the spinning-in-the-fog of trying to exist and survive in the midst of NRA's, but the life I led when it actually was my own life.

Perhaps there are people who change-- at whim, or on demand-- but I am not one of them. Despite the chaos of *Programs*, my personality, character, priorities, and goals did not change. Although I am existing in the middle of the wreckage caused by NRA's and 12-Step Programs, I am still the same person I was before boarding that bus on Chestnut Street.

"LIVING IN THEIR DISEASE"

A special note: a long-ago acquaintance summed it up accurately when he said "*You are living in their disease.*" This book should show exactly what it is like when normal people are caught up in the disease of addiction by having NRA's in one's everyday life.

The information here mostly consists of my own experiences-- experiences of a person who, with no knowledge of "substance-dependency issues," began associating with people who were involved with 12-Step programs, and was soon sucked into it myself. Initially, with "a good heart, but blind eyes," all it was to me was 'this woman is raising kids by herself- like I am!' and 'this other woman had an overbearing relative- I can relate to that!' with these and other similarities preventing me from noticing the majority had very serious problems.

I had been "dragged through Hell" before I learned about, or even heard the term, "the nature of addiction." Consequently, I attempted to relate to people with the same approaches and principles as I'd related to other people throughout my lifetime-- approaches and principles such as: treat people fairly; give people the benefit-of-the-doubt; deal with people in a straightforward manner; all it takes is communication; and, of all these mistakes, the biggest one: look at each person as an individual.

The catch: these approaches and principles are fine when we are interacting with normal people. They do not work when interacting with the NRA population.

So, basing my interactions on those approaches and principles, I went from seeking friendship to being sucked into something I knew nothing about, and had no place being. I found NRA's who presented themselves as 'friends'-- but were out to get something. I even found an NRA who, upon my clearly stating I wanted nothing to do with him, claimed we were 'in a relationship' simply because he said we were. I found attempting to free myself-- and my family-- from destructive situations resulted in everything from financial disasters to being on the receiving-end of criminal behavior to having a variety of disgusting lies told and spread about me.

Why? because the majority of NRA's have one focus: themselves. They do not care what extremes they must go to to get what they want-- or who suffers for it. Attempting to interact with NRA's as if they are "regular people" can lead to financial ruin, legitimate and family relationships being destroyed, being taken advantage of, being abused, ending up isolated with no one to turn to, and ending up in what they call 'hostage situations.'

The point: when I first began meeting individuals in 'programs,' I had no idea what I was up against. When I began attempting to extricate myself, I found it was like trying to free myself from quicksand.

In contrast, I've known people who sought help from other programs-- help to learn how to deal with the alcoholics/addicts in their lives; and, even more to the point, to learn how to do so without losing oneself and one's own life. If I, who never had a drug addict or alcoholic as a family member or loved one, experienced such misery, upheaval, loss, and destruction, I can not even imagine what people who do are going through-- people who not only love an alcoholic or a drug addict, but want that person in their lives.

I have found the only legitimate approach is like the New Hampshire motto: "LIVE FREE OR DIE." The NRA population has no qualms about expecting the latter of us-- whether it is literal death from extreme ongoing situational depression; 'death' of the human beings we are: human beings with dignity, personal selves, free will, and rights; or the 'death' of our hopes and futures-- it is rare to find an NRA who places any significance on whether or not another human being 'dies,' figuratively or literally.

Many years ago, a very wise person made a statement: "You must never lower your moral standards-- not for anyone, not for anything." It took a long time for me to realize that simply by having NRA's in my everyday life, I was indeed "lowering my moral standards." From the way I was treated to the wrongs I was expected to tolerate, to "guilt by association," I learned one does not need to do anything wrong in order to lower one's own moral standards.

Regardless of who you are, what you are, or how you are connected to this subject, you deserve better-- you deserve physical and emotional safety, and peace of mind; you deserve to have and express your own personal Self; you deserve the human dignity that only exists with free will; and you deserve bright hopes and futures. You do not deserve to spin in the web of 12-Step programs, unable to function and unable to get out. *As a human being, you deserve to LIVE FREE.*

part three

SO WHO ARE THE "EXPERTS"?

"The experts" can be found in two different categories--
and they are not the individuals who have spent years or decades
sitting in 12-Step meetings. While they may think they are, or
claim they are, even their own literature says they are not. 12-
Step literature clearly states even the most longterm "Oldtimers"
are no more 'experts' than Newcomers; they have no professional
knowledge or authority, and they do not know anything about
"others."

One category of experts are the professionals. I have
been granted permission by some professionals in the fields of
addiction, recovery, and cults, to reference their work in this
book.

The second category includes those who are "recovering
from" their 12-Step program experiences; such people can
clearly say "*This is what happened,*" and "*This is the way it was.*"

When I began writing this book, I had very little
knowledge of other people's bad experiences with 12-Step
programs. The people I encountered throughout the years who
did experience problems within the programs had no idea how to
deal with the situations, and did not deal with them at all. In
other words, they simply continued to suffer. My first encounters
with people who took a different course of action came a few
years ago: two young men and a middle-aged woman who, upon
taking one look at their first 12-Step meetings, walked away and
never went back.

The young men, who both managed to "get clean and/or sober" without any assistance, had simply dismissed "the programs" as nonsense. The woman, however, had made her decision to never attend another 12-Step meeting because of her experience at her first meeting: she related that 'some guy' had refused to keep his hands off her-- and, to make the experience even more distressing, the meeting regulars and oldtimers who were present simply watched the incident, saying and doing nothing. No one intervened in the woman's behalf, and she never went back. It may or may not be relevant, but the meetingplace where the woman had this horrible experience was the same meetingplace where, approximately a year later, I acquired a stalker-- along with a variety of program members who knew what was going on long before I did, and did nothing to help me.

Since then, many other people have commented about their experiences. I have decided to include some in this book-- both to give them the opportunity to speak, and to make it clear these kinds of experiences happen in 12-Step programs *everywhere.*

An important point, though: the people who came forward to say they wanted their experiences and opinions included in this book represent the tiniest minority; many others hesitated, stating they were *afraid* to speak up. It is one of those situations in which an old saying is accurate: do not judge anyone, if you have not walked in their shoes. From my experiences with former 12-Step members, it represents the largest part of the problem: men and women are afraid to openly say *'This and that is what happened to me' because* they are afraid of retaliation from those who harmed or wronged them. For these people, no amount of confidentiality and anonymity was enough for them to feel safe enough to speak out.

This includes men and women who were on the receiving end of violence and other atrocious behaviors. They have been *victimized twice*-- first by the way they were treated, and then by feeling they needed to remain silent. It is a clear example of how freedom of speech and justice do not exist within the programs-- and how many do not have it even after they leave.

Some former members have chosen to come forward:

A former member shares this:

"Born Again, but Not Born Yesterday"

The title of this contribution is synonymous with the *signature* I use on the certain, special websites which give people an opportunity to critique, criticize, and analyze 12-Step recovery programs. It aptly describes how I view myself in relation to any kind of (spiritual) group or, organization, that purports to be beyond reproach. This skepticism includes my having a dubious attitude towards sanctimonious *individuals*, as well.

Until I began attending AA (and Alanon) in the Midwest, I had not known what degradation at 12-Step Recovery groups truly was. Up until then, as a female in East Coast 12-Step groups, I had been subjected to relatively sporadic and infrequent episodes of marginalization and disrespect. The following is an extremely short synopsis of what happened when I moved to the Midwest a few years ago.

Generally speaking, America's Midwest is significantly behind the USA's coastal regions in its cultural attitudes towards women. This phenomena appears to be reflected in the Midwestern 12-Step groups in a very pronounce fashion. My initial mistreatment from AA and Alanon members happened simultaneously, commencing with an odd, lukewarm reception towards me, from the females, within my first few weeks of attendance at the local groups. This tentativeness towards me quickly intensified towards a more obvious aloofness.

Soon, I also found out first-hand that it was assumed that a woman spending time alone with a male, for any reason, and, in any place, even if other people were nearby, had to mean that there was an affair going on. I believe that the basis for this "irrefutable" presumption is that all women are insatiably starving for male attention. I can't imagine any paradigm being more degrading and belittling to women than this.

Additionally, here, in the Midwest, the unfounded belief that an affair is going on becomes an unbreakable dogma------if the affair is denied, the belief in its existence becomes strengthened, and the "guilty parties" become even more culpable. Any attempt to prevent further spread of rumor is viewed as more admission of guilt. This standard clearly exemplifies "The Scarlet Letter", and beyond, in its arrogant presumptuousness.

Something else I observed is that the supposedly, *voluntary*, hugs given between males and females at AA meetings become a mandatory "happening" of extreme mind-blowing drama. Among the men, getting hugs is an obsession. It is truly pathetic. On different occasions, I also was personally subjected to the inconspicuous, "accidental" brushing of males' hands on my "off-limit" body places.

Moving further along, I soon became a victim of "stalking", here, in Midwestern AA. After analyzing why it seemed that any attempt on my part to bring the perpetrator to justice would be met with futility, I concluded that "stalking" is indirectly enabled by the AA "good ol' boys" network; stalking's insidious nature is further abetted by inadvertent compliance from the females. This set-up is structured in a way that allows males to perpetrate against, and, cross females' boundaries without any interference from others. It is the same patriarchal mindset that still permeates the larger world, but, in 12-Step Groups it has a greater chance of surviving, due to the 12-Step groups' policies of anonymity and confidentiality.

In the "stalking" set-up and cover-up, we are primarily dealing with the complicity stemming from loyal friendships between the guys, especially if there is a "one-up", authoritarian relationship involvement between them. This entire process has been covered on the *"The New Twelve Steps – Expose AA"* and *"The Orange Papers"* websites, written by their membership and administrators.

Gauging from my experience, it's impossible for a lone woman to gain any ground in making accusations and getting assistance, as a stalking victim in Midwestern AA. The archaic gender-based peculiarities of this particular culture, along with my lack of personal support due to being far from home, are predominant factors in why this happened to me, and why I had no recourse.

The fact that anything of these proportions had NEVER happened to me in any 12-Step groups before I came to the Midwest speaks volumes. Women here are just now starting to become genuinely self-actualized. I know that "stalking" exists on the East Coast, but, I surmise that here it is rampant. Additionally, until AA members start to become *un-codependent*, and women more assertive, AA women will continue to be victims of "stalking", and other forms of predatory focus.

The most degrading aspect of my "stalker" experience was that he was the same man that AA members thought I was having a clandestine affair with. He psychologically capitalized on the rumors that were circulating, and, in turn, the gossipers cherished the fertile "dirt", all of this evolving into a self-feeding, vicious cycle. So, the atrociousness of not having my boundaries respected by this perpetrator was further compounded by the "Affair Dogma" that is ingrained in Midwestern AA members' belief-systems.

Moreover, this stalker was of the "erotomania" variety; once you see what they are doing and begin avoiding them at all costs, they make up twisted stories in their own minds so that your rejection of them, and your attempts at refuting rumors, actually validates that you are in love with them. You can imagine my rage and infuriating feelings of frustration at having absolutely no control over my public persona in AA.

I was also relentlessly pressured by Alanon's, "big cheese", to disclose what AA groups I went to. She demanded and insisted that I tell her. Of course, I didn't, as it was none of her concern. She may have been doing this to find out if I was the same woman that she had heard AA members in certain groups gossiping about. Her dictatorial intrusiveness, along with

Midwestern Alanon's general apathy towards anonymity, is a major reason why I no longer attend the Alanon groups here. No anonymity seemed to exist between the local AA groups and local Alanon groups. Every 12-Step group's member's personal business was up for grabs, or, at least it felt as such.

Fabrications were spread about me by another "double-winner" (AA/Alanon member) who had been (covertly) relapsing on pain pills. Although she later publically admitted to her "relapse", with this "act of humility" having been done at a large, holiday, AA forum, she never apologized to me for her participation in the convention of gossip against me. Apparently, she had not liked my *non*-melodramatic, logical approach to her "victimhood" issues, which I had given as feedback in our private discussions.

As part of my former, East Coast, experience, the majority of men with whom I had personally interacted in AA were, like me, learning boundaries and seeking healthy ways of having relationships. Many of them were on the same path as I, looking into our early childhood stuff, codependency and self-esteem issues, etc.

Although imperfect as all humans are, the men in East Coast AA had often become like surrogate fathers, uncles and brothers to me. I had phenomenal friendships with them, as kindred spirits, and remember them with love to this day. These AA men had comprised a major part of my social, spiritual and personal life. Alongside of this, a few of the WWII-generation of AA men had played an outstanding and instrumental part in my having had attained rock-solid sobriety.

To have gone from this supportive, "relaxed gender", environment to one in which every woman in AA is regarded as a potential threat to other woman, and who is viewed by the guys as a potential boost for their egos, was drastic. But, this seemed to be the accepted mode in the Midwestern AA groups. Invariably, the mate-seeking instinct in human nature will always be somewhat present, universally; however, the double standards towards women in 12-Step recovery groups need to be looked at seriously and thoroughly.

What was so striking was how the incidences had developed in an especially rapid, all-pervasive, over-lapping and concentrated manner. I was getting bombarded from all fronts. This is why I say that the still under-developed positive cultural trends for women in the Midwest are the primary mitigating factors in why this happened to me. Cultural differences notwithstanding, all of AA, and many of the other 12-Step Recovery groups, should get an overhauling in regards to women if they are to continue producing anything worthwhile.

Very fortunately for me, when these incidents had occurred, I had already (successfully) been in a variety of East Coast 12-Step Groups for over two decades. I had also been a professional addictions counselor for ten years, and had acquired outside help for my own early childhood issues. Due to my very negative experience in Midwestern AA, I no longer attend AA here, and, as aforementioned, nor do I attend Alanon, and have not for over two years.

*   *   *

Another former member says:

Maybe the ones with the longest sobriety were the ones most brainwashed and in the need of the most "rescuing."

I think the weirdest example is the time I went to an actual "AA Wedding." It wasn't called an AA wedding, but the bride, groom, all the attendants, ushers, audience members, were from our big AA group. And I remember feeling the hairs rise on the back on my neck, like...don't these people have non-AA family members? It was so weird. And I remember them talking about their commitment to recovery in the vows.

Their big sticking point: it's not AA, it's the people who are wrong. because soooooo many AA people blame the people whenever they had bad AA experiences. Like, you are silly to leave AA just because you had one bad experience, it was the person, not the program! I also remember them laughing, now that I think about it, about all the "crazy anti-AA" people out there.

I think I could be a good anecdote about how it sucks even when it's just regular AA.

We are not crazy. The program is: the execution of HOW they try to accomplish it is so messed up and psychologically damaging and unhealthy.

I want people to leave the program and live awesome, sober lives! It's SO POSSIBLE! I am LIVING PROOF!

*　　　*　　　*

One former member comments about the destructiveness of 'treatment,' as well as the 12-Step programs:

Maybe you can write about the whole process of going to rehab and how its a just a label and drug operation.
I wouldn't protest this if I saw it helping anyone, a third of them come in cause psychiatry got them addicted to drugs in the first place and almost everyone goes out psych labeled and medicated on something that they can never just stop taking without risking some nasty withdrawal reactions they were likely NEVER told about.

What are the numbers 85% relapse rate? 85 % now back to drinking drug of choice plus psych meds or new med withdrawal reactions added to the mix!

My story is simple, I learned psychiatry and all that chemical imbalance disease stuff is fraud, got resentments, and decided to get sober without it and was finally successful, this added to my resentment.

I never got any sponsor myself but was pressured to as it was a requirement to stay at the sober living and for many so is psych med compliance if its connected to a treatment center like mine was. I didn't want some stranger (sponsor) knowing everything about me-- being my lawyer, doctor, financial adviser, marriage counselor. Past addiction to alcohol or drugs does not qualify anyone for this!

*   *   *

Another person who left the 12-Step program has been blogging about the experience, and granted me permission to quote from the blogs:

AA came into my life at a time when I really believed I needed their help. I thought that they were "nice" because of their "love-bombing" outer shell. I can still see those smooth smiles and outstretched helping-hands. I saw little to fear. Beneath all of their "niceness" is a cold-heartedness and an agenda that they do not want so-called "newcomers," "pigeons," and/or "babies" to know about. Still, they extended a hand that was made to appear like friendship and concern to me in my initial exposure to The Program. I fell for it.

People having power over other people corrupts people... AA gives people a faux sense of power and authority over other people. It is unearned. It is misplaced. It is wrong and what's more is that it is very, very dangerous.

I was instructed by my sponsor and her sponsor, my so-called grand sponsor to tell her EVERYTHING I thought and did. When I failed to do this she said that I was "lying by omission." So, I slowly over time began confiding all of my thoughts and actions in her.

I was instructed to cut off or greatly limit my relationship with my family and especially my own mother.

This was a particular sore point for me because my mother and me have been the best of friends for years. In trying to please them I greatly limited my visits with my mother and talks on the phone.

This also forced me to limit my contact with my aunt who was also very close to my mother and to me. It was awful. I found myself in the strange position of trying desperately to please my sponsor(s) while at the same time trying not to break my mother's heart. Naturally during all of this I was being instructed and indoctrinated into AA in their usual fashion.

Can someone PLEASE tell me what is "spiritual" about breaking people down and manipulating them?

What is spiritual about stealing from people their sense of balance, well-being, self-determination, freedom of thought and self-will? Yes, I said it; self-will.

The longer I look at AA and NA from the other side of the fence now, the darker it all becomes.

Prior to leaving AA, I never imagined that our society would allow such heinous madness to persist openly and with so little opposition or uproar from our society.
I feel like I have had blinders on!

Does AA & NA Bullying Contribute to Violence and Suicides While Breaking National Laws Against Vulnerable Adult Abuse? The positive image most Americans have of AA and NA is unearned and misleading. Unknown threats to physical, emotional, mental and financial safety lie in wait for vulnerable adults and minors who enter twelve step based programs.

There are no background checks or safeguards in place which would identify what attendees among the members are of criminal intent, mental incompetence, violent nature, sexually deviant or are in some ways unscrupulous and abusive; but many are. AA and NA programs are not really programs at all and no vulnerable person, especially not teens belong at these meetings.

No accountability exists at these meetings. They are meetings of peers; a free for all of people with various alcohol, drug, mental, emotional and/or legal issues. Attendees of these meetings are not qualified to help people with alcohol-over-use, substance abuse or emotional/mental issues. No trained facilitators ever direct these meetings.

Often, attendance at these meetings does more harm than good for the many vulnerable adults and minors that attend them. In fact, many minors sent to these meetings end up as victims of the predators mandated to these meetings. The threat, however, does not end with the threat to minors, who as stated, have absolutely no place at these very adult meetings.
Vulnerable adults are just as susceptible to harm at these meetings as minors are. Exposure to alcohol and drugs results in making these individuals more likely to be victimized, traumatized, abused and bullied.

What AA and NA members proudly call, "tough-love" is merely a cowardly cover for emotional and mental abuse of disempowered individuals during times of crisis. When inherently troubled individuals are given power over other, less powerful and also troubled individuals, it is nothing more than a set up for abuse.

There are many instances where exposure to AA or NA results in violence, suicide attempts and actual suicides.

The victims are largely silent. Many suffer quietly. Some are dead. Due to the fact that so many of them are out of sight, we as a country can comfortably keep them out of our minds. Most of these people simply fade away and no one knows of the torment AA and NA injected to their lives. People deserve to know that AA and NA are potentially very dangerous places.

*   *   *

A former member says:

AA endangers the public safety, when it encourages attendance at its AA meetings, by claiming that AA is a safe and supportive group of common folks just like you.

Because to the contrary - all the while - and for many years - AA world service office knowingly recruited members with dangerous violent histories from jails and mental institutions, Thus AA IS not simply negligent, but entirely aware and fully liable, and cogently misleading, in not providing a decent moral warning to the public.

AA has a responsibility to warn the public that attendance at AA meetings statistically places individuals at a higher than average risk of being harmed by a many dangerous attendees including but not limited to, sexual molesters, murderers, domestic violence offenders, sociopaths, pathological liars, gamblers, identity thiefs, of any race, age, sex, religion, or creed. And no matter how long the member may be sober - the probability remains high and unreported.

I have no problem with men rehabilitating themselves, but I also don't mind being forewarned that my odds of offering a murderer a ride home from a publically promoted "safe self help group" were better known.

I would have left AA sooner and gone to a professional helper if I'd been informed that half of AA were ex cons and psychopaths. Some dear departed souls never had their right to know honored prior to having a choice.

*   *   *

Another former member shares her 12-Step program experiences:

I was "taken hostage" and stalked by people in AA too.
I was also given the ultimatum of homelessness or do what these people say.

I also suffer from clinical depression and since I have been out of AA I have had no second doubts about going to therapy for my personal issues and taking my prescribed medication. Six straight years of doing that and I have not had a compulsion to drink. But when I was in AA, there were periods of going off my meds and being told to listen to my sponsor instead of a licensed therapist, and I would eventually spiral down into a terrible bout of depression. I find that instead of helping me be well, AA hindered my recovery from depression, and from drinking.

I had cut off family, friends, social acquaintances, all in the name of "recovery." When I left, it was just me, my husband, and my children. I was feeling very alone and alienated. I was also out of touch with what had been going on with popular culture during the decade I was in AA.

One sponsor I had wanted me to make amends to someone who abused me, as if I had a part in my own abuse. When I spoke to a licensed therapist about it, she said I didn't have to put myself in danger or retraumatize myself by resuming contact with an abuser. But the sponsor told me to dump my therapist as she was telling me to go against the steps, and I did so. I am now reexamining the episodes of abuse through a different lens, and didn't have to make amends to a toxic person after all.

I do have some issues left over from having been in so long and indoctrinated so much, even though it has been 6 years away from the "program." But I am in counseling and continue to do well. I am certainly not miserable and sitting around craving alcohol, and making everyone around me miserable, like they told me would happen.

*   *   *

And another former member shares about her experiences:

I was 14 and it was around 1989. This was when insurance would easily pay for rehab and when schemes began with some rehabs "misdiagnosing" patients to keep them in rehab longer for the money.

At 14, after my rape, I began to get wild, I dated a cocaine dealer and began using cocaine. My mother found some in my jewelry box and had it tested since she did not know and did not want to tell my father until she was certain. It was a Sunday, my father reading Wall Street Journal as usual and my mom acted very unusual, I knew something was up. The door rang, I opened it only to see two big men dressed in suits, I turned around and my dad said I was going with them to rehab. I cried, begged my father but ended up going for 30 days. The rehab was right by my Middle School, I came there and found some other kids from my neighborhood there. We were all in shock, that was the first time I began to not eat. I starved myself and that became the cycle of my eating disorder. One night they took us to an A.A. meeting, not knowing anything about it, I walked into the smoke filled room and was terrified. I noticed a man who's face was disfigured, I wondered why but continued to listen. I felt uncomfortable, and I kept hearing how I'm an alcoholic and I can never drink again, I also heard horrible stories that really scared me. I was 14 after all and thrown into this adult group. They all scared me, afterwards someone walked up to our rehab group and said "You're all addicts, you can never drink or use drugs again". I remember thinking "What? What's going on? Who are these people? I'm 14!".

That was my first meeting of A.A.

I graduated High School and was accepted into college. I was told to go to A.A. I went for the first time as an adult, men hit on me, I tried staying with the women but they didn't seem interested. I felt out of place, confused, not sure if I was an addict or alcoholic. I went for about 3 weeks, then stopped. All was fine after that.

I was fine until I ran into this girl at the grocery store (I'll call her Kay) who I used to party with, we began talking and it was nice to have a girlfriend who I used to know. She seemed good and told me she was "in A.A." and had 3 years sober. Even though I was not close to her in the past, I must admit that after everything it was good to have a girlfriend to talk to. I told her about what happened with the drugs and she told me "You have to come to a meeting with me." I told her "A.A. is not my thing" and she replied "just try it out" so I did. I saw many people I knew there and thought it was okay at first, I got a sponsor which was hard to find since I have to take psych meds and most women did not want to sponsor me. They said "We take no drugs no matter what". I was confused since my meds did help me but eventually I found a sponsor. Before I knew it, I was getting coffee for her, delivering it to her house and running various other errands for her, all the while paying for it myself. She told me I'm powerless, I've done bad things and I need to be humble, grateful and trust in God. We began doing the Steps and when I went through my list and brought up the rape, she said my fault in it was that I was there. I found this to be strange and began to notice other strange things. I began to feel like I was in a cult, I felt so ashamed and not knowing why, I would relapse. I was honest with her and began to find a God of my understanding as she told me. I went to Buddhist meetings, church, everything. I was horribly depressed and my mom was worried. I did not mention I was in A.A. since I did not want her to know.

During this entire time Kay seemed to be more and more into my business, meaning my family, my ex boyfriend who hurt me and my ex husband. I began to notice how she was so into "saving me" as she was always around and telling people about me, even things I did not want others to know.

One day a person who I knew from years ago died of a drug overdose. I was devastated and very sad. After the meeting others would comment about how "That's what happens when you use again" and other unconcerned comments. I found it rude, out of place and then another person in A.A. died. It turns out he went off his meds and killed himself. I did not know him well but I was sad again and again, people made the same comments. i finally yelled after a meeting "What's wrong with everybody! He would probably still be alive if he was on his meds!" people just looked at me weird but I did not care. I decided to stop going to meetings. I called my sponsor and told her, I don't want to use but I'm not going to A.A. anymore. She said we could still be friends and we were until she yelled at me out of nowhere, only later to semi apologize saying she is bi-polar and is not on her meds. I forgave her and we stayed friends. Kay was furious that I stopped going, she began asking people if they've seem me, she would stop my my apartment, called me non-stop, it was a nightmare. I began to stop eating, I just couldn't eat for some reason. I told her I'm not using but my anorexia has come back. She already knew the challenges I had with this in the past and the hospitalizations due to anorexia.

I was on FaceBook and so was Kay, I kept her as my friend online. I was unaware that she had already contacted my mother via FB and was speaking to my mom and my step father. So Kay was communicating to my mother and then step father on the phone. She told my mom that I need an Intervention or I would die, saying that I was on drugs. My mother didn't know what to do (as she later told me) and that her husband believed I should "go away". He and Kay planned an Intervention, a detox facility and a mysterious rehab. Kay called a guy she had a crush on in A.A. to help with the Intervention we'll call Jake and also called someone I'll call Mark to help. Mark called me and said he had some food he wanted to drop off and asked if I would be home on Monday between 1pm and 3pm. I said yes and told him how I found some help with my eating disorder and how excited I was.

Monday came, I was expecting Mark and sure enough there was a knock on the door, I looked through the peep hole and noticed Mark but as I swung the door open, I noticed my mom, step father, Kay, Jake and Mark. I was shocked but so happy to see my mother. It then occurred to me that something was happening. They asked me to sit down and Jake began to tell his story and at the end he said they have a detox for me and a rehab for me to go into. I cried and said, "I'm not doing anything wrong, I'm just not eating!". Kay looked at me and said "No, your using", I cried out "No". My mother cried and I looked at her, then Jake said "If you don't go into this detox and rehab, you'll be homeless, your mother will not help you". My mother's look changed to a look of devastation, like something is off. I could not believe it- basically, I do what they say and they put my stuff in storage or I go homeless. My mom was helping me out financially at the time and I knew that meant no car insurance, cell phone, etc.   Little did I know that they considered taking my car which I paid for out of state and keeping it. Now remember, at this time, I had already been diagnosed with Complex PTSD, on medication and just trying to get help for my eating disorder. I gave in sadly and everyone drove me to another city close by for Detox. Kay took my cell phone and Mark took my car.

I entered Detox and after a drug analysis, no drugs showed up. I explained to the doctor there about my eating disorder, that I hadn't done drugs in 3 months. He said that I would have to get off my medication (against my doctor's orders) and he put me on Subutex- I had no idea what that was. I began vomiting, the next day my teeth were chattering, they had to get a mouthguard for me. I was sweating, unable to eat even if I wanted to and a psychological wreck from being without my meds. I was not allowed to call my doctor or my mother.

I knew I lost even more weight from vomiting and Kay said "You look great, it feels good to be sober huh?, I said "Whatever". Kay said that she could not find a 6 month rehab for me?! and that she found a sober living for me in the valley. She said that because of my "past" with eating, not a lot of places would take me for free. She managed to find a house with 20 girls in it that charged my mom $2,500. a month and I had to pay for groceries.

I asked Kay for my phone and she said that it's not part of my "treatment plan" which turned out to be *her* plan. I asked about my car and she said "Oh, Mark's driving it". I was livid, no wallet, no I.D., no cell phone, no money, nothing. I finally weighed myself after day 4 of being at the sober living, I had lost 15 pounds, 5'8" weighing 90lbs. I had no voice, I felt like I was in prison.

I was finally able to use the computer, I went to FB immediately and sent a friend a message, he was in AA and said he'll have "Clay" stop by, he has a sober living that may be different. Clay came by the next day, the staff was furious and I called my mom using his phone asking for her permission, she finally said yes. I went to Clay's sober living that day. I walked in and it was a relaxed vibe, I felt better. As the days progressed Clay would pick me up in his Maserati and take me to lunch since I had no money to eat, he made a pass at me and I refused. No more lunch after that, I told my roommate and she said that she has sex with Clay for a discount on the rent. There was a girl there who I kept running into by the bathroom, she was shooting up Heroin. It just all freaked me out, I just wanted to feel safe and nowhere seemed safe. Kay was enraged when she found out I left the other sober living and that I did not follow "the treatment plan". I went to local meetings and ran into someone I knew that now manages another sober living in Hollywood, a few days later, I went there. Clay had been paid already and had no problem with me leaving. I told Clay why, two months later I found out that it was shut down.

I went from place to place and this only made my PTSD worse. I finally have my own place, am doing well and got rid of all AA people.

*   *   *

And another former member talks about his experiences and viewpoints:

I did N.A for over ten years... in that time I had as many sponsors. A famous suggestion is to take your own inventory not others, however this is what most sponsors do....and it is painful and confusing. Recently there was a guy who had been touching up young vulnerable boys he was sponsoring- he has been arrested and hopefully will be charged. In the last years I've seen and heard so many bad stories that I can't even begin to put them here.

People are what they are and in the rooms of N.A and A.A you will find some of societies nastiest and sickest people. The thing that is almost laughable, if it wasn't so serious, is that the program teaches these people how to then act as spiritual guru's. I'm reminded of the sentence from the Bible that says 'if the blind lead the blind they both fall in the ditch' and this is so true of N.A. Take a look at long term members with 10 plus years....many will spin a good yarn as they've had plenty of practice and they want to look good but talk afterwards and you will find that they often lack social skills (even after all that work) and are most commonly some of the most self-obsessed, self-centered, self-agrandising and insecure individuals you will ever meet... most never have relationships as a result or if they do, they tend not to go the distance.

The danger with going and making it part of your lifestyle or plan (as I found out) is when you leave you feel like you've lost everything you once had and then you have to learn to talk normal English again. Being around miserable, moaning people will rub off on you.

Meetings are now nut houses (fascinating from a sociological point of view, as people talk very openly about all kinds of horrors) which are great places to score drugs and pick up vulnerable randy women for sex.....I have personally know two women who came in looking for help, got used for sex and then used drugs and died.

I really don't know what the solution is....and so I left, and I'm doing just fine on my own. I know this is long, however, I hope this is useful to someone out there. God bless you all and don't let the bastards get you down.

*   *   *

part four

5) Coercive Mind Control Tactics*

Terminology note: Today, mind control or brainwashing in academia is commonly referred to as coercive persuasion, coercive psychological systems or coercive influence. The short description below comes from Dr. Margaret Singer, professor emeritus at the University of California at Berkeley-- the acknowledged leading authority in the world on mind control and cults.

Coercion is defined by the American Heritage Dictionary as:
   1. **To force to act or think in a certain manner**
   2. **To dominate, restrain, or control by force**
   3. **To bring about by force.**

Coercive psychological systems are behavioral change programs which use psychological force in a coercive way to cause the learning and adoption of an ideology or designated set of beliefs, ideas, attitudes, or behaviors. The essential strategy used by the operators of these programs is to systematically select, sequence and coordinate many different types of coercive influence, anxiety and stress-producing tactics over continuous periods of time.

In such a program the subject is forced to adapt in a series of tiny "invisible" steps. Each tiny step is designed to be sufficiently small so the subjects will not notice the changes in themselves or identify the coercive nature of the processes being used. The subjects of these tactics do not become aware of the hidden organizational purpose of the coercive psychological program until much later, if ever. These tactics are usually applied in a group setting by well intentioned but deceived "friends and allies" of the victim. This keeps the victim from putting up the ego defenses we normally maintain in known adversarial situations.

The coercive psychological influence of these programs aim to overcome the individual's critical thinking abilities and free will - apart from any appeal to informed judgment. Victims gradually lose their ability to make independent decisions and exercise informed consent. Their critical thinking, defenses, cognitive processes, values, ideas, attitudes, conduct and ability to reason are undermined by a technological process rather than by meaningful free choice, rationality, or the inherent merit or value of the ideas or propositions being presented.

How Do They Work?
The tactics used to create undue psychological and social influence, often by means involving anxiety and stress, fall into seven main categories.

TACTIC 1
Increase suggestibility and "soften up" the individual through specific hypnotic or other suggestibility-increasing techniques such as: Extended audio, visual, verbal, or tactile fixation drills, Excessive exact repetition of routine activities, Sleep restriction and/or Nutritional restriction.

TACTIC 2
Establish control over the person's social environment, time and sources of social support by a system of often-excessive rewards and punishments. Social isolation is promoted. Contact with family and friends is abridged, as is contact with persons who do not share group-approved attitudes. Economic and other dependence on the group is fostered.

TACTIC 3
Prohibit disconfirming information and non supporting opinions in group communication. Rules exist about permissible topics to discuss with outsiders. Communication is highly controlled. An "in-group" language is usually constructed.

TACTIC 4

Make the person re-evaluate the most central aspects of his or her experience of self and prior conduct in negative ways. Efforts are designed to destabilize and undermine the subject's basic consciousness, reality awareness, world view, emotional control and defense mechanisms. The subject is guided to reinterpret his or her life's history and adopt a new version of causality.

TACTIC 5
Create a sense of powerlessness by subjecting the person to intense and frequent actions and situations which undermine the person's confidence in himself and his judgment.

TACTIC 6
Create strong aversive emotional arousals in the subject by use of nonphysical punishments such as intense humiliation, loss of privilege, social isolation, social status changes, intense guilt, anxiety, manipulation and other techniques.

TACTIC 7
Intimidate the person with the force of group-sanctioned secular psychological threats. For example, it may be suggested or implied that failure to adopt the approved attitude, belief or consequent behavior will lead to severe punishment or dire consequences such as physical or mental illness, the reappearance of a prior physical illness, drug dependence, economic collapse, social failure, divorce, disintegration, failure to find a mate, etc.

These tactics of psychological force are applied to such a severe degree that the individual's capacity to make informed or free choices becomes inhibited. The victims become unable to make the normal, wise or balanced decisions which they most likely or normally would have made, had they not been unknowingly manipulated by these coordinated technical processes. The cumulative effect of these processes can be an even more effective form of undue influence than pain, torture, drugs or the use of physical force and physical and legal threats.

How does Coercive Psychological Persuasion Differ from Other Kinds of Influence?

Coercive psychological systems are distinguished from benign social learning or peaceful persuasion by the specific conditions under which they are conducted. These conditions include the type and number of coercive psychological tactics used, the severity of environmental and interpersonal manipulation, and the amount of psychological force employed to suppress particular unwanted behaviors and to train desired behaviors.

Coercive force is traditionally visualized in physical terms. In this form it is easily definable, clear-cut and unambiguous. Coercive psychological force unfortunately has not been so easy to see and define. The law has been ahead of the physical sciences in that it has allowed that coercion need not involve physical force. It has recognized that an individual can be threatened and coerced psychologically by what he or she perceives to be dangerous, not necessarily by that which is dangerous.

Law has recognized that even the threatened action need not be physical. Threats of economic loss, social ostracism and ridicule, among other things, are all recognized by law, in varying contexts, as coercive psychological forces.

Why are Coercive Psychological Systems Harmful?

Coercive psychological systems violate our most fundamental concepts of basic human rights. They violate rights of individuals that are guaranteed by the First Amendment to the United States Constitution and affirmed by many declarations of principle worldwide.

By confusing, intimidating and silencing their victims, those who profit from these systems evade exposure and prosecution for actions recognized as harmful and which are illegal in most countries such as: fraud, false imprisonment, undue influence, involuntary servitude, intentional infliction of emotional distress, outrageous conduct and other tortuous acts.

6) From chapter two of *Releasing the Bonds: Empowering People to Think for Themselves* © 2000 by Steven Hassan; published by Freedom of Mind Press, Somerville MA:

Destructive mind control can be understood in terms of four basic components, which form the acronym BITE:

I. Behavior Control
II. Information Control
III. Thought Control
IV. Emotional Control

It is important to understand that destructive mind control can be determined when the overall effects of these four components promotes dependency and obedience to some leader or cause. It is not necessary for every single item on the list to be present. Mind controlled cult members can live in their own apartments, have nine-to-five jobs, be married with children, and still be unable to think for themselves and act independently.

THE BITE MODEL

BEHAVIOR CONROL

1. Regulate individual's physical reality:
    a. Dictate where, how and with whom the member lives and associates
    b. Control types of clothing that are permissible, colors, hairstyles worn by the person
    c. Regulate food and drink allowed or rejected
    d. Impose sleep deprivation
    e. Financial exploitation, manipulation, or dependence
    f. Restrict leisure, entertainment, vacation time
    g. Commit major time for indoctrination and group rituals

h. Require permission for major decisions
i. Insist that thoughts, feelings, and activities be reported to superiors
j. Control rewards and punishments
k. Discourage individualism, encourage group-think
l. Instill obedience and dependency

INFORMATION CONTROL

1. Deception:
   a. Deliberately withhold information
   b. Distort information to make it more acceptable
   c. Systematically lie to the member

2. Minimize or discourage access to non-cult sources of information, including:
   a. Internet, t.v., radio, books, articles, newspapers, magazines, other media
   b. Critical information
   c. Former members
   d. Keep members busy so they don't have time to think or investigate

3. Compartmentalize information into Outsider vs. Insider doctrines
   a. Ensure that information is not freely accessible
   b. Control information at different levels and missions within pyramid
   c. Allow only leadership to decide who needs to know what and when

4. Encourage spying on other members
   a. Impose a buddy system to monitor and control members
   b. Report deviant thoughts, feelings, and actions to leadership
   c. Ensure that individual behavior is monitored by group

5. Extensive use of cult-generated information and propaganda
   a. Misquotations, statements taken out of context from non-cult sources

6. Unethical use of confession
   a. Information about sins used to dissolve identity boundaries
   b. Past sins used to manipulate and control

THOUGHT CONTROL

1. Member required to internalize the group's doctrine as truth
   a. Adopting the group's 'map of reality' as reality
   b. Instill "black and white" thinking
   c. Decide between "good vs. evil"
   d. Organize people into "us vs. them"

2. Use of loaded language-- for example, thought-terminating cliches

3. Only so-called good and proper thoughts are encouraged

4. Hypnotic techniques are used to alter mental statements

5. Memories are manipulated and false memories are created

6. Thought-stopping techniques, which shut down reality testing by stopping negative and allow only so-called good thoughts, are used:
   a. Denial, rationalization, justification, wishful thinking, etc.

7. Rejection of rational analysis, critical thinking, constructive criticism

8. No critical questions about leader, doctrine, or policy allowed

9. Alternative belief systems viewed as illegitimate, evil, or not useful

EMOTIONAL CONTROL

1. Manipulate and narrow the range of feeling

2. Emotion-stopping-- like thought-stopping, but blocking feelings like homesickness, anger, doubts

3. Make the person feel that problems are their own fault-- never the leader's fault

4. Excessive use of guilt
    a. Identity guilt
    b. You are not living up to your potential
    c. Your family is deficient
    d. Your past is suspect
    e. Your affiliations are unwise
    f. Your thoughts, feelings, actions are irrelevant
    g. Social guilt
    h. Historical guilt

5. Excessive use of fear
    a. Fear of thinking independently
    b. Fear of the outside world
    c. Fear of enemies
    d. Fear of losing one's salvation
    e. Fear of leaving the group or being shunned by the group
    f. Fear of disapproval

6. Extremes of emotional highs and lows

7. Ritualistic and public confession of sins

8. Phobia indoctrination: inculcating irrational fears about leaving the group or questioning the leader's authority:

a. No happiness or fulfillment
b. Terrible consequences
c. Shunning-- fear of being rejected by friends, peers, and family
d. Never a legitimate reason to leave-- those who leave are weak, undisciplined, unspiritual, worldly, brainwashed, etc. etc.

"Behavior control is the regulation of a person's physical environment (habitat, companions, food, sleep) and conduct (tasks, rituals, other activities).

"Behavior control may include sleep deprivation, restricted diet, invasion of privacy, separation from friends, and isolation."

"Information control begins during recruitment, when (cults) withhold or distort information. If the recruiter is a stranger, the person believes he has made a new friend."

"A cult's doctrine is seen as absolute truth, the only answer to a member's problems."

7) Profile of the Sociopath

Glibness and Superficial Charm

Manipulative and Cunning
They never recognize the rights of others and see their self-serving behaviors as permissible. They appear to be charming, yet are covertly hostile and domineering, seeing their victims as merely an instrument to be used. They may dominate and humiliate their victims.

Grandiose Self of Self
Feels entitled to certain things as "their right."

Pathological Lying
Has no problem lying coolly and easily and it is almost impossible for them to be truthful on a consistent basis. Can create, and get caught up in, a complex belief about their own powers and abilities. Extremely convincing and even able to pass lie detector tests.

Lack of Remorse, Shame or Guilt
A deep seated rage, which is split off and repressed, is at their core. Does not see others around them as people, but only as targets and opportunities. Instead of friends, they have victims and accomplices who end up as victims. The end always justifies the means and they let nothing stand in their way.

Shallow Emotions
When they show what seems to be warmth, joy, love and compassion it is more feigned than experienced and serves as an ulterior motive. Outraged by insignificant matters, yet remaining unmoved and cold by what would upset a normal person. Since they are not genuine, neither are their promises.

Incapacity for Love

Need for Stimulation
Living on the edge. Verbal outbursts and physical punishments are normal. Promiscuity and gambling are common.

Callousness/Lack of Empathy
Unable to empathize with the pain of their victims, having only contempt for other' feelings of distress and readily taking advantage of them.

Poor Behavioral Control/Impulsive Nature
Rage and abuse, alternating with small expressions of love and approval produce an addictive cycle for abuser and abused, as well as creating hopelessness in the victim. Believing they are all-powerful, all-knowing, entitled to every wish, no sense of personal boundaries, no concern for their impact on others.

Early Behavior Problems/Juvenile Delinquency
Usually has a history of behavioral and academic difficulties, yet "gets by" by conning others. Problems in making and keeping friends; aberrant behaviors such as cruelty to people or animals, stealing, etc.

Irresponsibility/Unreliability
Not concerned about wrecking others' lives and dreams. Oblivious or indifferent to the devastation they cause. Does not accept blame themselves, but blames others, even for acts they obviously committed.

Promiscuous Sexual Behavior/Infidelity
Promiscuity, child sexual abuse, rape, and sexual acting out of all sorts.

Lack of Realistic Life Plans/Parasitic Lifestyle
Tends to move around a lot or makes all encompassing promises for the future, poor work ethic but exploits others effectively.

Criminal or Entrepreneurial Versatility

Changes their image as needed to avoid prosecution. Changes life story readily.

8)   THE THREE STAGES OF GAINING CONTROL OF THE MIND

1. UNFREEZING:
   a. Disorientation/confusion
   b. Sensory deprivation and/or sensory overload
   c. Physiological manipulation:
      1. Sleep deprivation
      2. Privacy deprivation
      3. Change of diet
   d. Hypnosis
      1. Age regression
      2. Visualizations
      3. Storytelling and metaphors
      4. Linguistic double binds, use of suggestion
      5. Meditation, chanting, praying, singing
   e. Getting the person to question his or her identity
   f.   Redefining the person's past-- implant false memories, forget positive memories

II. CHANGING
   a. Creation and imposition of a new identity, step by step
      1. Formally within indoctrination sessions
      2. Informally by other members
   b. Use of behavior modification
      1. Rewards and punishments
      2. Thought-stopping
      3. Control of environment
   c. Mystical manipulation
   d. Use of hypnosis and other mind-altering techniques

1. Repetition, monotony, rhythm
e. Use of confessionals and testimonials

III. REFREEZING
a. New identity reinforced, old identity surrendered
1. Separate from the past; decrease contact or cut off friends and family
2. Give up meaningful possessions and assets
3. Engage in cult activities, move in with members
b. New name, clothing, hairstyle, language, and family
c. Pair up with new role models, buddy system
d. Ongoing indoctrination

9) Jack Trimpey, one expert in the field of addiction and recovery has also had plenty to say on the subject:

Addiction Recovery Groups (RG's) are Hazardous to your Life, Your Health, Your Mental Health, Your Liberty, Your Civil Rights, Your Safety, Your Dignity, and Your Pursuit of Happiness!

The addiction recovery group (RG) is an invention of Alcoholics Anonymous (AA), an expansionist, religious organization patterned after the now-defunct, evangelical Oxford Group. AA's 12-Step philosophy conflicts sharply with all of the world's great religions, contradicts sound concepts of mental health, and has no legitimate place in any of the trusted helping professions.

The 12-Step program of Alcoholics Anonymous does not work with substance addictions, and poses serious risks to your health, safety, family relationships, and general well-being.

The recovery group is like a pool filled with non-swimmers. Whether you can swim or not, they will pull you down in order to survive.

RG philosophies usually conflict sharply with traditional moral precepts, such as right and wrong, good and evil, or other original family values. Meetings focus entirely upon philosophical matters, never upon how to efficiently quit an addiction. In fact, the groups will prevent people from taking aggressive, independent action on the problem, labeling such behavior as "denial" or "dry-drunk" or "pink cloud" or "stinking thinking."

If something doesn't make sense to you, don't attempt to believe it! The more you attempt to "work the program" of AA/NA, the more you risk lasting harm to your self-concept and your family relationships. AA is an *identity change organization.*

RECOVERY GROUP DISORDERS ARE REAL:
(in part):
- Profound self-doubt. Doubt in your ability to do things you once did with ease. Doubt of your own thought processes. Uncertainty and indecision in simple matters. Doubt of simple truths you always believed in. Doubting your own motives, or the motives of others you know well. Conflicted preoccupation with the meaning of life, the nature of reality, the reality of God, even though those matters were resolved satisfactorily earlier.

- Women, in particular, should avoid all recovery groups. Women are not weaker or deficient in their ability to self-recover from intoxicants. Neither men nor women benefit from forming dependencies on others who are struggling against addictions.

Home-based recovery is far more appropriate and efficient for women, who may then develop other positive social affiliations. Women, however, are quite vulnerable to exploitation by "thirteenth stepping," the AA tradition of groupers obtaining sexual gratification from other members. In the recovery group, consensual sex is difficult, since the members are there under duress, and are taught that their lives depend upon assimilation into the recovery group. When women are mandated into recovery groups by courts, they are being subjected to rape. The recovery group is a predatory cult in the first place, using addiction as a lever to gain mastery over desperate newcomers, so it is not surprising that sexual exploitation is prevalent in RG's.

- By calling yourself "an alcoholic," you are identifying yourself as one who does not know right from wrong, who cannot learn from past errors and mistakes, and who at any time may drink or use drugs inexplicably, anti-socially, and self-destructively. You are describing yourself as a walking time-bomb, whose word is not to be trusted. You are saying that you are genetically inferior in a way that exempts you from moral judgment and conduct. This changes your standing in society, in your family, as an employment or insurance risk, and before the law.

- The 12-step recovery group movement is anti-family, just as with any other cult.

The self-indulgence of alcohol or drug addiction is said to be a "family disease," in which spouses and even children share in the responsibility of a parent's substance abuse. Your life's problems will be traced to your parents and ancestors, and you will be told you are congenitally defective.

You will be expected to tell bad stories about your earlier years, seeking perpetrators in your family who "abused" you and caused you to suffer as an adult.

You will be told that your family cannot understand you unless they also accept the addictive disease concept and become involved in a 12-step program such as Al-Anon. If your spouse attends Al-Anon, he/she will be advised to regard you as a sick person even if you are abstinent.

They will create mistrust and emotional distance in your family if you don't attend enough meetings, or don't submit properly to the

12-step program. Al-Anon uses the disease concept as a lever to keep you coming back to meetings, and to make loyal members of your family. They are not interested in your abstinence, which they dismiss as insignificant unless you attend meetings.

Families often break apart on account of AA cult loyalties, just as religion sometimes comes between family members. Children, in particular, are vulnerable to serious disorientation from the disease concept of misbehavior, and to the demands of social cultism on the family unit.

This is a partial list of risks to your well-being posed by the recovery group movement. While the 12-step recovery group movement is the worst offender, all recovery groups carry similar risks in varying degrees.

10)   The title of Steve Salerno's 2005 book says it all: *SHAM: How the Self-Help Movement Made America Helpless.* Mr. Salerno's book offers a wealth of useful information; some stands out as being most relevant to 12-Step program experiences:

Victimization and Recovery have relentlessly encouraged ordinary people with ordinary lives to conceive of themselves as victims of some lifelong ailment that, even during the best of times, lurks just beneath the surface, waiting to undo them.

You say you don't remember anything terrible being done to you as a child? You're 'in denial.' You're 'repressing,' which is framed as dysfunction in its own right-- so you're damned if you do, damned if you don't.

The late 1980s and 1990s witnessed the astonishing rise of "repressed memory syndrome," wherein great hordes of reasonably well-functioning adults who had never before recalled a single moment of childhood trauma suddenly began recalling, en masse and in great detail, lengthy patterns of childhood abuse... the memory itself proved spurious-- either implanted or otherwise induced... or "autosuggested..." Even when such allegations prove false, lives can be ruined.

In the normal course of American life, truly awful things happen to comparatively few of us... (but) Many of us now renounce ownership of our lives.

11) One of the most comprehensive books on the subjects of addiction and recovery, by Dr. Stanton Peele, makes both aspects of the problem crystal-clear with the title of Chapter 6: "What is Addiction and How Do People Get It? Values, Intentions, Self-Restraint, and Environments."

12) Dr. Sandra L. Brown, MA saferelationshipsmagazine.com

What is a Pathological?

You may have heard the terms Psychopath or Sociopath.
These are characteristics common to these individuals:

As children, they have the "WIIFM" attitude-- "What's In It For Me?"-- which by adolescence has transformed into manipulating, lying, conning- to gain what they want by any means necessary.

They have learned how to "read" people-- and use this to exploit people.

They believe that laws, conventional standards, morality, and the rules which normal people live by, do not apply to them.

They have no conscience. Everything is a "game"-- and human beings are nothing more than objects through which to gain what they want.

Their normal emotional growth has been stunted. While it is rare for a pathological to be emotionally older than fourteen, their adolescent behavior coupled with the manipulation and conning they have developed and practiced through experience may be confusing to someone who does not understand what he or she is up against.

If anyone will get away with a con or a criminal act, it will be the Pathological... This ranks as the "Eighth Wonder of the World"-- how pathological people can con their way out of the most vicious deeds and often never pay in any way for their behavior.

13) NRA'S AND "CODEPENDENCY"

I requested, and received, written permission from a group known as Codependents Anonymous, to include some of their material. Please bear in mind that my opinions on 12-Step programs does not include this group. Instead, CoDA appears to be a legitimate group that truly wants to help people.
The most important point, as it relates to the popular 12-Step programs, is there are two very distinct "categories": there are individuals who, one way or other, become victims; and there are those who seek out individuals to victimize.
In the References section, I have included a link to the CoDA website. However, when it comes to untangling the insanity of NRA's, this group has done an excellent job of clarifying what "Codependent" NRA's are all about, *and* what they are looking for.

342

People who are in danger of becoming involved in "codependent relationships" tend to exhibit these characteristics:

DENIAL PATTERNS:

I have difficulty identifying what I am feeling.
I minimize, alter, or deny how I truly feel.
I perceive myself as completely unselfish and dedicated to the well-being of others.
I lack empathy for the feelings and needs of others.
I label others with my negative traits.
I can take care of myself without any help from others.
I mask my pain in various ways such as anger, humor, or isolation.
I express negativity or aggression in indirect and passive ways.
I do not recognize the unavailability of those people to whom I am attracted.

LOW SELF-ESTEEM PATTERNS:

I have difficulty making decisions.
I judge what I think, say, or do harshly, as never good enough.
I am embarrassed to receive recognition, praise, or gifts.
I value others' approval of my thinking, feelings, and behavior over my own.
I do not perceive myself as a lovable or worthwhile person.
I constantly seek recognition that I think I deserve.
I have difficulty admitting that I made a mistake.
I need to appear to be right in the eyes of others and will even lie to look good.
I am unable to ask others to meet my needs or desires.
I perceive myself as superior to others.
I look to others to provide my sense of safety.
I have difficulty getting started, meeting deadlines, and

completing projects.
I have trouble setting healthy priorities.

COMPLIANCE PATTERNS:

I am extremely loyal, remaining in harmful situations too long.
I compromise my own values and integrity to avoid rejection or
anger.
I put aside my own interests in order to do what others want.
I am hypervigilant regarding the feelings of others and take on
those feelings.
I am afraid to express my beliefs, opinions, and feelings when
they differ from those of others.
I accept sexual attention when I want love.
I make decisions without regard to the consequences.
I give up my truth to gain the approval of others or to avoid
change.

AVOIDANCE PATTERNS:

I act in ways that invite others to reject, shame, or express anger
toward me.
I judge harshly what others think, say, or do.
I avoid emotional, physical, or sexual intimacy as a means of
maintaining distance.
I allow my addictions to people, places, and things to distract me
from achieving intimacy in relationships.
I use indirect and evasive communication to avoid conflict or
confrontation.
I diminish my capacity to have healthy relationships by declining
to use all the tools of recovery.
I suppress my feelings or needs to avoid feeling vulnerable.
I pull people toward me, but when they get close, I push them

away.

I refuse to give up my self-will to avoid surrendering to a power that is greater than myself.

I believe displays of emotion are a sign of weakness.

I withhold expressions of appreciation.

In contrast, the NRA's who seek vulnerable people tend to exhibit these characteristics:

CONTROL PATTERNS:

I believe most people are incapable of taking care of themselves.

I attempt to convince others what to think, do, or feel.

I freely offer advice and direction to others without being asked.

I become resentful when others decline my help or reject my advice.

I lavish gifts and favors on those I want to influence.

I use sexual attention to gain approval and acceptance.

I have to be needed in order to have a relationship with others.

I demand that my needs be met by others.

I use charm and charisma to convince others of my capacity to be caring and compassionate.

I use blame and shame to emotionally exploit others.

I refuse to cooperate, compromise, or negotiate.

I adopt an attitude of indifference, helplessness, authority, or rage to manipulate outcomes.

I pretend to agree with others to get what I want.

I use terms of recovery in an attempt to control the behavior of others.

14) In recent years, various websites and forums have appeared to inform the public and support former members. One forum, Expose AA, offers the following information:

What Is Deprogramming?:

Exercising and retraining the mind with the intention of abandoning or relieving oneself from rigid beliefs and controlled thought that were developed from outside sources.

Why Deprogram From A.A.?

The main theme in AA and NA is powerlessness, and developing a pattern of thinking that is adverse to self-efficacy.

How Did This Happen?

AA was founded by two alcoholic members of an early 20th-century Evangelical Christian cult called the Oxford Group. The OG's mission was to bring members under their control by offering them God's Miracles in exchange of a process in which they surrendered their lives and confessed their sins and weaknesses to the group.

15) *from HAMS: Harm Reduction for Alcohol*

AA is most successful at recruiting and retaining males of low I.Q. And educational attainment who have dependent personality types. AA is a very good fit for people with dependent personality types because the 12 Steps function by making people totally dependent on AA.

It is unfortunate that bright and independent thinkers who question the AA program are told that their thinking is diseased, failing people with independent personality types, higher I.Q.'s, and higher educational attainments-- i.e. the majority of people.

What is the greatest shame is people who suffer the most from AA are usually the brightest, most independent thinkers there.

Moreover, most women find AA is damaging, rather than helpful, because they are in need of personal empowerment-- whereas AA specializes in 'breaking down big egos.'

16) Dr. Janja Lalich, professor of Sociology, states:

Anger is a normal and healthy reaction to the hurt and assaults that you experienced. Anger is the most appropriate response to abuse and manipulations.

It fortifies your sense of right by condemning the wrong that was done to you. It gives you the energy and will to get through the ordeal of getting your life back together.

Suppression of anger contributes to depression and a sense of helplessness. You must be allowed-- encouraged, even-- to express appropriate moral outrage. It will enable victims to assert their inner worth, and their sense of right and wrong.

Even implicitly denying victims' need to express moral outrage shifts blame from victimizers to victims.

17) Dr. Sam Vaknin has produced a wealth of material that is relevant to many of our experiences; the information follows in

the References section of this book. Dr. Vaknin granted
permission for me to quote some material from his website:

How to spot an abuser:

Is there anything you can do to avoid abusers and narcissists to
start with?
Are there any warning signs, any identifying marks, rules of
thumb to shield you from the harrowing and traumatic experience
of an abusive relationship?
Imagine a first or second date. You can already tell if he is a
would-be abuser. Here's how:

Perhaps the first telltale sign is the abuser's alloplastic defenses–
his tendency to blame every mistake of his, every failure, or
mishap on others, or on the world at large.

Is he hypersensitive, picks up fights, feels constantly slighted,
injured, and insulted? Does he rant incessantly? Does he express
negative and aggressive emotions towards the weak, the poor, the
needy, the sentimental, and the disabled? Does he confess to
having a history of battering or violent offenses or behavior? Is
his language vile and infused with expletives, threats, and
hostility?

Next thing: is he too eager? Does he push you to marry him
having dated you only twice? Is he planning on having children
on your first date? Does he immediately cast you in the role of
the love of his life? Is he pressing you for exclusivity, instant
intimacy, almost rapes you and acts jealous when you as much as
cast a glance at another male? Does he inform you that, once you
get hitched, you should abandon your studies or resign your job
(forgo your personal autonomy)?

Does he respect your boundaries and privacy, or does he ignore
your wishes? Does he disrespect your boundaries and treats you
as an object or an instrument of gratification (materializes on

348

your doorstep unexpectedly or calls you often prior to your date)? Does he go through your personal belongings while waiting for you to get ready? Does he text or phone you multiply and incessantly and insist to know where you are or where you have been at all times?

Does he control the situation and you compulsively? Does he disapprove if you are away for too long? Does he interrogate you when you return? Does he hint that, in future, you would need his permission to do things – even as innocuous as meeting a friend or visiting with your family?

Does he act in a patronizing and condescending manner and criticizes you often? Does he emphasize your minutest faults (devalues you)? Does he call you names, harasses, or ridicules you? Is he wildly unrealistic in his expectations from you, from himself, from the budding relationship, and from life in general?

If you have answered "yes" to **any** of the above – stay away! He is an abuser!

Abuse by proxy:

If all else fails, the abuser recruits friends, colleagues, mates, family members, the authorities, institutions, neighbours, the media, teachers-- in short, third parties – to do his bidding. He uses them to cajole, coerce, threaten, stalk, offer, retreat, tempt, convince, harass, communicate and otherwise manipulate his target. He controls these unaware instruments exactly as he plans to control his ultimate prey. He employs the same mechanisms and devices. And he dumps his props unceremoniously when the job is done.

One form of control by proxy is to engineer situations in which abuse is inflicted upon another person. Such carefully crafted scenarios of embarrassment and humiliation provoke social sanctions against the victim. Society, or a social group become the instruments of the abuser.

Abusers often use other people to do their dirty work for them. These - sometimes unwitting - accomplices belong to three groups:

I. The abuser's social milieu

Some offenders - mainly in patriarchal and misogynist societies – co-opt other family members, friends, and colleagues into aiding and abetting their abusive conduct. In extreme cases, the victim is held "hostage" - isolated and with little or no access to funds or transportation. Often, children are used as bargaining chips or leverage.

II. The victim's social milieu

Even the victim's relatives, friends, and colleagues are amenable to the considerable charm, persuasiveness, and manipulativeness of the abuser and to his impressive thespian skills. The abuser offers a plausible rendition of the events and interprets them to his favor. Others rarely have a chance to witness an abusive exchange first hand and at close quarters. In contrast, the victims are often on the verge of a nervous breakdown: harassed, unkempt, irritable, impatient, abrasive, and hysterical.

Confronted with this contrast between a polished, self-controlled, and suave abuser and his harried casualties – it is easy to reach the conclusion that the real victim is the abuser, or that both parties abuse each other equally. *The prey's acts of self-defense, assertiveness, or insistence on her rights are interpreted as aggression, lability, or a mental health problem.*

III. The System

The abuser perverts the system - therapists, marriage counselors, mediators, court-appointed guardians, police officers, and judges. He uses them to pathologize the victim and to separate her from her sources of emotional sustenance - notably, from her children.

Forms of Abuse by Proxy

Socially isolating and excluding the victim by discrediting her through a campaign of malicious rumors.

Harassing the victim by using others to stalk her or by charging her with offenses she did not commit.

Provoking the victim into aggressive or even antisocial conduct by having others threaten her or her loved ones.

Colluding with others to render the victim dependent on the abuser.

But, by far, her children are the abuser's greatest source of leverage.

18)   Donna Andersen, author of Lovefraud, and www.lovefraud.com, composed a detailed open letter to attorneys whose clients have been victimized by sociopaths. However, the information in Ms. Andersen's letter is equally applicable for anyone who wants or needs to know what these situations are really like. Portions of the letter are as follows:

All sociopaths are social predators, and live by exploiting others.

What you need to understand about sociopaths

1. A sociopath's prime objective is power and control. All they want is to win.

2. Sociopaths love the drama of court because it gives them an opportunity to win. They do not consider the possibility that they may lose. If they do lose, they view it a bump in the road, and figure out how to attack the target again. Forcing the target to incur steadily mounting legal expenses is considered a win.

3. Sociopaths lie. They lie convincingly. They have no qualms about lying in court documents or on the witness stand.

4. Sociopaths manipulate other people to lie for them. These witnesses may not know they are lying—they may simply believe everything that the sociopath has told them, because sociopaths are so convincing.

5. Sociopaths feel no obligation to follow court orders or the law. They only follow court orders or the law if they perceive an advantage in doing so. But they are experts at figuring out ways to use the law to further their objective, which is to crush your client.

How people become targets

Sociopaths are always on the lookout for people they can use. The sociopath begins the exploitation, while simultaneously ramping up manipulation to keep the target under control. This may involve:

- Isolating the target from his or her support network
- Emotional, psychological, verbal, physical, sexual or financial abuse
- Gaslighting—making the target doubt his or her own perceptions

What you need to understand about the target

Involvement with a sociopath is like living in a black hole of chaos. Your client, the target, has probably had every aspect of his or her life disrupted:

- Career interrupted
- Finances ruined
- Health compromised
- Home and property neglected
- Relationships shattered

19) Michael Samsel, RN:

VIOLENCE DEFINED:

Consent can only occur where refusal is safe and respected. Casual onlookers can easily overlook the violence in a situation because they see submission and mistake it for consent. A 'well-behaved' survivor is often on the receiving end of considerable 'silent' violence.

STALKING

Stalking includes all actions aimed at eliminating the survivor's privacy. Examples are: frequent phone calls, being upset if calls aren't returned very quickly, insisting that the survivor call to check in frequently, questioning about all activities, not allowing partner to have relationships with a person of opposite or preferred sex, not allowing partner to keep conversations private, not allowing partner any private or alone time, opening partner's mail, checking their phone log or directory, cancelling appointments for the survivor (in contrast to never *making* appointments for the survivor), going through the survivor's purse or dresser, asking others to keep an eye on partner, questioning others to reconstruct partner's movements, following partner, not allowing partner to go alone to an activity only they are interested in, not allowing a partner to go somewhere the batterer doesn't want to go, showing up unannounced or uninvited, showing up very late or very early, showing up at a workplace, etc... In extreme cases, primary aggressors have installed video surveillance, recording devices, or computer programs that track computer use.

ISOLATION

Isolation has two purposes. One, to keep the survivor away from anyone that she might, in the mind of the primary aggressor, abandon him for. It is not unusual for primary aggressors to try to keep their partner from all males. Two, isolation keeps the survivor away from anyone that may influence the survivor to leave, use boundaries, or respond to the primary aggressor differently. This often includes her entire family, and most of her friends. Often isolating actions will be rationalized by the primary aggressor stating they don't like the person. But isolation is about controlling the survivor's access to the person she likes or from whom she receives support.

HARASSMENT

Harassment is 1) a pattern of unwanted contact that robs the survivor of privacy, and the ability to relax and feel safe, or 2) a pattern of interfering in the survivors relationships with others.

The survivor has been intimidated and options taken away.

GASLIGHTING

Gaslighting describes actions that 1) make another person believe he or she is crazy, and 2) discredit the person by making others think they are crazy.

BOUNDARIES

Boundaries are also known as limits-- they are not products of negotiation Boundaries are decisions that protect fundamental safety or integrity, indicating what one will and will not tolerate.

The difference between control and boundaries is that control is meant to make others what you want them to be but boundaries make it safe for us to be ourselves.

A primary aggressor will not respect boundaries. If a survivor tries to set boundaries, it may very well increase her danger.

QUOTES ABOUT POWER

Secrecy and silence are the perpetrator's first line of defense. if secrecy fails, the perpetrator attacks the credibility of his victim. If he cannot silence her absolutely he tries to make sure no one listens.

20) Writer Lori Soard, in her article "Real Life Villains and Sociopaths-- You Can't Win," offers the following information and advice:

Know your enemy: Sociopaths manipulate, lie and scheme against you. They think nothing of spending 10 hours a day on the phone, or in person, telling anyone and everyone lie after lie about you. Your reputation may be in tatters by the time they are done.   According to therapist Martha Stout in *The Sociopath Next Door,"* sociopaths have no remorse. They do not feel sorrow when they destroy your life.

Don't play the game: Once a sociopath targets you, the situation turns into a game for him or her. Your attempts to "fix" the situation with rational conversation is seen as weakness by the sociopath. She will feel she is winning and will amp up her efforts, even twisting your words and using them against you. A sociopath will never stop attacking your reputation in the most ruthless manner possible.

Most therapists agree that sociopaths cannot be treated effectively. Instead, take steps to protect yourself and your family.

21)   *And, speaking of "experts," an "internal memo" written by a General Service Trustee of a 12-Step program states, in part:*

COMPLAINTS HAVE BEEN RECEIVED ABOUT GROUPS OF MEMBERS AND INDIVIDUAL MEMBERS WHO ARE INVOLVED IN THE FOLLOWING BEHAVIORS TOWARD

OTHER MEMBERS AND OTHER GROUPS IN THE FELLOWSHIP:

ACTUAL OR IMPLIED VIOLENCE,

BULLYING,

INTIMIDATION,

STALKING,

THREATENING BEHAVIOR,

VERBAL, EMOTIONAL, AND SEXUAL ABUSE.

THERE IS CONFUSION ABOUT TAKING LEGAL ACTION AGAINST PERPETRATORS BECAUSE THE VICTIMS THINK THEY WILL BE BREAKING ANONYMITY,

FEAR RETRIBUTION

AND THAT THEY WON'T BE BELIEVED.

REFERENCES

1) WHERE DO WE GO FROM HERE: CHAOS OR COMMUNITY? 1967; Martin Luther King, Jr.

2) Dr. Richard Gardner

3) www.orange-papers.org

4) Without Conscience: The Disturbing World of the Psychopaths Amongst Us, by Robert D. Hare, PhD.;

Copyright 1993. Copyright Guilford Press. Reprinted with permission of The Guilford Press

5) www.factnet.org/ Dr. Margaret Thaler Singer

6) Steven A. Hassan- author of:
Releasing the Bonds: Empowering People to Think for Themselves (2000);
Combatting Cult Mind Control (1990);
Freedom of Mind: Helping Loved Ones Leave Controlling People, Cults, and Beliefs (2012)
www.freedomofmind.com

7) www.macafee.cc

8) Kurt Lewin

9) Jack Trimpey, who, with his wife Lois, cofounded
Rational Recovery
https://rational.org/index.php?id=35%20
and the AVRT© system.

10) Steve Salerno: SHAM: How the Self-Help Movement
Made America Helpless

11) Stanton Peele, PhD.: The Diseasing of America: How We
Allowed Recovery Zealots and the Treatment Industry to
Convince Us We Are Out of Control

12) Dr. Sandra L. Brown, MA
saferelationshipsmagazine.com

13) www.coda.org
(The Patterns and Characteristics of Codependency may not
be reprinted or republished without the express written
consent of Co-Dependents Anonymous, Inc. This
document may be reprinted from the website
www.coda.org (CoDA) for use by members of the CoDA

Fellowship.

14) www.expaa.org

15) HAMS: Harm Reduction for Alcohol

16)   Dr. Janja Lalich-- sociology professor, and coauthor of "Captive Hearts, Captive Minds: Freedom and Recovery from Cults and Abusive Relationships."

17) Dr. Sam Vaknin, author of "Malignant Self-love - Narcissism Revisited" and other books about personality disorders (www.narcissistic-abuse.com)

18) Donna Andersen, author of Lovefraud.com

19) Michael Samsel, R.N.

20) Lori Soard: www.lorisoard.com

21) Internal memo from a 12-Step program

ADDITIONAL REFERENCES

www.orange-papers.org

www.expaa.org

12-STEP HORROR STORIES: TRUE TALES OF MISERY, BETRAYAL, AND ABUSE IN AA, NA, AND 12-STEP TREATMENT (2000); Rebecca Fransway part five

AFTERWORD

When I began writing this book in October, 2011, my knowledge of other people's experiences was minimal. That changed. Men and women throughout the United States have related their own personal experiences in 12-Step programs-- experiences which clearly meet the definition of "horror stories."

My experiences are by no means unique-- and by no means uncommon. People who turn to 12-Step programs for help, friendship, answers, solutions, often find themselves in dangerous situations with dangerous individuals-- and no one to turn to for assistance. There have been various incidents of murder; rape and sexual assaults are very common; and, what has been the universal experience of countless numbers of men and women: *psychological abuse.*

Because of these experiences, many former 12-Step program members suffer from, are receiving help for, and cope with depression, anxiety disorders, and even Post-Traumatic Stress Disorder-- not because of their 'childhoods,' not because of their 'relationships,' not because of their 'pasts,' *but because of their experiences in these Programs.*
Many former members have also been attempting *deprogramming.* As most average people cannot afford professional services for this often-misunderstood process, there are few resources other than individuals trying to work these issues out themselves, seeking help from support groups and similar contacts. The fact is the abuse and psychological tactics

that occur within the programs are so widespread and so extreme that it brings a new meaning to the word *"recovery."*

What it comes down to: is there any legitimate reason human beings should be in the position of tolerating all kinds of abuses or worse, the destruction of their families, the destruction of their lives-- and feel they must either remain silent or put themselves in further danger?

One would think that in the United States of America, human beings not only have "certain unalienable rights," but that those rights must be taken seriously.

other books and ebooks by C. A. Sheckels:

Seekers

Taking Back Your Life After Sexual Assault

The Battered Women's Handbook

Effective Grieving

What Your Children Need From You- and Why